NOTHING GOOD
WILL EVER COME OF IT

NOTHING GOOD
WILL EVER COME OF IT

A HISTORY OF PARLIAMENTARY
MISGIVINGS, MISJUDGMENTS AND
MISGUIDED PREDICTIONS

PHIL MASON

WARNER BOOKS

A *Warner* Book

First published in the United Kingdom
in 1993 by Warner Books

Copyright © Philip Mason 1993

The moral right of the author has been asserted

A CIP catalogue for this book
is available from the British Library

ISBN   0 7515 0370 3

Typeset in Goudy Old Style
by 𝐀 Tek-Art, Addiscombe, Croydon, Surrey

Printed and bound in Great Britain
by Clays Ltd, St. Ives plc

Warner Books
A division of
Little, Brown and Company (UK) Limited
165 Great Dover Street
London SE1 4YA

CONTENTS

INTRODUCTION

What does the phrase 'the march of history' conjure up in the mind? Whatever one's preferred or favourite period of history might be, however different it is from those which precede or follow it, it will almost certainly have one thing in common with all those others – the idea of progress. We are accustomed to seeing the 'march' of history as a relentless story of social advance, the unstoppable crusade of reason eradicating the iniquities and unfairnesses of earlier, less enlightened ages, the inevitable triumph of 'common sense' over outmoded or bigoted ideas. It is not particularly surprising that this should be so. It makes sense that we should find it psychologically more comfortable to believe that the world which has been bequeathed to us by our ancestors is the result of a rational plan, a deliberate scheme rather than a hotch-potch of accidents, lucky or unfortunate. Although not surprising, it is nevertheless still rather odd, because if we thought about it we would know that our own world – which will be our children's past – rarely bears any hallmarks of being a rational or deliberate progression towards a better tomorrow. We in fact seem to, and largely do, proceed by accidents, lucky or unfortunate. Bad ideas get accepted because of a temporary majority in their favour; good ideas flounder because they get poorly presented. But what is bad? What is good? It is in order to wipe out this confusing uncertainty that the picture of the past we create for ourselves has always tended to have an air of inevitability and purpose about it, and that we have been moving consciously and determinedly from a poorer state of affairs to a better state of affairs: the march of progress.

To a modern mind, this feeling of being part of a constant uplifting progress is most commonly manifested by the expression of genuine disbelief that anyone could have seriously objected to aspects of life which we now take for granted – rights such as the right to vote secretly at elections; the right, indeed, for all to vote at all, women included; the right to education, and for it to be free; unemployment benefit, pensions, and all the other facets with which we pride ourselves today as the symbols of a civilized society. In their time, all these were issues of radical and unprecedented change. They were resisted by many through arguments which ranged from prejudice of varying degrees of rationality to dire (and often entertainingly bizarre) prophecies of consequent doom if the reform succeeded.

All innovations succeed through tireless advocacy by committed people. Our traditional histories make us familiar with them: Wilberforce against slavery and child labour, the Pankhursts for women's suffrage, Florence Nightingale for hospital reform, Elizabeth Fry for prisons. Less familiar are the detractors, those who resisted the urge for change – often with equally cogent reasoning – those who thought that the very fabric of society was about to be torn for ever in incalculable ruin.

'Nothing Good Will Ever Come Of It' is the first book to restore the balance. Here we survey over a century and a half of history's march, from the French Revolution to just a generation ago – arguably the greatest period of sustained social change in human history. We shine a new light on the past. We illuminate corners which are rarely inspected any more. We recall the controversies to try to show that the past was not the smooth triumph of wisdom over ignorance, or that it was only a matter of time before 'common sense' prevailed. Putting the other sides of the argument back into the limelight shows that matters were a little more finely balanced than we might believe they were today.

The resulting concoction will shock, amuse, entertain and, we trust, instruct. For while the reader ridicules those quoted here from the safe certainty of knowing what in the end happened, we should remember that they had no such luxury. We should perhaps dilute a little our own perception that what has happened happened because it had to happen. In reality, history is no great unfolding of an ordained truth or a predetermined path of progress. In all the great issues covered here, there was *as seen at the time* no self-evidently 'right' side to the argument. *Our* writing of history created that optical illusion. As we re-read the opposing arguments from the cosy certainty of looking back, we must remember that nothing was inevitable. With both sides of the argument aired, we can usefully ask ourselves afresh how we might have voted on each at the time. Any of them could have gone the other way given different circumstances. The point is that on most occasions there were arguments of equal logic to those which eventually won out. Each reader can now come to their own conclusion as to whether history came out right. Who then, also, will feel confidently able to pick the 'right' side in some of our own contemporary controversies?

The arguments are no ramshackle collection of the thoughts of just anyone. Where better to observe the ebb and flow of social evolution than the daily columns of the official record of Parliamentary debates, *Hansard*? '*Nothing Good Will Ever Come Of It*' has been compiled from the most comprehensive study ever made of the countless millions of words uttered in the hallowed chambers of the Palace of Westminster. We are a fortunate nation to possess such a rich source that, volume after successive volume, links in seamless union the changing years, decades, centuries. Fortunate indeed – since Parliament on more than one occasion doubted the wisdom of ever providing a record of its debates. According to Lord Althorp in 1834, the record would become so voluminous: 'that it would not find readers; it must be in great measure perfectly uninteresting to the public'. It still may not be everyone's idea of bedtime reading, but a trawl through *Hansard* pays rich dividends, as we trust what follows will show.

ONE:
SLAVERY

'A Most Ruinous Measure'
The Abolition Of The Slave Trade

The movement for the abolition of the slave trade was the first significant 'social' crusade to emerge from that urge for Enlightenment which began to take hold in the last decades of the eighteenth century. Although not directly addressing the *principle* of slavery, both sides knew that the greater question was at stake. As a certain precursor to attacking the system itself, it became the battleground upon which the essence of the practice of Man having ownership over Man was contended. With the immorality of slavery implicitly accepted by a successful abolition of the trade, the later struggle for the emancipation of existing slaves would become a drier, desultory affair, couched chiefly in terms of arid economic evaluations and disputes over levels of compensation, all conducted in an aura of a foregone conclusion.

The great polemics of the crusade against slavery were thus aired in the initial contest to outlaw the trade. There was great substance resting in the balance. The abolitionists were attacking one of the lynchpins of the country's economic success and the mainstay of its colonial achievements. Britain dominated the transatlantic trade – British ships accounted for well over half the number of slaves transported annually. Only France, with a quarter, came anywhere near as a rival. In all, since its start in earnest in the late seventeenth century, the best estimates suggest that between 8 and 10 million Africans were shipped to the Americas; at its peak the trade carried 100,000 a year. On average, a plantation slave survived ten years – if they managed to reach the Caribbean alive: death rates during the trip were often as high as a quarter of the complement.

By every account, it was a wretched business, but the battle against it was to be long and hard fought. Led by the indomitable Wilberforce, who introduced motions on abolition almost every year for two decades, it pitched a small band of moral campaigners against one of the most powerful economic forces of the day. Right may have been on the side of the abolitionists – who could doubt it today, or ever imagine it had ever been doubted – but the opponents of abolition did not rest their case solely on amoral arguments of economic necessity and the balance sheet but advanced with plausible logic powerful countervailing moral positions, maintaining that the trade, albeit distasteful, was in fact in the best interests of all concerned. As the debate simmered down the years – nineteen were to pass between Wilberforce's first motion in 1788 and the eventual abolition, and a further twenty-five before slavery itself was stopped – it was by no means as self-evident as it might appear today that abolition was the only moral outcome.

One of the earliest lines of argument was that nothing would make worse the lot of the existing slaves than an abolition of the trade.

> Nothing I am persuaded could tend more to render the negroes on the plantations discontented than an assurance that their labours were not to be alleviated by the arrival of additional assistance.
>
> (Sir William Young, 1796)

> The negroes in the West Indies do not desire the abolition; for they consider any obstacle to the importation of new slaves as a prolongation and increase of their present hours.
>
> (Mr Ellis, 1797)

Only increased frustration among the plantation workers could result and would deal a devastating blow to the system.

If you were to stop all future importations, such a measure must give a very strong turn to the minds of the negroes now upon the islands; they might well say, if you think that the situation of slavery is so dreadful that you will not allow any more of our countrymen to be made slaves, why are we to continue slaves still? If the abolition of the trade rests entirely on the reasons of humanity and justice, the same principle would lead as far as entire emancipation. If then by abolishing the trade you could convince the negroes in our islands that their state was much more shocking than ever they had before considered it, the only consequence would be that they would be more ripe for insurrection which would bring an additional danger upon the colonies.

(Sir William Pulteney, 1805)

The negroes, who had always been accustomed to look to a reinforcement of strength by the purchase of Africans as a boon to themselves and an alleviation of their labours in cultivating the plantations, would become discontented; and as they could not distinguish between the nice refinements of justice, that discontent was likely to ripen into resistance to their masters when they found that they alone were to be the objects of slavery. The white population of the islands [would be] diminished and the security against external and internal dangers thereby destroyed; no adventurers would hereafter be found to hazard their lives in an unwholesome climate because the stimulus was taken away.

(Mr Hughan, 1807)

A sudden abolition of the trade for African negroes would yet farther defeat its purpose of humanity held out to us and produce the most unequivocal oppression and misery of the slaves in the ... islands. ... The actual state of the negroes in the colonies, their proportions as to sex and young and old [were such that] the negroes neither do nor can multiply by natural

means, circumstanced as they are at the present hour. ...
Under such circumstances, the slave trade being suppressed
and negroes decreasing the first year in the smallest percent-
age, that decrease must become progressive and accelerate
from year to year; for as his numbers become less, his labour
becomes more, from time to time falling heavier on the
negroes who remain. How cruelly the measure of suppressing
at once the trade for slaves from Africa might operate in
relation to the slaves actually on the plantations of the West
Indies is not readily to be conceived in all its extent of misery
or not to be conceived without horror.

(Sir William Young, 1791)

It would also encourage thoughts of eventual liberation.

How impolitic then is it to raise doubts and questions in their
minds upon the subject of emancipation, for to that this
question ultimately leads and how pregnant with danger is
such conduct to our colonial interests and possessions. ...
Under these circumstances, it becomes the House to say at
once to the world that they are resolved not to adopt a system
which can only lead to the most injurious consequences and
thus to put an end to discussions which have already and
which evidently must have the very worst effect upon the
minds of the negroes.

(General Gascoyne, 1805)

The equation was clear: you could not abolish slavery
without immense ruin to planters; and you could not
abolish the trade without conferring moral obloquy on the
practice of slavery itself – so the trade perforce had to
continue in the interests of maintaining the security of the
colonies.

But even if Britain bit the bullet and took the honourable course, other less principled rivals would step into the

breach. Far from contributing to the welfare of slaves, abolition by Britain would actually worsen their prospects.

> Would the interests of humanity, would the advantage of the coast of Africa be [served by abolition]? Certainly not. The trade would still be carried on; the supply would be obtained with the difference that now the trade is conducted under the control and regulation of this House whereas then it would be carried on by other nations free from all the salutary and humane regulations enforced by the parliament of this country. ... A precipitate measure would take out of the hands of this House the means of alleviating, by proper regulation and control, the miseries with which the trade is attended.
>
> (Mr Dundas, Secretary for the Colonies, 1799)

This self-pious line was to be repeated again and again.

> If this Bill were to pass, the trade would be carried on by other nations and the miserable slaves would therefore be again exposed to all the miseries from which the wise and humane regulations under which the trade has been conducted by British merchants have relieved them.
>
> (Sir William Young, 1804)

> Unless [proponents] can give security that the rest of Europe would not take this trade up when we should drop it, the purpose of humanity will be so far from being answered that it would be defeated by our putting out of our control that power which we use with moderation and giving it to others who will exercise it with cruelty.
>
> (Earl Temple, 1804)

> Instead of benefiting the cause of humanity it will injure it exceedingly. What was given up here would be adopted elsewhere without any of the humane regulations established

by this country.

(Sir Robert Peel (the elder), 1806)

I doubt whether even a concurrent [i.e. all countries] abolition of the slave trade would erect the Utopia in Africa which the imagination of the abolitionists has projected; but a *partial* abolition, an abandonment of that small share which we now carry on for the sake of our old colonies and which we carry on under the strictest regulations for the prevention of abuses, cannot pretend to have the smallest effect towards that object. It has the double disadvantage of precluding the hope of our ever bringing about a concurrent abolition and of inviting our rivals to assume, as soon as they can, our place in the trade infinitely to the disadvantage of Africa in point of humanity.

(Mr Hibbert, 1807)

Britain could not absolve itself from its sins by unilateral action, by, simply, desisting and looking the other way.

When my vote is solicited for an abolition of the trade in question ... as far as it relates to Great Britain only, I would wish at least previously to be convinced that while Britain loses, Africa will gain. ... Great Britain may abandon her part of the trade but cannot abolish it. If Great Britain suddenly withdraws from this commerce, as Pontius Pilate, she hath washed her hands indeed, but is she thence the more innocent of what follows? If her intervention would have prevented what follows, Great Britain is not the more innocent. [There is] incontrovertible proof that the nations of Europe and the United States of America are crowding to this trade for slaves and wait but its suppression on the part of Great Britain to rush on the coasts of Africa in competition for the share of traffic thus newly opened to them.

(Sir William Young, 1791)

Life was never meant to be easy.

> I have heard a great deal of kidnapping slaves and of other
> barbarous practices. I am sorry for it, but it should be recol-
> lected that these things are the consequence of the natural law
> of Africa and instead of declaiming against it we should
> endeavour, like wise men, to turn it to our advantage. ... I
> acknowledge it is not an amiable trade but neither is the trade
> of a butcher an amiable trade and yet a mutton chop is,
> nevertheless, a very good thing. I cannot help doubting the
> propriety of the motion; and the more I consider the subject
> the more I am persuaded that it is an improvident and unwise
> measure. ... Parliament cannot abolish the trade; we might
> relinquish it, but to whom? – to France, Spain, Holland and
> other countries who would take it up and share it among them.
> The trade would still be continued and without the humane
> regulations applied to it by the English. ... I must acknowledge
> that the slave trade is not an amiable trade but I will not satisfy
> my humanity at the expense of the interests of my country and
> I think we should not too curiously inquire into the unpleas-
> ant circumstances with which it is perhaps attended.
>
> (Mr Grosvenor, 1791)

A correct perspective had to be kept on the issue.

> I am very far from denying that many acts of inhumanity have
> been committed in the transportation of slaves to the West
> Indies [but] it would be unreasonable to expect among that
> class of people concerned in the African trade a degree of
> moral perfection that is not to be found in Great Britain itself.
> Ought the records of the Old Bailey to be considered as a fair
> criterion by which to estimate the character of the English
> nation? ... I do declare, in the most solemn manner, that I
> consider the negroes in the British West Indies to be in as
> comfortable a state as the lower orders of mankind in any

country in Europe. Before the agitation of this question, their minds were at ease and they were perfectly contented with their situation. ... There is more wretchedness and poverty in the parish of St Giles in which I live than there is in the whole of the extensive colonies that now are, and formerly were, under the dominion of Great Britain.

(Mr Baillie, 1792)

There was a danger that the spirit of the age was unslipping too readily its bonds with the past and with dangerous portents for the future.

We do not find in the Parliamentary History ... the least tendency to such wild and destructive doctrines as the present. No, they are reserved for this age of novelty and innovation, and for the temper and disposition of a certain description of people which are amply manifested by the publications of the most inflammatory and dangerous tendency with which our daily papers are crowded and disgraced. I am perfectly satisfied that the question before this House is only an introduction to greater evils. ... The abolition of the slave trade will be an absolute breach of the compact that ties the colonies to the mother country; and being founded on injustice, and contrary to the spirit and meaning of the laws of England, will meet with universal resistance.

(Mr Baillie, 1792)

The situation of the negroes in the West Indies colonies is equal, nay superior, to the condition of the labouring poor of this country. They are better fed and more comfortably accommodated. ... The best of the negroes does not in general perform half as much labour as even the most indifferent of our labourers.

(Mr Fuller, 1804)

I come into the House with an unimpassioned vacancy of head

and heart, but with all my might I would oppose [abolition]. We have by want of temperance and of prudent conduct lost America. The House should beware of being carried away by the meteors they have been dazzled with.

(Mr Drake, 1791)

The country ought to be loath to apply double standards.

It is no more than the law of this country; for what are the convicts that are annually transported to Botany Bay but slaves?

(Duke of Clarence, 1799)

With respect to the charge of injustice upon the African merchants ... no such charge can apply for they only buy slaves whom the African states thought proper to dispose of. ... The African states are as competent to transport such offenders as we are those whom we send to America or Botany Bay. ... The right of the African princes is recognised by the practice of our own country.

(Mr Fuller, 1804)

The major weakness, it was maintained, in the campaigners' case was their detachment from the reality of the slaves' lot.

There does not exist a more happy race than the slaves in our colonies if any trust is to be placed in outward appearances which universally indicates cheerfulness and contentment. ... History, ancient and modern, proves the universal existence of slavery in all countries of Africa inhabited by negroes and that this system prevailed ages before the commencement of the European slave trade. ... Three-fourths of the negroes are in a state of slavery [in Africa]. Such then being the state of the population ... where the inhabitants are totally ignorant of any other distinction than that of master and slave, how will the condition of these slaves be ameliorated by the extinction of one branch only of the trade. The European trade in slaves is derived from that description of individuals who are slaves in their own country and if put an end to not one less will exist in Africa.

(Mr Hughan, 1807)

The fact therefore is that this measure cannot produce any reduction in the number of slaves in Africa and not one less will be exported from that continent; a temporary interruption of the trade might perhaps take place and involve the objects of it in horrors on the coast to which they are not during its continuance exposed.

(Mr Hughan, 1807)

Behind this last sentiment lay the key to one of the main planks of the argument against abolition: that the trade was in fact to the distinct advantage of the African.

The whole body of the people in all parts of Africa [are] in the condition of absolute slavery. [Citing an example of an African king who was about to execute captured prisoners of war], the King of Kasson, having received information of the French traders on the Senegal river, spared the lives of the captives ... and sent them thither for sale. On this occasion at least, the slave trade promoted the cause of humanity, for it can hardly be doubted that the king of Kasson's prisoners would have shared the same fate as the other [dead warriors] if avarice had not prevailed over revenge in the mind of the savage king.

(Mr Edwards, 1798)

The abolition of the slave trade would cause many Africans to be murdered since there would be no sale for the prisoners of war.

(Mr Thornton, 1798)

The slave trade tends in a very considerable degree to lessen this waste of human blood and the kings of the country instead of slaughtering their captives now sell them to the nations of Europe. They are conveyed from a country of barbarous superstition to a land of civilization and humanity. In my opinion therefore, the clamours against the trade are groundless.

(Mr Henniker Major, 1798)

The state of Africa is composed of small hostile tribes in the lowest state of barbarism, of different religions and languages; [where] there must be frequent wars; and where there are no regular establishments to guard and maintain prisoners [and] no parole of honour to exchange; the history of mankind is undenied to this point. What can the savage do to debarrass himself of his prisoner but put him to death? ... What then is the effect of this Bill? ... That within your own dominions which you wish to protect you will cause cruelty and slaughter and in the other parts of Africa you will increase the demand for slaves and every atrocity and enormity you complain of.

(Earl of Westmoreland, 1799)

The Africans are accustomed to slavery in their own country and the taking them to another quarter of the globe is therefore no great hardship.

(Sir William Young, 1804)

The state of the slaves in Africa is truly deplorable and therefore taking them away, particularly to the English colonies, is a relief to them.

(Mr Fuller, 1804)

The abolition of the slave trade would be the scourge of Africa; as a planter I wish it to take place; but as a cosmopolite I desire its continuance out of humanity to the inhabitants of the coast of Africa.

(Mr Petrie, 1799)

So noble! A rich vein of such altruistic concern for one's fellow man was mined, without hint of self-interest, for all it was worth.

[I have] reason to apprehend a sanguinary result of abolishing the slave trade ... [from the] occasional famines in the interior country, from the droughts and from the horrid devastations by locusts, when the people, from very necessity become cannibals, or sell their supernumeraries who aggravate the famine and must otherwise starve or be put to death....

... a surcharge of wretchedness and of depravity as resulting from the measure proposed is what I augur and what I deprecate....

By humanity being the principle as applied to this question, I should suppose humane treatment and consequences of more goodness and more happiness to be the object. 'No', say these wonderful orators, 'a traffic in human flesh is not a moment to be borne with; let it be carried on by whom it will; let it be aggravated by all the miseries incident to a contraband trade of life and fever under the torrid zone; let the consequences of Great Britain suppressing suddenly her share of it be what they will; the national honour, glory and character require that suppression; the consequences are not at our door.' My answer is short: my conscience tells me that the consequences are at our door.

(Sir William Young, 1791)

[Do the proponents] suppose that the slave dealers or merchants in [Africa] will march these poor creatures back to the different places where they were born or had been brought and deliver them again to their parents or relatives? If that is not the case, I fear they will be murdered as the easiest way of getting rid of them when there is no longer any mandate or means of disposing of them.

... abolition will be attended with great cruelties and massacres.

(Mr Rose, 1804)

The outcome affected more than just the slaves. Try as they might, opponents could not abstain entirely from reflecting a little self-concern. Apocalyptic visions were offered as to the effect on the whole fabric of the nation.

The abolition of the trade will ruin the West Indies, destroy our Newfoundland fishery, which the slaves in the West Indies support by consuming that part of the fish which is fit for no other consumption, and consequently, by cutting off this great source of seamen, annihilate our marine.

(Alderman Watson, 1791)

The time in which we live will constitute an awful period in the history of the world; for a spirit of subversion is gone forth which sets at nought the wisdom of our ancestors and the lessons of experience. Those ranks and gradations which constitute the strength and the ornament of society are everywhere broken down; and the lowest of mankind are raised to a level with the greatest, the most virtuous and the most enlightened. In such a conjunction, the [abolitionists] come forward and propose measures which in their consequences will raise the standard of rebellion in the West India islands. [They] tell the poor innocent negroes that they are unjustly and inhumanly brought into their present condition and of course that they have nothing to do but to murder their masters and plant the tree of liberty on their graves ... if [Mr Wilberforce] proceeds, he will raise a consuming fire which will not be extinguished until both classes are exterminated.

(Mr Edwards, 1798)

[Abolition had] consequences of which I am persuaded will prove fatal to the best interests of this country. As soon as France makes peace with this country ... her first object will be to get complete possession of the slave trade and if she succeeds in that object it will soon appear that she had got possession of an engine that will work the downfall of the naval superiority of this country.

(Earl St Vincent, 1807)

The French ... are foremost for [the slave trade's] continuance and extension. It is apparent therefore that if we are disposed to sacrifice our African trade, other nations will not enter into so ruinous a plan. Will [the French] suffer a trade upon which their whole commerce turns, to languish? No: they will thank us for our mistaken ideas of humanity and will profit by them! The disadvantage would be ours; the advantage would be theirs! ... I think it does not require much penetration or judgment to detect and expose the fallacious doctrine of those who would attempt to abolish what other nations encourage and protect....

[There was even the risk that] our present wild, fanatical manner of conducting this speculation may alienate the affections of our colonies who, through a deluge of blood, may work out for themselves another independence.

(Colonel Tarleton, 1792)

The very existence of the country was at stake.

By an abolition, several hundred ships, 7,000 sailors and some millions of industrious mechanics will lose their employment and be rendered worse than useless; for a sudden chasm of this sort will undoubtedly be productive of the most dangerous consequences to society. ... If with an imprudent temerity we daringly strike at the root of our commerce, we undermine our present advantages, destroy our future expectations and the representatives of the people will be guilty of suicide upon the laws, the prosperity and the constitution of England.

(Colonel Tarleton, 1792)

A decade and a half later, in the middle of a desperate war

against Napoleon, the now promoted General Tarleton was as pessimistic as ever.

> At all times I have thought this a most ruinous measure. ... Are not, I would ask, our principle means of security derived from our seamen and these are in great measure ... procured by the trade of Liverpool? It is not a little astonishing, therefore, to hear one say that this is the time for abolishing a trade which supplies us with so many seamen. Is the time when we are engaged in such a war as the present, a war in which so many seamen are required, upon whom we rest as our chief security, is this a time for such a measure that goes to complete the ruin of one of the chief nurseries from which our seamen and consequently our measures of security are in great measure derived? This measure is certainly founded on the opinions respecting the rights of man which have produced so much horror and devastation all over the world.
>
> (General Tarleton, 1805)

From the earliest days of the campaign, opponents had seen nothing but the direst consequences.

> If slavery is abolished, the negroes will suppose themselves on a footing with their masters and then an end will be put to all order, management and safety. If the measure is carried into execution, I think we might as well give up our colonies and islands entirely at the same moment.
>
> (Mr Stanley, 1791)

> With regard to the emancipation of the slaves, I have only to say that the opinion of those who have the best local information on the subject is that such a measure would produce the downfall of the empire.
>
> (General Gascoyne, 1807)

Let the House consider the importance of these colonies to the general interest of the nation and then weigh consequences. The West India trade composes one third of the whole amount of the trade both import and export of Great Britain. Put not this great stake to hazard.

(Mr Hughan, 1807)

In short, no-one would win.

[There would be] the ... ruin of the British Empire resulting from it. As to Africa, this measure will produce no benefit to that country for there will not be less slavery after our abolishing the trade than before it; in the West Indies it will tend to produce discontent among the negroes; to individuals it will be a great loss and injustice and will prove ruinous to numbers who have a claim to the protection of this country. France and other rival nations will most probably refuse to imitate our example and will redouble this traffic to our ruin.

(Mr Williams, 1807)

An interruption of the trade would strike at the heart of the entrepreneurial spirit of the country.

The principle [of abolishing the trade] is founded in injustice and every clause is replete with tyranny and oppression. ... The Bill will also terminate all spirit of adventure, all incitement to industry, all thirst of emulation, for hitherto it has been the hope of overseers to rise in the world as soon as they had obtained that employment and the means they had of doing so was by saving a portion of their wages to purchase two or three negroes which they let out to the planter for hire....

... Every gentleman of character and fortune will be liable to lose his reputation, to suffer in his estate and be separated from his wife, his children, his country and his dearest connections.

(Sir William Young, 1796)

If the last sentiment about the misfortunes destined to
befall the distressed planter smacked of any similarity to
those which were inflicted on every slave transported from
Africa, the irony was completely lost on the speaker.

Legislators, it was argued, owed a duty to those planters
whom they had earlier encouraged to do precisely that for
which they were now being pilloried.

> How far is the House justified in putting an end to a trade [in
> slaves] after it had encouraged the produce of certain com-
> modities [in the West Indies] depending upon the trade and
> altering the course in which so much money is invested?
>
> (Earl Temple, 1804)

> It would be unjust towards those who were encouraged to
> cultivate the colonial wastes to deprive them of the means.
> The negroes enjoy complete protection and their property is
> better secured than our own for they pay no taxes.
>
> (Mr Dent, 1799)

> Parliament which has always countenanced the trade ... can-
> not, without a breach of faith, [outlaw it].
>
> (Colonel Tarleton, 1791)

> It is not at all clear that it is just for the mother country to treat
> the colonies in the way she has, by first giving legislative
> encouragement to the traffic in question and afterwards, when
> large properties have been embarked in them, endeavouring
> thus to put a stop to it and thereby involving in beggary and
> ruin those who have risked their property and thereby added
> greatly to the wealth, prosperity and aggrandisement of the
> whole empire.
>
> (General Gascoyne, 1806)

It was a powerful joust at the conscience of the government. If that was not enough, they were not backward in coming forward in the cause of the slaves themselves. Piety knew few bounds when the planters essayed forth on the limitless harm that would be done to those whom the campaigners professed to be helping.

> The effect of the creditor pressing on the planter will be fatal to the slave. ... Slaves are liable for seizure for debts in default of other goods and chattels; and in a sale of slaves, under such circumstances, there is no provision to guard against the separation of families. ... Doth not such separation constitute a principal share of that very extreme of outrage on the rights and feelings of human creatures which [campaigners] strongly deprecate in Africa? Why institute new causes of such separation in the West Indies? ... I have shown that the cause of humanity is no gainer by such precipitate undertakings.
>
> (Sir William Young, 1791)

The campaigners' new-found concern for the welfare of slaves came in for solid attack throughout. The moral-cum-religious basis of the case received predictable counter blasts from those who searched in vain amongst the authorities so frequently used to bolster the abolitionists' arguments. Indeed, in those very same authorities, opponents found grist for their own mill.

> I read as an authority that slavery is not incompatible with Christianity and religion the opinions of the Bishop of Gloucester, St Paul and several other saints [who] in their writings make mention of bondsmen without adducing any arguments against the commerce in slaves.
>
> (Mr Stanley, 1791)

[Quoting Leviticus 25: 44-46*] The above clearly proves that
*For footnote see next page

slavery has from the earliest times been countenanced and
authorised by religion itself.

(General Gascoyne, 1806)

In the sacred books I can find no such authority [that religion
outlaws slavery or its trade]. In the Old Testament, the slave
trade or the sale of men is spoken of indifferently just as other
trades....

... in the Epistle of Paul to Philemon, Paul sends back
Onesimus ... who was Philemon's slave and had run away from
his master – he sends him back, I say, to resume his station
without one word expressive of his disapprobation of slavery
or in vindication of Onesimus who had fled from it.

(Mr Hibbert, 1807)

A favourite riposte was, simply, that slavery had got a bad
press.

It is absurd to suppose that the merchants whose profit arises
from the number of healthy Africans they land in the West
India islands would not attend to their own interests and take
every possible care to preserve their health.

(Lord Rodney, 1788)

Of the hardship which the negroes suffer I really know nothing. They have, on the contrary, considerable means of comfort. They have it in their power to save money; but this
money they prefer spending in wakes and other meetings

---

* Both thy bondmen and thy bondmaids, which thou shalt have, shall be of
the heathen that are round about you; of them shall ye buy bondmen and
bondmaids. Moreover, of the children of the strangers that do sojourn among
you, of them shall ye buy ... and they shall be your possession. And ye shall
take them as an inheritance for your children after you, to inherit them for a
possession; they shall be your bondmen for ever.

where they enjoy themselves according to their own peculiar
customs.

(Mr Fuller, 1804)

I am persuaded that the negroes in the West Indies are in
general cheerful and happy. They are fond of ornaments: and
I appeal to the observation of every gentleman whether it is
the characteristic of miserable persons to show a fondness for
finery?

(Colonel Phipps, 1791)

However strawlike was the clutching, at the end of the day
there was always the self-evident conclusion that it was the
Africans' own fault.

I have never heard the Africans deny their mental inferiority.
They have never hesitated to confess to me that they could
not vie with Europeans in talent or knowledge. In matters of
ingenuity or calculation, they are no match for the inhabitants of the other quarters of the world. ... If [they] had been
capable of civilization, they could easily have been able to
drive off their coasts a few African slave ships and thus have
prevented the original establishment of the trade. Something
in the internal circumstances of the country must then have
favoured the establishment of the system.

(Mr Fuller, 1804)

Is it pretended that the mere possession or use or transfer of a
slave in Africa is unjust or inhuman? Is it unjust? By all the
laws and customs of Africa existing from the remotest antiq-
uity it is authorised; and the abstract rights of man cannot be
profitably applied to societies existing under established laws.
What is consistent with those laws must be accounted just. Is
the same thing in Africa inhuman? Surely not. We have
abundance of evidence to prove that during famines which are

frequent in Africa, multitudes of the natives fly to slavery as a refuge and without it must inevitably perish. ... Here is Africa ... inviting the slave trade, not the slave trade seducing Africa.

(Mr Hibbert, 1807)

The emancipation of the negroes appears impolitic and impracticable. Civilization is progressive, and precedes the grant of freedom. ... They are perfectly resigned to their situation and look for nothing beyond it.

(Mr Vaughan, 1792)

The natives of Africa are not yet sufficiently matured by civilization to receive their liberty and freedom; emancipating those who are not sufficiently enlightened to understand and feel the blessings of liberty would be like putting a sword into the hands of a madman.

(Mr Peel, 1794)

There really was no alternative.

The West Indies cannot be cultivated by Europeans whose constitutions will not bear fatigue in that climate. It is therefore necessary, if they are to be cultivated at all, it must be by some other class of the human species, who being natives of warm climates, are able to endure that degree of labour and fatigue which no Europeans can do in that climate. ... Some say that it is much better to employ free negroes than slaves and that the labour of free men would be more productive. This is however only a supposition, a mere theory. The fact is known to be that the natives of warm countries are not naturally disposed to labour. In warm countries the climate produces the means of subsistence with so little labour that they have no necessity and consequently no inclination for laborious work, and for that species of labour which is necessary for raising sugar and other colonial produce it is absolutely necessary to use something of compulsion. It might appear to some to be a great hardship to compel men to labour but it is the common condition of the lower orders of society.

(Sir William Pulteney, 1805)

One of the last debates on the successful Bill which finally abolished the trade offered a crystallization of all the interweaving doubts and concerns which had shaped the decades of resistance.

Taking into view on the one hand the radical barbarous internal situation in Africa, the inadequate and incomplete object of that abolition which is proposed by the Bill and, on the other, the magnitude of the danger to the colonies, I am of opinion that the remedy is worse than the disease and we are incurring a most fearful risk without the power or the means of extending to Africa the practical benefits of those principles of justice and humanity on which the Bill is speciously founded....

... [I view] with fearful anxiety [abolition] leading, necessarily leading, to a fatal paroxysm of disaffection and insurrection and to a renewal of those revolutionary horrors from the effects of which Europe is not now free and which will live in the recollection of mankind, an awful lesson of the dangerous effects of innovating schemes ... and a just and powerful motive for a reverential deference to those long established habits and institutions which may be reckoned the foundation of national prosperity and happiness. When the negroes in the islands learn that the parliament has pronounced their condition to be unjust and inhuman and that they are not to be benefited by the Bill, it will be sufficient to animate them to a spirit of discontent and a desire of redress from which a scene of misery and horror may be contemplated equal in enormity to that which has lately disgraced the character of France. And can it be the policy of Great Britain to encounter all these fearful hazards from a doubting chance of benefit to the native

> African who is in a situation not to be benefited by your exertions, a situation of hopeless and hereditary slavery?
>
> (Mr Browne, 1807)

The House of Lords had the last say. On the last day of the last debate, one peer sought to put into perspective the magnitude of the change that was about to be made.

> Nothing good can be expected from it. ... I would venture to say that it is to the existence of the slave trade that your Lordships are indebted for their being now sitting in this place. Our existence depends on the strength of our navy and the strength of our navy is chiefly derived from the slave trade ... The town of Liverpool alone now sends out a greater number of privateers than were employed by the whole of the country against the enemy in the time of Queen Elizabeth.
>
> (Earl of Westmoreland, 1807)

In the end, though, it was to no avail. Having passed the Bill, the leader in the House put a different gloss on the act just done.

> [I] congratulate the House on having now performed one of the most glorious acts that have ever been done by any assembly of any nation in the world.
>
> (Lord Grenville, 1807)

POSTSCRIPT

The abolition in British colonies of the practice of slavery itself followed, but not until the passing of almost another three decades and then with immense caution. An Act in 1833 – twenty-six years after the trade was outlawed – gave the slaves legal freedom but at the same time apprenticed them to their former owners for a further seven years before they could become free agents (a relaxation from the government's initial proposal for a twelve-year scheme). The long preparation was an essential safeguard in the eyes of the reluctant abolitionists. As early as 1824 the concerns had been laid bare.

To let in the full light of freedom on eyes scarcely unsealed, eyes from which the scales of bondage have not yet been purged away would indeed be a perilous experiment. It would indeed be a fatal gift. To be safely enjoyed it must be gradually and diligently earned. ... This condition is the legitimate stimulant of laudable industry and the best corrective of ambitious desire. No effort of an individual and no enactment of a legislature can relieve human nature from the operation of this condition. To attempt to shorten the road between desire and attainment is nine times out of ten to go astray.

... I am fully persuaded that freedom when acquired under the regulations prescribed by government will be a more delightful as well as more safe and more stable possession than if it were bestowed by a sudden acclamation. In dealing with the negro, Sir, we must remember that we are dealing with a being possessing the form and strength of a man but the intellect only of a child. To turn him loose in the manhood of his physical strength, in the maturity of his physical passions, but in the infancy of his uninstructed reason would be to raise up a creature resembling the splendid fiction of a recent romance [Frankenstein]. ... Such would be the effect of a sudden emancipation before the negro was prepared for the enjoyment of well-regulated liberty.

(Mr Canning, 1824)

I am not an advocate for ... premature abolition. The evils of such a course would, I feel, be more noxious than the evils of slavery itself. It has always been my opinion that the emancipation of the mind should precede the emancipation of the body. Religion and education should prepare the way for the approach of freedom.

(Bishop of Bath and Wells, 1826)

For some, the whole idea was never likely to be successful.

The dangerous delusion under which so many [abolitionists] labour is [that they] presume [the slave] to have attained a degree of civilization from which he is yet far removed, that he has acquired those habits which will render him an industrious labourer if he were free and that he regards freedom with the same feeling as we do, instead of considering it, as he really does, in no other light than as a total cessation from any employment.

(Mr Burge, 1832)

If the slaves are liberated it will be impossible that the negro and the white man can live together because it is out of the question that the whites can possess their property while the others possess greater force, both from their congeniality to the climate and their immensely greater numbers. Will the black man then cultivate sugar which the advocate of his cause contends is the cause of the loss of human life? If the negroes are liberated, where are we then to get sugar? The consequence will be that we shall not only lose the capital already sunk but our money must go to foreigners for sugar and we shall have no other sugar than that produced by slave labour: for let it be relied on – there will not be one slave less and we shall lose that power of ameliorating the condition of the negroes we now possess which will be totally out of our power with respect to Cuba, the Brazils and other colonies belonging to foreign nations. I will go further and say ... we should renew the slave trade because these foreign colonies, in order to keep up the supply, will still carry on the trade.

(Mr Baring, 1831)

This was not the first time he had offered his thoughts to the House on the subject.

> The question of the actual emancipation of the slaves is one which appears to me to be attended with the greatest difficulties. [If, as was intended, any child born of a slave would be a free person], if these children are born free, who is to take care of them? One of the greatest advantages of the abolition of the slave trade is that it tends to an improvement both in the condition and in the treatment of the negro females and children: it gives an interest to the master [in the absence of replacements from Africa] in rearing the children and in taking proper care of the mother while she is breeding. But if you do away with the interest of the proprietor in the offspring, which undoubtedly will be the effect [of gradual abolition] all this beneficial result of the abolition of the slave trade immediately ceases.
>
> ... If any measures are taken for abolishing slavery ... they must have the effect of endangering the peace and tranquillity of our colonies. If we are to arrive at a free black population, the inevitable consequence will be that the whole of the islands would be lost to this country; there would be an end to our colonial system. It would be absurd to suppose that a free black population ... would consent to continue to devote their labours to proprietors.
>
> (Mr Baring, 1823)

As ever with compromises, the eventual scheme of emancipation also had its critics for falling between two stools.

> Under [the plan] the negroes will be too much freemen to be coerced as slaves and they will be too much slaves to be actuated by the motives that actuate freemen.
>
> (Mr Hill, 1833)

Two:
Children

'A LIBEL ON THE HUMANITY OF PARENTS'
THE SUPPRESSION OF CHILD LABOUR

To the twentieth century mind nothing perhaps so starkly embodies our comforting sense of distance and progress from the cold brutality of early Victorian times than the subject of children and in particular child labour. How could one possibly have held with humanity the notions regarding the exploitation of children for profit that were the mainstay of the industrial revolution in early nineteenth century Britain? From today's perspective there is no questioning it: the early Victorians and their predecessors are pictured as callous, cruel and heartless. At the time, things seemed a little different and it was by no means only greedy factory owners who protested against reform.

In the first half of the century, the interests of the young and vulnerable were advanced on two complementary fronts – the ponderous development of education provision (as we see later in this chapter) and the increasing regulation of the emergent master of the age, the factory owner. Both began about the same time, but the attack on child labour relentlessly outran the compensating efforts in education. This left for much of the century whole generations in limbo, barred from wage earning but still without any widely available possibility of educational advancement to offer hope for the future. It made for no easy transition. At the time, the deprivation of working opportunities for children seemed to many quite rational minds as an imposition on the liberties of the nation without any real consequential advantages. There ensued a debate sustained over decades which brought forth from both sides mutually conflicting medical evidence about the actual conditions in mills and factories and their effects which children endured, a debate which generated much heat but little light – neither side was ever going to be persuaded from the righteousness of its own position.

Progressively hours were shortened and the minimum age at which children could be employed was raised. The first modern Factory Act in 1819 fixed for children aged nine a limit of twelve hours a day (!). It only applied to cotton mills. Elsewhere in other factories and in the mines children as young as six and seven put in more hours a day than most adults do now. It was to be 1891 before the age limit for employment was raised to eleven; it only reached fourteen as recently as 1920.

While history came down on the side of the reformers against child labour, perhaps because the reformers had also on their side the not insignificant ally of sentiment, the bare bones of the argument, stripped of such sentiment, offered a more finely balanced tussle, one that to the impartial observer of the time would have been no easy one to pronounce upon. The proposition, it had to be acknowledged, represented a fundamental shift of responsibility from the parent – who, it might be assumed, should know best – to the anonymity of the State and what were often disparagingly perceived as 'do-gooders.'

> [I protest against] the principle of legislating for the regulation of the authority of parents over their children, who must be best aware of the quantity of work those children are able to bear and who must undoubtedly feel most for their distress. Such a proceeding is a libel on the humanity of parents.
>
> (Mr Curwen, 1816)

At the dawn of the age of government intervention in the private affairs of the population it was not an inconsiderable argument.

[Such intervention] is an imputation on the feelings of parents to suppose that they would suffer their children to work to the prejudice of their health; and it is also an imputation on gentlemen at the head of manufactories to suppose that they would compel children to make excessive exertions.

(Mr Curwen, 1816)

[I ask] whether it is possible that individuals in the situation of parents, who it must be generally admitted have some portion of the milk of human nature where their offspring are concerned, should seek to wean away the health and spirits of their children by over-exertion?

... [I wish to] remark upon the propriety of legislating between the parent and the child: it goes to say that those of the poor order are not fit to be trusted with the management of their own children.

(Mr Curwen, 1818)

The theme of these opening gambits was stark and simple. Who knew best – parent or government?

The object of the Bill is said to be the protection of children's health and morals against the rapacity both of their parents and masters. This is as much to say that Parliament will no longer trust parents with the care of their own children.

(Lord Stanley, 1818)

A whole battery of moral questions were raised by this development.

[It] strikes directly against that established principle which gives the parent the labour of his child during his minority so long as he gives him adequate support. The result of such a regulation must inevitably be that the children will cease to be employed and that their parents will lose the value of their labour while the children are consigned to unprofitable idleness. ... Masters might avoid any inconvenience by employing in their works only men and women, but what can the children do when their means of support are taken away? At present parents find a difficulty in bringing them up well even by the united produce of their labour. The difficulty will be much greater when the children themselves are prevented from contributing anything towards their own support. It should be considered what effect the measure is likely to have upon morals. Limiting the hours of labour cannot tend to improve them. On the contrary, it will only give more opportunities for idleness and all the bad consequences arising from it.

(Lord Stanley, 1818)

I cannot comprehend how it is possible, by legislative enactments, to supply the place of parental affections [on] behalf of the child. I doubt ... whether Parliament can protect children as effectively as their parents.

(Mr Hope, 1832)

Legislation dictated by feelings and affections, however amiable or benevolent unless strictly under the control of the reason and the judgment, is not the best means for securing the welfare and happiness of those for whom the feelings are most interested.

... It is the parent who makes the contract and sanctions the work of the child; [no-one] can feel a stronger safeguard for the child than the natural affection of the parent. If the master and parent conspire together, as it is alleged they do, to overwork the child, what contrivance has the ingenuity of the authors of this Bill devised to prevent them? What substitute has it invented for parental affection? What protector and guardian has it found out who, stimulated by a stronger impulse than the love of the parent and armed with more than a father's inquisitorial powers, should continuously watch over the hours of labour and of rest?

(Mr Hyett, 1833)

There was a plausible double strand to the argument. First, that government should not busy itself in the freely entered into transactions of the people; and second, and even harder to refute on objective grounds, such intervention would actually result in more, not less, harm – however well-meaning the intention.

> Every parent is the natural guardian of his child. It is too much, perhaps, to take that guardianship out of the parent's hands by the interference of the House. If a parent derived assistance to the amount of 8 shillings a week from his child's labour, it might seem cruel and unjust to deprive him of it.
>
> (Lord Lascelles, 1818)

> I object [to such reform] but so far from considering myself an enemy of the children who are the objects of the proposed [measure], I reckon myself their friend [since] they are improved in health, number and comfort by the free disposal of their labour. If their hours of working are reduced, their wages likewise must be reduced and then they might be exposed to the hardships of want. Two sets of children will be employed to do the labour of one and half of their present wages can then only be allowed them.
>
> (Earl of Rosslyn, 1819)

The result, he added, was only too clear.

> Under the present system the children have labour, food and clothing; under the proposed one they will have idleness, poverty and wretchedness.

And the ripples would spread wider throughout society.

Will morals be improved as degrading poverty advances? Will education spread when wages become lower? Will manners become more civilised and will religion penetrate the masses when discontent has taken the place of prosperity and when ease and comfort have given place to despair?

(Sir James Graham, Home Secretary, 1844)

I must say that practical benevolence is more praiseworthy than mistaken humanity.... See then the blessed effect of the change – the price to be paid for the purchase of 'moral' feeling. Morality is all very well; but will it flourish in beggary and starvation?

(Marquess of Londonderry, 1842)

It was often difficult, critics said, to know whose interests were being pursued – the children's or the self-satisfaction of those who set themselves up as their benefactors. What particularly rankled with opponents of reform was that it was very easy for reform-minded moralizers to introduce change when they bore none of the costs. Only those whom they purported to be 'saving' paid the price. How easy it was to be moral at someone else's expense.

[The reformers] deprive parents of the right to dispose of the time of their children to the best advantage. ... [They] go to the length of saying to the parents of children, 'Your necessities drive you to send your children to work, yet we will deprive you of that power of augmenting the means of subsistence for your family without, at the same time, providing you with a substitute.' ... I think that there is something very inconsistent in such legislation.

(Mr Villiers, 1836)

I mistrust that interference on behalf of the poor which the poor are themselves to pay for.

(Dr Bowring, 1836)

Furthermore, it was not only those deprived of work who would suffer. The lot of those left would also be that much worse.

> The result must be that the [adult] operatives, unable to bear this greater reduction in the wages of the children below [the minimum age] will be compelled to work their children above that age a greater number of hours than before ... and adults instead of obtaining relief might have to work for fourteen or sixteen hours. This will prove more injurious than the existing system.
>
> (Colonel Torrens, 1833)

But at root it was the interests of the children which were being compromised.

> I protest against [any reduction in hours] since I believe that it would be to inflict the most grievous tyranny upon those who having only their labour to sell have a right to make the most of it. Great injury will thus be done to manufacturers but double injury to those employed in them.
>
> (Mr Poulett Thomson, 1836)

Time and again the argument returned to the central issue which such reforms posed – who knew the interests of the people best: the people themselves or this anonymous, do-gooding State?

> As a general principle I think nothing should be done by means of legislation to draw out of their usual channels, out of those channels into which they will naturally flow, capital and labour, forcing and seducing them into other channels which they do not naturally seek.
>
> (Lord Brougham, 1842)

People were quite well able to make these judgments themselves.

It becomes us to consider in what way such a trade or employment [as manufacturing] is pernicious. If it is merely disadvantageous to the interests of the persons concerned in it, ... if we thought that the persons employed in such a trade might earn more or might be better off by engaging in another, in that point of view legislation has no right whatever to interfere between them and their occupation. Their interest is their affair.

... I remind the House that we are making laws to bind the labouring classes of the community and not intended to affect the rich. We are rearing up a power to attack not the strong but the weak, not to control the great but to crush the feeble.

(Lord Brougham, 1842)

A little less plausible was the contention that factory owners possessed a self-regulating sense of fair play.

It is generally expedient not to interfere with free labour. For on what is that principle founded? On the knowledge that by leaving the regulation of the labour in the hands of the master, if he works his labourer too hard, that labourer can resort to some other employment.

(Mr Wynn, 1818)

There was though a hint of logic in the argument against such an all-encompassing approach the reformers sought. The age of a child was no sure indicator of a certain number of hours' work capacity.

The fault ... is the fixing a limit to the exercise of labour which is much the same as if one size of shoe is ordered to be made for every foot. The only rational course of proceeding is to leave

labour free and then the time of labour will be properly
regulated between the employers and the employed.

(Earl of Lauderdale, 1818)

I contend that those person who are acquainted with the
management of cotton factories are much better able to judge
of what regulations are fit to be adopted than those who know
nothing about the practical effect of the existing law.

(Mr Philips, 1825)

Much more to the point, and much more persuasive an
argument, was the fear of opponents that the good owners
(who needed no chastisement) would comply anyway while
the bad, for whom the draconian laws were being framed,
would simply evade the regulations and steal a march on
the honest traders.

I sincerely believe it will go far to drive the most respectable
and humane manufacturers ... out of their establishments
which will fall by degrees into the hands of the less scrupulous
and the less humane.

(Mr Hyett, 1833)

Unless the Government inspection schemes were effective
– and the thought of squads of official factory inspectors as
the inevitable consequence of such intervention filled
many more Members with greater despair than the act of
regulation itself. Despite whatever army of snoopers the
Government created, the shady trader would always find a
way to circumvent any law which did not coincide with the
general interest but which went contrary to it.

We prohibited foreign trade, but the smuggler came, a public
benefactor, though a breaker of the laws – and tumbled down
the barrier that legislation had raised against friendly communication. So laws to regulate wages and hours of labour and

conditions of contract are merely cobwebs broken through at will, because it is in the interest of master and servant that they should be broken.

(Dr Bowring, 1836)

For some, taking the wider view, the insidious spirit of the age for meddling in other people's affairs was a growing curse on society.

There is a Quixotic spirit abroad at the present day which singling out a few of the abuses to which human nature always will be liable ... rushes on to remedy them with breathless haste, regardless of the dangers it might inflict on those whom it wishes to relieve....
... Are we in these days of liberty of thought and liberty of action to recur to the olden time of chartered guilds and exclusive companies, prescribing ... the hours of manufacture? There is indeed in the present day a zeal, I might almost say an excessive lust, of legislation, a mania for making little laws for little occasions when we ought rather to be doing our best to be getting rid of those which are causing the mischief.

(Mr Hyett, 1833)

On the Bill to abolish what perhaps comes most readily to modern minds as the evocation of the harshness of the age – child chimney sweepers – the debate was widened on this point. Opponents maintained that what the reformers were doing was something more than mechanical regulation of working practices. They were attempting to enforce morality by Act of Parliament. It was a subtle but by no means easily dismissed argument.

I object to the Bill because it is not fit for the legislature to lay down rules of humanity to individuals; because by doing so, the very principles of humanity will be rooted up: for greater

cruelties will then be practised than any which the Bill goes to
provide against.

(Earl of Lauderdale, 1819)

The simple point was that by legislating on certain themes,
others not covered would become, as it were, sanctioned by
default. It would remove people's natural power of recog-
nising right from wrong and put all life's relations on the
black and white scale of legislative enactments. Anything
not expressly forbidden would be deemed permissable.

It is impossible to legislate on subjects of this kind. ... [It]
originates in a mistaken spirit of humanity, the attempt to
enforce which by law [will produce] effects the very opposite of
those which are intended. If the legislature attempts to lay
down a moral code for the people there is always a danger that
every feeling of benevolence will be extirpated.

(Earl of Lauderdale, 1819)

'A GOOD AND NOT A GABBLING PEOPLE ...
IS WANTED'
EDUCATION

As with many of the areas of life we touch upon in this volume, the notion of state education – from virtually the cradle of birth to the coming of age, compulsory and ranging over as many subjects of learning as the mind can comprehend – would have been unimaginable even to the most respectable and forward-thinking early Victorian MP musing on ways for the improvement of the people. Perhaps more clearly than any other part of our national life, the basis of our education system, until at least the late 1980s, still reflected the feelings, prejudices and concerns of the Victorian age when even amongst education's most avid proponents there was a persistent and remarkable degree of caution about reform. The consensus of Government and non-government Members alike from the earliest times right down to the great milestone Act of 1870 was to avoid as far as possible the state getting involved at all in educating the people of the country. Education, it was universally declared and acknowledged, simply was not a responsibility to which the state was beholden. The toiling classes learned their skills for future life in their apprenticeships which traders provided, and the churches dispensed spiritual and moral guidance; what more could be needed? For the vast majority of the nation's young, 'education' was to be little more than that, and only that, which was necessary for making one's way in one's station in life. Anything beyond that was unwarranted extravagance. The concept of using education to *improve* one's station in life was viewed with a wariness bordering on paranoia as dangerous and subversive of the settled structure of society.

Hence, such education as did go on – and it would always

largely confined to the basics of reading, writing and arithmetic – proceeded on a charitable or voluntary basis, by philanthropists or religious societies. (The latter were activated in part by the pragmatic realization that the Word could be spread that much more widely and permanently if the Word could actually be read by those whom they sought to win over. There was waged a vigorous tussle between the Established church and the Non-conformist sects for the hearts and minds of the nation, and education formed a major plank in the strategies of both sides – the former to retain, the latter to convert, adherents.)

Slowly – ever so slowly – the need for a better educated populace crept up on legislators, if for no other reason than that by the late 1860s huge massed industrial cities were taking shape all over the country, the electoral franchise was about to be widened still further and the fear of a growing urban class, illiterate and uneducated, began to outweigh the apparent prudence of self-denial by the State. But still the Government maintained an arm's length distance. Until the most recent years of this century, the concept of central control of education was a foreign one: education began, grew and was intended for decades to remain, a locally organized, locally provided service. That it even got that far was, for some, one of the most detrimental developments the nation could contemplate.

The earliest attempt to establish publicly funded education came in fact as part of a scheme intended primarily to reform the then equivalent of the social security system, the Poor Law. To try to reduce the burgeoning claims for relief, a modest plan in 1807 had the foresight to see that some degree of tuition for children of ordinary classes would, in the long run, aid their prospects of getting work and thus take them off the poor register. The scheme envisaged free education for two years to be taken at any time their parents chose between the ages of seven and fourteen. This was enough, though, to raise the fundamental objections of opponents.

> To carry the system of education to the labouring poor ... will, I fear, tend rather to raise their minds above their lot in life and by no means strengthen their attachments to those laborious pursuits by which they are to earn a livelihood, pursuits to which, at present, there exists throughout the poor of the country a very strong reluctance. If therefore care is not taken to blend with their education early habits of industry I fear that schooling will rather injure than serve them in result.
>
> (Mr Rose, 1807)

> I do not think ... that the occupiers of lands and houses should be taxed in order that all the children in the country should be taught to read and write, especially when it is doubtful whether writing will be of any real use.
>
> (Mr George Vansittart, 1807)

Far from being a constructive measure, it was guaranteed to be fatally disruptive to the existing order of things.

> [The notion is] more pregnant with mischief than advantage to those for whose advantage it is intended and for the country in general. For however specious in theory the project might be of giving education to the labouring classes of the poor, it will, in effect, be found to be prejudicial to their morals and happiness; it will teach them to despise their lot in life instead of making them good servants in agriculture and other laborious employments to which their rank in society has destined them. Instead of teaching them subordination, it will render them factious and refractory, ... it will enable them to read seditious pamphlets, vicious books and publications against Christianity; it will render them insolent to their superiors, and, in a few years, the result will be that the legislature will

find it necessary to direct the strong arm of power towards them
and to furnish the executive magistrates with much more vigorous laws than are now in force. Besides ... it will go to burden the
country with a most enormous and incalculable expense and to
load the industrious orders of society with still heavier imposts.

(Mr Giddy, 1807)

It was barely a decade since the biggest naval mutiny the
country had ever seen. Surely the lesson of that near fatal
event for the security of the nation should be heeded.

Instruction is gaining ground by very rapid strides through the
country, perhaps too rapidly. Is the day labourer ... happier for
being instructed in reading and writing? Does the House not
recollect the mutiny at the Nore [where] the mutineers had
daily and nightly meetings [where] they employed themselves
in reading the newspapers and other publications [which]
tended much to the consequences which ensued?

(Sir T. Turton, 1807)

Besides, on the whole parents did not want it.

In many places there is a disinclination in the lower orders to
send their children to school merely for education. If this Bill
is now to be adopted, it will incur a great expense in the
erection of schools without producing much practical benefit.

(Mr Rose, 1807)

From the ages of 7 to 14 in the country places [parents] can
send their children into the fields and gain something for the
better support of their families; ... if deprived of this advantage
they will come sooner upon the parishes for relief.

(Mr Simeon, 1807)

One practical difficulty for opponents of education was

that in Scotland there already existed a system similar to that now proposed for England and which, on all the evidence, appeared to be rather successful. Such evidence did not deter the English doubters who argued away the Scottish example with ingenious aplomb.

Certainly Scotland does form an exception [where schools exist] but it can bear no analogy to the education of the people of England. The Scotch are a people that do not appear to be educated for remaining at home, they being in general inclined to move beyond their country. Their education would render them totally discontented if they did not travel into other countries. If they remained in their own country they would become extremely dissatisfied with their situation.

(Sir T. Turton, 1807)

Prejudices against education persevered for decades. In the 1830s one with so wide an appreciation of the state and character of the country as William Cobbett (he of the celebrated rural rides tour of the English provinces) could still offer a narrow view on the subject.

[I] could not consent to take from the people one single farthing in the way of taxes, directly or indirectly, in order to teach the working classes reading and writing. I am sure I should not be accused of a wish to degrade them or to deprive them of any advantages, but I think the word education is much mistaken. Education is the knowledge necessary for the situation of life in which a man is placed. Take two men for instance – suppose one of them to be able to plough and the other able to plough and make hurdles and be a good shepherd. If the first man knows how to read as well as to plough and the other man does not know how to read, even then I should say that the latter is the better man.

(1833)

He had a particular distaste for the new brand of disseminators who would be let loose on the country, 'that new race of idlers' he called teachers.

> What reason is there to tax the people for the increase of education? It is nothing but an attempt to force education – it is a French, it is a Doctrinaire Plan, and I shall always be opposed to it.
>
> (1833)

If that was not enough, could it be shown that such education as had gone on in the voluntary system had done any good?

> All this increase of education has not been productive of any good, and I venture to say that there is not a single country gentleman who will not say that the fathers of the last generation made better labourers, better servants and better men than their sons of the present generation. This proves that the labouring classes are much better without that intellectual enjoyment which [educators] are anxious to provide for them than they are with it.
>
> ... What ... is the state of crime ... now as compared with its amount at the period [when] the education of the lower orders of the people began? Why the proportion is now at least four, if not seven, times as great as it was when education commenced. ... Within the same period too, the number of bastards had increased to a most prodigious extent, so that in this respect, the morality of the people can not be said to have been advanced by education.
>
> ... It is a good people and not a gabbling people that is wanted in the country, and this smattering of education will only raise the labourers of this country above the situations best suited to their own interests and those of their families. It will put into their heads that they were not born to labour but to get their living without it.
>
> (Mr Cobbett, 1834)

The bottom line was clear.

> In short, if all are to be scholars, it will be necessary for the
> whole population to shut up their mouths and determine to eat
> no more. The interference with labour will be [the] very worst
> course which can be pursued by the legislature. By useful
> employment the youth gains habits of obedience and industry,
> but send him to school, to a drunken master or to a sober
> conceited coxcomb of a schoolmaster and he will only learn
> habits of idleness and become too great in his own conceit to
> labour.
>
> (Mr Cobbett, 1834)

As late as mid-century, fundamental doubts persisted.

> The true object of education is not to make men learned but to
> make them good men and good subjects. Education wrongfully
> imparted has only the tendency of making the criminal a more
> clever criminal.
>
> (Mr Borthwick, 1846)

The nub of the question was that there were wider issues to
consider than merely the intellectual advancement of children.

> Those who are at all conversant with agriculture know that if
> we deprive the farmer of the labour of children, agriculture can
> not be carried on. There is no machinery by which we can get
> the weeds in growing crops out of the land. It can only be done
> by the employment of children, and if that employment is
> stopped the land will be choked with weeds, the crops will
> much decrease and a national calamity will be the result.
>
> (Mr Ball, 1856)

And was it all, in fact necessary?

> I do not agree with those who are continually denying the education [level] of the English people – I think they are as well instructed as the people of any other country. There are 450 million letters sent through the Post Office annually; and who wrote them? Not the upper or middle classes but clerks and persons in subordinate situations.
>
> (Mr Hadfield, 1856)

From the earliest days a continuing theme of those who opposed state interference was that it would discourage the healthy voluntary spirit so evident in the country.

> I am entirely opposed to the interference of the State in matters connected with the education of the people. ... I believe, indeed, that State interference has done more to retard than to advance popular education, for it stops those voluntary efforts which have produced such mighty effects when left alone.
>
> (Mr Hadfield, 1856)

> The number of schools has been most extensively increased and though the voluntary exertions of individuals have not, perhaps, gone quite so far as might be wished, yet they have been very considerable. The consequences of the Government interference will, I fear, be to put an end to them. ... If that should be the case ... nothing can be more fateful to the cause of education.
>
> (Lord Althorp, Government spokesman, 1833)

> If there be one principle more certain than another, I suppose it is this, that what a people is able to do for itself, their government should not attempt to do it for it. For nothing tends so much to strengthen a people – to make them powerful, great and good – as the constant exercise of all their faculties for public objects and the carrying on of all public works and

objects by voluntary contributions among themselves.

(Mr Bright, 1847)

[Government funding] will absolutely arrest the vast progress now being made [and] run the risk of cutting the throat of a system which, if it has not done all the good that can be wished, has unquestionably effected a vast amount of good and [in its place] set up a system of local or State education to be supported by an enormous taxation.

(Mr Henley, 1855)

I cannot help thinking that it would be impossible for the ingenuity of man to devise a scheme better calculated [than the voluntary approach] to adapt itself to the wants and the wishes of the country. It is a scheme of non-interference on the part of the Government – it is a scheme by which we only seek to stimulate and to aid local efforts. Nobody need avail himself of it who does not desire it and those who are prepared to conform to its requirements derive from it the greatest advantages. Under these circumstances we ought to hesitate before we run the risk of prejudicing a system which has already met with so much success.

(Mr Liddell, 1856)

A typical argument turned logic around and maintained that harm, not good, would ensue.

[State education] means the contravention of the principle of independence and spirit which happily exists throughout our population. ... [It will] break down their spirit and destroy their independence of mind. We all know that the poor do not set much store now on what they do not earn or purchase by their own free will and the House should not lightly tamper with or do anything to impair that feeling.

... Either [State education] will be inoperable and then it

will be useless to pass [the Bill] or it would be operative and
then it would affect the system of education established in this
country in a most mischievous – perchance in a most fatal –
manner.

(Lord John Manners, 1855)

At least one old grandee felt that the instinctive good
disposition of the captains of industry was all that would be
necessary.

I hope public money will only be required as a stimulus to local
exertion; I hope the affluent who are connected with the great
seats of manufacture who have derived and are deriving their
wealth from the manufacturing industry of the country, that
they will insist upon reserving to themselves the gratifying
duty of promoting the social improvement of the working
classes and providing for them the means of rational amusement and
recreation.

(Sir Robert Peel, 1841)

It was not altogether clear indeed that any practical alternative to the voluntary approach existed. The notion of
imposing extra rates on the ratepayer to pay for education
seemed illogical.

[It is] proposed to support the schools by an educational rate to
be raised in those districts which, from poverty or want of zeal,
do not make sufficient provision for the educational requirements of the people. But it is evident that a poor district is not
the fittest field for the imposition of a fresh tax and it is equally
clear that such a measure must be calculated to increase the
hostility to an educational provision of a district in which that
hostility was already but too strongly developed.

(Mr Liddell, 1856)

The premise was that either people would be doing it voluntarily under the present system or, if they were not, no enforced system would be able to make them do it. It was all best left to individual choice. The modernizing world would encourage its own market for skills naturally.

> I believe that the poor man keeps his children at school so long and so long only as he believes is necessary to fit them for the station they have to fill in after life. ... Every railway, every telegraph and factory creates a new demand for skilled labour ... The incentives to education are therefore daily increasing, and I can not help thinking that we might look with far greater confidence to the operation of these natural causes than to any compulsory enactment for the extension of this great blessing.
>
> (Mr Liddell, 1856)

But even if it could be done, the sensibilities of the British people would not put up with it. The fact had to be faced that the commitment of public funds to education would inevitably herald that which was anathema to all: compulsory attendance.

> The State, having entered into a compact with the ratepayers, will be bound to take care that their money is not wasted and that can only be effected by obliging the children – at whatever cost to their parents – to frequent the schools. The injustice of such a proceeding is palpable. £3m – £4m represents the annual value of the wages earned by the children of the poor. ... The time might come when compulsory education will be a necessity of the State but when that period arrives it will be difficult to evade the claim of poor parents to be compensated for the loss of their children's wages.
>
> (Lord Robert Cecil, 1856)

The 'threat' – for no less a sense of foreboding coloured the debates on the issue – of compulsion had been a feature of opposition from the earliest days.

> I disapprove entirely of compulsion [which] might considerably check the spontaneous charity of many individuals; another objection is that it is teaching the persons relieved that they might claim as a right that relief which they might be taught to look upon as a favour.

(Mr Sturges Brown, 1807)

> I do not believe, either on the part of Her Majesty's Government or on the part of any other association of men ... or on the part of any individual who has education at heart [that] there can exist any intention of promoting any legislative measure ... for the purpose of making the education of the people compulsory on the people (God forbid! unless it intended to make education hateful to the people).
>
> ... I do not believe ... it will be possible if desirable, or desirable if possible, to establish a system of compulsory education in this country.

(Lord Brougham, 1837)

Education was, and would ever remain, a private matter between parents and their children.

> I think that there ought to be in no time, in no country, whatever might be the constitution of the country and the state of society, any positive and direct compulsion as to the education of the people. ... If I were required to prove that compulsion ought not to be introduced, I would ask any man who calmly reflected upon the subject, how dangerous a thing it would be, upon whatever grounds we put it, whatever temptation there might be for extending education, whatever risk there might be in the continuance of ignorance, whatever

might be the duty on the part of the parents to educate their children, whatever mischiefs might arise or whatever consequences might infest the whole community from the breach of that duty of parents – I would ask that man to consider how delicate, how perilous a matter it would be to usurp the parental office by public authority and prescribe, by a command of the State, fortified perhaps by the penalties attached to a civil offence, the line of parental management which the father and mother should pursue in taking care of the offspring which Providence and nature has committed to their care? Another answer against the compulsory principle, if indeed any other is wanting, is that it is a violation of individual liberty – it is a tyranny ... declaring that in order to educate people we would enslave them, that in order to diffuse instruction amongst them we would contract their liberty and introduce a system which would be intolerable to the citizens of a free state and only fit (if fit at all) for a country ruled by a despotic government where liberty being little known slavery is the more bearable.

(Lord Brougham, 1837)

This noble Lord, who had as recently as three years earlier been Lord Chancellor, the chief Government Peer in the Upper House, went further still.

The ... general rule I am disposed to lay down ... is not only that there should be no compulsion exercised and no interference on the part of Government as regards who should or who should not be educated at all, but that there should be no power given to the Government to educate the people – that is to say, that its interference should be excluded beyond what was absolutely necessary. With regard to the question of what course of education ought to be chosen, I would look with the greatest jealousy at the Government of any country in deciding it. It appears to me nothing more or less than tyranny for any government to have the power of ... deciding the number of schools to be established, the kind of instruction to be afforded in them, the mode of teaching to be adopted and the description of books to be read.

(Lord Brougham, 1837)

Proponents of education pointed to the continent and to the awesomely emerging Prussia which had for centuries benefited from a national compulsory system. For opponents, the very example was reason enough *not* to follow suit. Compulsion was portrayed as un-English and would never be acceptable this side of the Channel.

I do not think such a system would be palatable in this country. ... [a] system of national compulsory education might do very well for a country in which the Government is truly despotic but I do not think that it would do well for such a nation as ours. I do not think that it would do for a country like this where the people have been taught for many years to depend upon their own exertions and we see the proud result of those exertions. ... [In Prussia] notwithstanding [that] the people have been brought up under a compulsory system of education for the last three hundred years, yet the people were wanting in morality and good order and ... the children attending the schools are the most vicious I have ever seen in any country.

(Sir B. Hall, 1847)

I have been asked why not compel the people, as in Prussia, to accept the benefits of education? To this I beg to reply that the people of England can not be compelled to accept this or anything else. ... The greater the efforts made to force an Englishman to do something that he does not like, even if good for him, the more violent will be his resistance. To make education compulsory will be to make it hateful to the people of England.

(Lord Brougham, 1847)

The general pattern of warnings was to urge the country to tread carefully before improving a system that seemed unwanting of repair, for fear of obtaining in its place:

> ... that great, gigantic, crushing, illiberal and intolerant system which I call a compulsory system of education.
>
> (Mr Hope, 1851)

Like other reforms, once made there could be no turning back: there would be a permanent, and it went without saying detrimental, scar on the character of the nation. Compulsory education could only mean the infection of the country with 'foreign' practices.

> There is a French word 'surveillance' which I can hardly translate into English but which implies an inspection of, a watching of, a prying into private affairs by Government servants, and something very like that system will be created for it will be necessary to go into every farmhouse and make enquiries with respect to the education of every boy under the age of fifteen. ... That which is now proposed for the best of purposes may be prostituted to the worst and we may, if we agree to these Resolutions, in the endeavour to attain an end perfectly legitimate and proper, narrow or suspend the boasted liberty of the people of this country.
>
> (Sir James Graham, 1856)

As intimated earlier, the sheer economics of the issue were an unanswerable obstacle.

> I believe it will be found ... that the wages of the children of farm servants amount to at least one-fourth of the entire wages of a farm; and here you call upon this class of persons to pay a new rate and to sacrifice one-fourth of their wages. Such a proceeding, I hesitate not to say, will spread confusion and

dissatisfaction throughout your whole rural population.

(Sir James Graham, 1856)

I am persuaded that for the welfare, for the respectability, for the very existence of the labouring classes, it is absolutely essential that their sons should be permitted to obtain employment at the earliest moment at which employment would be profitable to them and at which they can, by earning wages, relieve the wants of their families. The period of greatest difficulty in the life of a labouring man is that which occurs between the period of his marriage and the period at which his eldest son attains an age at which it is possible for him to earn money for his own support. This is the real period of agony to the labourer. If we prolong it by saying that two, three or four years more should be taken from the useful labour of his sons for the purpose of making them persons of more literary knowledge, we would inflict the greatest possible injury upon every labouring man in the country; we would force his family into the workhouse ... and we would destroy that sentiment of independence and self-respect which we ought to uphold. Continuous labour is of infinitely more value to a poor man than literary instruction which fits him neither for one thing or another.

(Earl Ellenborough, 1856)

Despite the unremitting feeling against assuming responsibility, public money was being directed, albeit tentatively, to supporting local exertions. The first government intervention was in 1833 when a grant of £20,000 (about half a million at today's values) was voted, which local authorities throughout England and Wales could apply to for help with building or repairing schools. From such an acorn, the vast edifice of modern public education was to grow.

Three central issues dominated the education world throughout the nineteenth century as the system of state-supported schooling grew. As intimated earlier, religion as an early motivator of education was always close to the surface, and there was a continuing controversy between the established Church of England and the Non-conformist sects over their relative rights in State-funded schools as regard religious teaching. If anything this aspect overshadowed all the others as *the* issue as the two sides fought for the very soul and bedrock of the educational system. The modern reader, though, reading the debates now feels little of the passion that was generated and can appreciate barely at all the importance of the issue that was felt to be at sake. The two other features of the debate are, by contrast, much more 'understandable' to the twentieth century mind and for this reason we focus on these. They concern two fundamentals of education which we take for granted today, but which in their time were hotly disputed tenets of the system: that attendance at school should be compulsory and that education should be free.

The advocates of education earnestly believed that only when education was turned from a voluntary option to a statutory requirement would the youth of the country benefit from what it had to offer. As early as 1858 the notion was on the agenda and already receiving stiff opposition.

> Any attempt to compel will only throw back the cause of education. ... I trust therefore that the good work [of the voluntary system] will not be marred by the interference of a compulsory system of education which will be found to be a Papacy as tyrannical as that of the Vatican.
>
> (Mr Hope, 1858)

The rationale was simple.

> Independence is of more importance than education and if the wages of the child's labour are necessary either to keep the parents from the poor-rates or to relieve the pressure of severe

and bitter poverty, it is far better that it should go to work at the earliest age at which it can bear the physical exertion than that it should remain at school.

(Mr Lowe, 1862)

Opponents viewed with concern the trend that was developing.

I look with alarm at the increasing tendency of the House to extend legislation beyond its natural province. We seem, step by step, to be introducing a system of minute surveillance over the private interests of the people for which our only precedents are those afforded by the police restrictions of other lands.

(Mr Buxton, 1860)

The debate rumbled on until the seminal Act of 1870, the first substantial piece of educational legislation and the first to acknowledge that education was a public service, permitting local school boards to levy rates in order to build schools and employ teachers at public expense. The Act also ushered in the notion of compulsion, but in a half-hearted way. It was not imposed nationally, but each school board could decide for itself whether compulsion was necessary in its own area. Even this was sufficient to raise the sharpest hackles.

[The Government] proposes to enforce the building of schools and to compel parents to send their children to them before [they] have come to appreciate the education which is to be forced upon them. [This departs from all the principles operating now and establishes] a press gang system instead.

(Lord Robert Montagu, 1870)

The spectre of state interference in such private affairs was anathema to many.

By this measure the state goes into every family, imposes new duties on the parent [and] declares and enforces duties of which the parent was before unconscious. It interferes with parental rights and responsibilities; it forbids to the parent the earnings of the child; it imposes a tax instead; it organizes society for purposes and in a manner to which we as a people have never been accustomed.

(Mr Winterbotham, 1870)

It would be entirely impracticable.

What an immense amount of extra police the proper working of this measure will require. Take the town of Liverpool alone. It is calculated that there are in Liverpool 80,000 children of whom 20,000 never attend school while the attendance of 10,000 others is too irregular to be of any use. How are we to find the means of looking after these 30,000 children? There will be, of course, a great army of police with power as we have heard ... to enter houses to see whether the children are at school. But still compulsion will be impossible. In Liverpool it is said there are 20,000 removals in the course of the year; how are the police to follow up these families through their removals and see that all their children are continued at school? How are the police even to know what children there are? There must evidently be an authoritative list; there must be a compulsory registration of births – a thing which the people of England will never stand nor this House of Commons sanction. Then there must be another registration of daily attendances at school; and an army of police clerks must compare these lists daily and schedule the discrepancies.

... I maintain that in the first place it is wrong in principle for the state to compel children to go to school; and in the next place that it is impossible. In some localities, it is true, the difficulties might be slight but one general law cannot be made for the whole country; such a law is impossible.

(Lord Robert Montagu, 1870)

The whole idea was simply 'un-English', as this sardonic commentator evocatively poured forth.

> It is a great thing, no doubt, always to be able to find a policeman when you want him, although he may be engaged in peeping through your own keyhole. It is a great thing to find your life mapped out for you by authority and fenced about with a thousand penalties; but the country to which we belong has grown so great in defiance of this system, in defiance of these principles – and we are still blind and old-fashioned and bigoted enough to rejoice that we are not a drilled nation, that we are not registered and inspected and certified from the cradle to the grave, ... we are still foolish and prejudiced enough to rejoice that we are free. Yes, free to do a great many things which may not be for our good and to neglect a great many things which might be for our good ... for in that freedom there is life and it is this free life which ... makes it a prouder thing to be an Englishman than to be a Bavarian.
>
> ... the amount of police interference which would be required in order to carry into operation a law flagrantly at variance with the tastes and habits of the people no-one in this country can say, for no-one in this country has tried.
>
> (Mr Leatham 1870)

But there was an even more cruel obstacle.

> A poor man barely able to keep himself out of the workhouse is often dependent on the labour of his children for 30 per cent of his weekly income. ... I will allege that the effect of a fine levied for non-attendance or even of compulsory attendance at school will be to condemn his children to starvation and himself to the poorhouse....

But there was a silver lining of sorts, since, he continues:

... the magistrate will have no choice but to let him off. By-and-by ... the system of compulsion will break down.

(Lord Robert Montagu, 1870)

It was the practical, undeniable effects of compulsion on the whole family that agitated some of the most persuasive critics.

It is in my opinion most unjust and tyrannical to prevent a poor man in the receipt of only ten shillings or fifteen shillings a week from supplementing that small sum by means of the earnings of his children. ... It is all very well to say that a poor man who does not send his children to school should be fined but he will probably have no money to pay the fine. How under these circumstances will the moral condition of the country be elevated by sending the father to gaol to associate with con-victs and the mother to the workhouse?

(Sir Rainald Knightley, 1870)

Some truly heart-tugging themes were pressed upon these wicked legislators.

I do not believe that there is any greater moral training for a child than that which accrues from his taking home his half crown or three shillings a week knowing that he is thereby adding to the comforts of home. The practice tends to unite a family together in bonds that never are broken; and of all the beautiful things which are to be seen in the habits and condi-tions of the poor, perhaps the most beautiful is the care and love they have for each other which is greatly fostered by this plan of allowing the early earnings of the child to contribute to the comfort and happiness of the family.

(Mr Gathorne Hardy, 1870)

All this moral fibre building was to be cast off, to be replaced by an iniquitous attack on the family instead, making criminals out of parents, splitting the home and, perhaps most heinous of all, taking away responsibility from those who should know best and giving it to the anonymous State.

> This legislation is, I believe, opposed to all the instincts and traditions of the people – it is introducing a tyrannical interference with domestic life which the people of this country will be very slow to approve. It involves a substitution of State in lieu of domestic control.
>
> (Mr Lowther, 1870)

The result could hardly be good for education itself. Paradoxically, compulsion, critics held, far from enhancing the status of education *reduced* the sense of importance people would attach to it. Parental responsibility would now be off-loaded onto the State, and they would no longer see any need to be concerned about it themselves.

> The principle [of compulsion] is one which the House ought not to encourage as this is nothing more or less than the substitution of the State for the parental authority and thus removing from the parents the responsibility which they ought to bear.
>
> (Mr Lowther, 1870)

> The best way to induce the poorer classes to send their children to school is to make it clear to them that to send them there is for their advantage.
>
> (Sir Charles Adderley, 1870)

This last principle, logical in its own terms, was not as innocent as it might look, at least as far as Sir Charles personally was concerned, for he had earlier revealed his own slant on the subject all too clearly; this gives a very different angle to his comment.

Education is not so much the imparting of knowledge as the training that will fit a child for the work to which his station will probably call him. Many years at school are not possible or required for the labouring class. ... I therefore deprecate all unnecessary compulsion.

(1870)

Thus, ingeniously, compulsion could be opposed both by those who felt education to be so good that it ought not to be forced but discovered by its own virtues and by those who felt education to be so irrelevant to so many that it ought not be inflicted on the unwilling and, by definition, unneedy.

Far removed from such philosophical gymnastics, the practical down-to-earth problems also looked logically unassailable. Given unwilling parents:

... it will be in [the child's] interests that he should be expelled and the boy will probably have no objection. How ... can discipline be maintained?

(Mr Cave, 1870)

Despite all the alarums, the dam was breached in the 1870 Act. It was to be ten more years – 1880 – before compulsion was made obligatory for all children. In the years which intervened until that moment, critics continued their resistance along familiar lines.

To deprive parents absolutely and at once of the earnings of the children will create great dissatisfaction throughout the country and make them discontented with the Education Act and this is an evil to be carefully guarded against. It will increase the pauperism of the idle pauper and his child will not see why he is not always to be maintained at the expense of [the State.]

(Colonel Barttelot, 1874)

This growth of Government interference was most un-healthy.

> [We] have been too much in the habit of adopting systems of legislation which make that penal which has never before been considered a crime.
>
> (Mr Birley, 1874)

> With regard to the mass of the people, I believe they might easily be led but they cannot be driven, and there is nothing they more dread than official meddling and interference.
>
> (Mr Scourfield, 1874)

It was easy, one critic said, to be generous with other people's money as the Government continued to raise more and more through rates to support public education. Not only was it was all too extravagant, it went against the national grain.

> If we search the statute book we will find no legislation couched in a spirit so offensive and un-English as this Education Act [of 1870]. Of all the despotisms and tyrannies with which men can be afflicted, there is no tyranny so oppressive and no despotism so intolerable as the despotism of the pedant and the tyranny of the prig.
>
> (Mr Sandford, 1875)

This sense of Government knowing best was becoming increasingly worrying.

> Much as I value education, I value the liberty of the subject more. I believe the father of a family is the best guardian of the interests of his family. … Generally speaking, the interests of the family will be better consulted by its natural head than by the State which will be a very bad substitute.

... For my part, I cannot see how far State interference is to be carried once it is begun. There are people who wish the State to step in and say what we are to eat, drink and put on; and although, in many cases, individuals might form erroneous opinions on these matters, still it is far better that the State should leave to a free people the free exercise of a free, if erroneous, opinion.

(Mr Sandford, 1876)

There is nothing more to be deprecated or that people resented more than minute and vexatious interference. The world is so constituted that it does not like disagreeable people and certainly the people connected with the administration of education seem to have the art of making themselves more disagreeable than any other persons in the kingdom.

(Sir John Scourfield, 1876)

The whole sorry business was memorably deplored by one member of the House of Lords who rued the day the children were coralled into school.

It has been said that children should be kept at school until 14 years of age; but the amount and the importance of the labour which lads between 10 and 14 can perform should not be ignored. Since the present educational system has come into operation, the weeds have very much multiplied in Norfolk which was once regarded as quite the garden of England, weeding being peculiarly the work of children whose labour is cheap, whose sight is keen, bodies flexible and fingers nimble.

(Earl Fortescue, 1880)

If compulsion opened such a can of worms, the principle of making it free as well was even more contentious, and not solely confined to the practical matter of cost. Most opponents continued to feel that this was simply not an obligation that should be taken from the parent and provided unquestioningly, on demand, by the State. The reality, though, was fairly starkly self-evident: once education had been made compulsory, it was difficult *not* to make it free – unless the courts were to be clogged up by a costly and probably unproductive pursuit of non-payers.

Most arguments centred on a subtle thesis, far removed from the hard practicalities. They were conducted on a much more lofty plane. This was a question not of daily minutiae of parents paying up but a much more fundamental principle going to the very heart of the individual citizen's position in regard to the State. As early as 1852 the theme emerged.

> I think it would be a great misfortune if the parent is taught that it is not necessary that he should contribute to the education of his children and that their education will be carried on entirely by the State. I think ... that the establishment of ... schools entirely as free schools would be not an improvement but would tend to make these schools of less use than they are and the payment of small sums by parents is rather an incentive to them to look after the education of their children.
>
> (Lord John Russell, 1852)

A more vigorous approach followed.

> [The working classes] are sensible enough to value their independence and will be ashamed to be paid out of the rates for the performance of their paternal duties. ... Those who are not too poor to pay the school fee do not like to have those fees paid for them. The working man already sees that the one thing necessary for his children and for their advancement in life is education; but to give education gratuitously will only degrade the education so given in the estimation of the parents.
>
> (Lord Robert Montagu, 1870)

The notion that one valued what one paid for and dismissed as valueless what one received for nothing was a compelling argument for years. In 1870 even the architect of the great Education Act of that year, William Forster, confessed that he was not prepared to go this far. That Act provided for relief from the school fee (which was notional anyway and usually a penny a day) only for those who could demonstrate inability to pay. In Foster's view:

> It would be a very dangerous thing for us to begin, at any rate, by establishing the principle that we take upon ourselves as the State the burden of the education of the children of any portion of the population. If we were broadly to lay down the principle that the State ought to pay the cost of the education, we would in effect say to the great body of parents throughout the country, 'We think it our business rather than yours to educate your children,' and I do not think we would be serving the cause of education by allowing such a belief to be spread abroad.
>
> (1870)

Others concurred.

> My own belief and that of the majority of school managers in England is that parents slighted education that is perfectly free but learn to value and take an interest in the instruction of their children when some small payment is demanded from them.
>
> (Sir Henry Selwin-Ibbetson, 1870)

> By casting education down before the people as an alms we will degrade rather than elevate it in [parents'] eyes.
>
> (Mr Miall, 1870)

It was to be more than twenty years before all school fees were abolished at publicly-funded establishments. That came in 1891. The range of predictions with which the government was deluged in the meantime was frighteningly diverse and left no doubt that the very morals of the nation would be compromised by any such move.

> It is in my view inevitable that to provide free education for the children of the middle classes would be to sap the independence of such classes in the same way that the independence of the wage-earning class has been sapped to a certain extent by the system already pursued. ... The general public opinion in England ... supports those who are anxious to return to the old English habit of self-help and who think that a certain amount of higher education might be too dearly bought at the cost of a spirit of independence and self-reliance.
>
> (Earl Fortescue, 1880)

> I venture to assert that this is not a measure which is promoted with the idea of improving the education of the country. ... People in the poorest rank of life continuously speak with pride of having made sacrifices in order to give their children the best education they can. Is it not well that we should encourage amongst our people the idea that in making sacrifices to give their children a good education they are doing what is right and proper? Is this a feeling to be lightly checked or eradicated? We want to improve the thrift, the self-reliance and self-restraint of the people and I ask if free education will tend to improve those qualities in the masses of the people?
>
> (Mr Bartley, 1891)

The answer expected was: 'clearly not.' But if this did not convince, a yet more alarming vision presented itself.

> We ought ... to be very careful and more than careful at a time when ... the population is increasing at a most appalling rate and increasing especially in its most thriftless elements that

One can almost hear Mr Bartley turning – perhaps revolving rapidly – in his grave at the modern education system that was to develop from these nineteenth century beginnings. Would he be anything less than apoplectic at the sight today of teenagers being schooled in how to fill out social security forms?

> Education is an enormous benefit but self-reliance is a greater benefit still and although education may be silver, self-reliance is golden. There is no true system of education unless it teaches people to be self-reliant and self-dependent.
>   ... The real goal [of national life] to be striven after ought to be so to order affairs and so to legislate that the mass of the community may earn sufficient to pay for their wants and for all the duties which they have taken upon themselves.
>
> (1891)

Perhaps the last word should go to one critic who espied in this measure a logical inconsistency which in the twentieth century would be resolved – but in the direction deprecated by him.

> I do not agree with the argument that because education is compulsory it must be free. If that argument must be followed, we should also pay for the clothing and the food of the children.
>
> (Mr Lawrence, 1891)

Almost every aspect of educational development which went to produce what we today take for granted was objected to with unremitting hostility when it first came on the scene. If the modern debate about the content of the national curriculum is fresh in our minds, it is only an echo of far earlier, and more fundamental, controversies. There was to begin with general antipathy to the idea of going beyond the confines of the basic 'three Rs'.

Whereas there were formerly only three subjects for which grants were made [by the Government] – reading, writing and ciphering [i.e., arithmetic] schools are now entitled to grants if their pupils can satisfy the examiners in literature, which means learning by heart a certain quantity of English verse – say a hundred or two hundred lines ... Next comes mathematics, Latin, French, German, mechanics, animal physiology, physical geography, botany and last – as much the best of all – domestic economy. ... I confess to a very strong dislike to the whole of these additions. I cannot pretend to say that I see any advantage in them at all. I am entirely sceptical on the subject. The great advantage of giving grants for reading, writing and ciphering is that the child's knowledge can easily be tested. These are things which cannot possibly be got by 'crams'. They are arts, so to speak, which people either do or do not know; and which you can test by means with which cram can have nothing to do. ... But the moment you get to such subjects as animal physiology, physical geography, mechanics and the like, there are certain phrases which can be got by heart ... which will convey to the Examiners the idea that a pupil possesses knowledge which he does not in the least possess, simply by the use of catchwords.

... I am entirely sceptical as to the advantage of examining children in that way in things which they are really unable to grasp. It will not only not do good but it will do positive harm and will tend to introduce a system which cannot be sufficiently deprecated.

(Viscount Sherbrooke, 1880)

None less than the Bishop of Exeter agreed.

Such systematic smattering does not cultivate the intelligence of the child but merely cultivates its memory in filling it with a knowledge which well deserves to be called 'cram' because in a very little time afterwards it is entirely forgotten.

(1880)

The essentials were neglected in favour of:

> ... a mere cramming the memory with the vocabulary of
> sciences and alphabets of unmastered foreign languages for
> evanescent show and deceitful prizes on examination.
>
> (Lord Norton, 1880)

For stridency of view, nothing could compare with Mr
Sandford's contribution.

> I object to algebra, Latin, French and German being taught to
> poor children at the expense of their neighbours. Champagne
> and truffles are good enough things in their way, but I am not
> going – neither is it necessary – to give them to paupers; but
> this is precisely an analagous case to teaching algebra, Latin,
> German and French to persons who do not require such
> instruction and who cannot afford to pay for it.
>   ... One of the first duties of education is to teach the poor
> to work. ... Those who are acquainted with the working of the
> [Educational] Board system in south London inform me that
> its result has been to disorganise the whole of the children –
> the girls are unwilling to enter service and the boys are
> unwilling to work. I consider it a most dangerous thing to
> convert a nation of labourers into a nation of clerks.
>
> (Mr Sandford, 1876)

He was an old adversary of the progressive age.

> The character of the education given to pauper children by
> these school boards ... will surprise many hon Gentlemen.
> They are to be taught reading, writing and arithmetic, the
> history of England, geography, elementary drawing, music,
> domestic economy, algebra and geometry. I do not think it was
> ever intended by the legislature that pauper children should
> receive such a high class education. I have heard of a school in

Mayfair where a girl had been taken from her needlework to attend a drawing class. Of what possible use can a knowledge of drawing be to young women intended for domestic service – except to enable them to caricature their mistresses....

Our colonies are calling upon us to give them labourers and not clerks and I protest against the miserable gentility inculcated upon those who are taught that it is disgraceful to work with their hands and who are ashamed of the horny hands of manual labour. It is the sure sign of the decay of a country when people look down upon useful manual labour and the sort of education I have described is certainly not that which ought to be carried out by compulsion.

(Mr Sandford, 1875)

Even the great Forster could urge caution just four years after his mould-breaking Act.

It is most important that we should not provide too high an education at the expense of the public.

(1874)

Some years earlier, similar doubts had surfaced – along with a doom-laden vision of the future.

I contend that Parliament has no right to tax the people for anything beyond elementary instruction. To remove barriers which a man himself in after-life will be unable to surmount is a fair and legitimate object; but further than that we ought not to go. It is said that the instruction should be carried so far as to give the people of the humbler classes a love for books: but what was the kind of books that these classes loved? ... The books they chiefly read are works of fiction and romance. If it is sought to give them a taste for any higher class of literature they must not only be supplied with books but with places in which to read them; and if we attempt that I do not know how far we might have to carry the expense unless we mean to resort to the system of the ancient Romans who gave games to the people for the purpose of amusing them and keeping them quiet.

(Lord Lyveden, 1862)

No child in the kingdom, however poor the parents, ought to be debarred on account of poverty from receiving an education which is necessary to keep it from poverty or crime. I do not, however, think it is the business of the State to force it upon the children any more than it is our duty to force upon them food or anything else. That is the duty of the parents.

(Mr Dillwyn, 1861)

Notwithstanding the views earlier recorded that only the rigorous 'testable' subjects should be taught, some objected to the very concept of examination itself. Redolent of arguments which would sweep through the educational establishment just over a century later, Earl Fortescue told the House of Lords:

A great majority of the school teachers throughout the country deprecate these frequent examinations not only as being very costly and troublesome but very depressing to slow children and repressing in their operation upon quick children.

(1881)

Another was convinced that:

Education, generally speaking, in the proper sense of the word is sacrificed to examination. ... Education is given into the hands of two classes of specialists – the examiners and the crammers and everything is directed to the examinations.

(Earl Wemyss, 1890)

All sorts of atrocious maladies could be traced to this

competitive environment.

> One most important feature of the subject ... is the effect produced on the health, not only on the present but of the coming generations. ... Dr Avery says, 'the effect on girls of over-mental strain is great. They grow up highly nervous women, giving birth in case of their marriage to weak and deteriorated offspring.'
>
> (Earl Wemyss, 1890)

Just to show that nothing was excluded from the sceptics' eye, we conclude with this broadside against perhaps the most elemental of modern educational principles – the classroom based on age.

> I hope and trust that the regulation as to grouping will be struck out as inoperative for any purpose of good. ... It is utterly absurd to talk of ranging children in a ... school according to their age instead of according to their proficiency. We might as well group the children according to weight as according to age for the latter is in reality no test of intellectual progress. ... If such [grouping by age] is adopted in a school nothing better can be expected than that it should tumble to pieces; for it will crush all competition and emulation among the children and bring them all to one melancholy dead level. ... I think we must come to the conclusion that carrying out this proposal is utterly impracticable if the good discipline of the school is to be kept up. The scheme, I contend, will be found to work great injustice in the case of scholars whose talents have advanced when in the school to a position beyond their years.
>
> (Lord St Leonards, 1862)

THREE:
POLITICS

'Wild And Undigested Schemes'
Parliamentary Reforms

The reform of Parliament constitutes the longest and most consistent of all the themes of change during the last two centuries. For modern Britons brought up in an age where the right to vote is taken for granted as an unquestionable one, it is sometimes cautionary to remind ourselves that such a position was only achieved for all adults as recently as 1928. The road to that objective is strewn with tireless, often thankless efforts, apparently doomed to futility in their day, but serving gradually to erode away the uneven fabric of the old order, albeit at times at a rate of glacial proportions. The battle was many-fronted: in the early days the fight was to increase the number of towns which enjoyed the privilege of returning MPs to the House of Commons and to widen the qualifications which had to be met for citizens to be granted the vote where elections took place. The qualification battle was to reach its peak of crisis in the campaign for female suffrage, but not before another major front had opened up on the way electors voted – the struggle for the Secret Ballot.

At the start, just after the end of the Napoleonic War, the central issue was the overhaul of the arcane system of representation in the Commons, which until as late as 1830 produced a House two-thirds of whose members acquired their seats by patronage, through anomalies such as 'pocket' seats where the nobility had an absolute right under ancient charters and prerogatives to nominate and return candidates; or 'rotten' boroughs where the electorate was bizarrely small and manageable through bribery or intimidation in these days of open voting when electors were required to declare their choice in public at the polling station. The extreme example of the abuses was Old Sarum, an uninhabited area of grassland in Wiltshire which had just seven absentee voters credited to it but returned two members to the Commons. Cornwall sent forty-four MPs to Westminster; the whole of Yorkshire just two; growing cities such as Birmingham, Leeds and Manchester returned not a single member.

In all, out of a total population of some 16.5 million in 1831, only some 440,000 (or two and two-thirds per cent) enjoyed the privilege of a vote. The defensibility of such a system would, it might be thought, have taxed even the best minds: not a bit of it. The objections flooded down whenever the 'R' word – Reform – was uttered. Even the faintest hint was guaranteed to set alarm bells ringing and dire warnings followed quickly in their train.

Although the first wholesale attempt to remedy matters – the Great Reform Act of 1832 – added just 217,000 voters (making a national electorate of four per cent), the seismic implications of the change could not be disguised by the modesty of the actual numbers involved. For both sides, the fundamental breach in the defences of the old system had been made. For supporters of reform it was only the start of the long haul towards universal suffrage. For their opponents, it was a step from which there could be no going back to the 'good old days'. And 'good old days', they maintained, were exactly what had been sacrificed by the precipitous move. It challenged the whole sanctity of order and good administration. There had been no doubt from the earliest mootings of reform that nothing advantageous could be derived from altering the present state of affairs. For those in authority, the impetus to change had received a fatal boost by the events across the Channel in 1789. The French Revolution set off a chain reaction of responses both amongst those hankering to emulate the essence (if not the actuality) of the revolution in Britain and amongst those who saw their role to preserve the structure of society from turbulent upheaval. During and in the wake of the Napoleonic Wars, a prominent plank in the anti-reformers' platform was that the British system, however oddly it might be constructed, had served the country well:

> I deprecate the wild notions which are so industriously diffused respecting the necessity and practicability of a radical reform in the representation of the people in parliament. ... When I find a greater degree of security, a greater degree of civil liberty and a purer administration of justice prevailing than in any other part of the world, I cannot bring myself to put these blessings to hazard by the inconsiderate adoption of wild and undigested schemes of reform.
>
> (Sir J. Pulteney, 1810)

> That the constitution as it at present exists is productive of great blessings need not be argued because few, very few indeed, will be found to deny the fact. It produces more freedom, more security, more prosperity, more glory, more happiness to those who have the fortunate lot to live under it than any government that ever existed in any other country. Wisdom and prudence then obviously dictate that before you put these inestimable blessings to the risk by any change, you should be satisfied that grievances exist of such magnitude as to counterbalance the danger of the experiment ... the frame and character of the constitution ... is not a simple machine but one of delicate movements, complicated and difficult to be understood, in which one spring works upon or checks another almost imperceptibly; a machine therefore with which it is dangerous to meddle since the alteration or removal of the slightest part may derange the whole and ... urge it to destruction. We know at present that it works well....
>
> (Sir John Nicholls, 1817)

It would be a clever, and almost irrefutable, argument of the debate down the years that it was wiser to stick to the devil we knew than gamble it all on untested theories (untested at least in Britain – it became a common ploy to point to the horrors of the French experience as indicative of what we could expect if the common people were admitted to the private game of government). Why put all we have at risk when any right thinking person could see that our ways admirably met our requirements?

> To perform properly, [Parliament] should collect and combine the wisdom, the integrity, the independence and the knowledge of the commonality of the realm. For its wisdom, it should collect men of the first talents; for its integrity, those of high character; for its independence, men of competent property; and for its knowledge, enlightened persons of all descriptions – statesmen, landed proprietors, merchants, manufacturers, lawyers, naval and military officers, men of letters and of general information. The House as at present constructed is thus composed.
>
> (Sir John Nicholls, 1817)

If the Old Guard were prepared to accept that on the face of it the system looked odd in parts, they were not disposed to follow the logic through to the extent of agreeing to change.

> [There] is inequality, it is true; and if you were now forming a new constitution you probably would not introduce such [anomalies]. But finding the constitution existing, the proper question to be asked is what is the practical inconvenience? Is Cornwall better taken care of or are its interests more attended to than those of Yorkshire? ... By no means, for it is the true principle of the constitution as well as the actual feeling of the members of this House that when seated here they are not the agents or attorneys or deputies of the places which chose them but that

each and every of them represents the whole and every part of the commons of the United Kingdom.

(Sir John Nicholls, 1817)

The logic of the argument was that it was immaterial that the citizens of Birmingham, for example, did not elect their own member. They were able to rely on the good sense of a distant Cornish borough to ensure that a candidate capable of protecting their interests was safely returned to the House. Whether the good voters of Cornwall, or any other electorate, in practice had any but their own interests at heart when they made their choice was not a point which proponents of such arguments seemed prepared to question. For the likes of Sir John, the motto was, tamper at the nation's peril.

If we sacrifice the blessings which the nation enjoys in order to gratify the caprice or soothe the insolence of the disaffected – if we put to the risk the best interests and the substantial happiness of the country ... we shall neither retain the respect of the wise and the contented nor put an end to the demands of the dissatisfied. No – let us stand firmly by the constitution if we value its blessings or wish for its permanency. ... The slightest scratch may produce a mortal wound....

(Sir John Nicholls, 1817)

[The present system] has exhibited England conspicuous among the nations for its religious and moral feeling, rich in its character, highly educated and scientific, cultivated like a garden, leading the world in commerce and manufacture, the first naval power, second to none in courage and military prowess. There can be no risk therefore in continuing under a constitution which has achieved such results: but there is great risk in altering it. ... Every sensible and honest man must admit that no constitution of government ought to be lightly changed nor unless it be clear beyond any reasonable doubt that important benefit will arise from such change. ... The principle once admitted, it opens the door to perpetual changes and paper constitutions according to the supposed interest or passions of contending parties. If there be any odium on the subject ... it should rather attach on those who seek change and not on those who support an established constitution admitted by all to have worked a considerable portion of good to the country.

(Sir Edward Hyde East, 1823)

For some, little fault at all could be found in the system:

[It] comprised nearly all those who possessed any landed property and whose birth, intelligence and means of information enabled them to judge of men and measures and to select those as their representatives whose talents were best calculated to do honour to their choice and confer lasting benefits on their country.

(Mr Ross, 1826)

And it quite reasonably excluded:

persons in the lowest classes of society ... whose utter want of education ought to exclude them from taking any share in the task of selecting legislators.

(Mr Ross, 1826)

For him, it was:

hallowed by ages yet unimpaired by time; ... I must consider any material and uncalled for alteration in this edifice as little short of sacrilege. I tremble lest the contagious example once set, we should not know where to arrest our progress. ... The plan [for reform] is fraught with fallacy and replete with danger.

(Mr Ross, 1826)

Fallacy and danger were two sentiments which featured
overwhelmingly in the anti-reformers' armoury. Far from
being simply empty catchphrases with which to lambast
their naive and reckless opponents, they were planks in the
argument which were cogently explored and which, perhaps surprisingly, still strike a chord today. The essence of
the position was that insulated from the vagaries of unin-
formed public opinion and possessed of such talents as the
good breeding of the higher orders of society endowed, the
House as presently constituted was best placed to serve the
interests of the nation.

> Among the greatest evils arriving from Parliamentary Reform
> I do not hesitate to class the immediate effect it will give to the
> will of the people upon the votes of this House, and conse-
> quently upon the decisions of the legislature and upon the
> measures of the government. ... It must be recollected that
> occasions now and then occur on which the people are very
> violent; and when they are very violent they are in general
> very wrong – occasions on which all other considerations give
> way to a momentary passion and the great mass of society
> assume the character and feelings of a ferocious ignorant mob.
> They clamour for peace when peace would be disgraceful; they
> ask for war when war would be impolitic or unjust. ... It is on
> occasions like these that we feel the advantage of having a
> House of Commons which speaks itself to the average and not
> to the fluctuations of public opinion, which is the faithful
> portrait of the national character in its ordinary attitude
> of dignity, sedateness and repose, not the mirror in which
> those transitory but disgusting forms are reflected which it
> assumes when under the dominion of ignorance, prejudice and
> passion.
>
> ... What the present composition of parliament enables
> us to do is ... to separate the real permanent sense of the people
> from their hasty passing impressions and to keep up that right

of appeal from present passion to future judgment which is necessary in order to preserve us from all the horrors and absurdities of democratical government.

(Mr Ward, 1812)

George Canning, eminent former Foreign Secretary and Prime Minister to be, was of similar view.

The House of Commons owes to the people a manly but not a servile obedience. ... We should not watch the eye, nor bend to the nod nor crouch to the unspoken will of the multitude, but [be] proved in the plain path of undeviating independence....

... A just sympathy with the people and a reasonable attention to their desires is no doubt the duty and must ever be the inclination of this House. The people, unquestionably, can reason fair when they have time; but, as notoriously their first impulse is feeling, I do not think it would be politic or for the interest of the country to have this House quite subject to popular control. ... If we do, some more cunning and ambitious visionary will take advantage of the tumult to place himself on the throne. We would soon see popular commotion end in military despotism and find philosophical disquisition superseded by practical oppression.

(Mr Canning, 1810)

Where [the House] depends on the popular voice without any extraneous control, in times of public disturbance or high political excitement, elections turn on one single consideration – one all-devouring, uncompromising pledge is administered [by voters] as a touchstone to the merits of every candidate. Talents, character, reputation, cannot for a moment uphold their possessor. ... How would such consequences operate here where the very essence of our constitution is its principle of balances and counterpoises; where from the combination and opposition of conflicting elements the harmony of the whole is extracted?

... The [present] House conforms itself to every change, slowly and reservedly it is true but not on that account the less surely or the less safely. It is certain, ultimately and in good time, to receive the impression of every prevailing impulse. ... Hence it is that no House of Commons violently departs from the track of its predecessors. ... It is this perpetuity of principle, this consistency of conduct, this moderation in the exercise of its power that I wish to preserve inviolate to this House.

(Mr Denison, 1826)

The increasingly popular belief that somehow mere numbers had any part to play in the system was, it was argued, a misleading fallacy.

[The Englishman] will find [such ideas] wild and illusive theories. He will find the principle of individual will powerful and efficient to the destruction of every individual and of every community, [and] to every good purpose null and void. He will find that those rights which entitle all to an equal share in the government are rights which only serve to remove them from useful labour, from sober industry and from domestic connections and which abandon them to be the slaves of every idle caprice and of every destructive passion. The government which adopts such principles ceases to be a government; it unties the bands which knit together society; it forfeits the reverence and obedience of its subjects.

(Mr Pitt, Prime Minister, 1793)

The new-fangled notion of equality of man, and the inevitable consequence which flowed from it that simple majorities of numbers should decide issues, was too much for many old hands.

To apply these metaphysical arguments as rules of conduct are, in my opinion, like turning a mill by the power of music or raising a wall by a tune.

(Mr Windham, 1793)

The premise was, simply, illogical.

[Since] men will see [the merits of an argument] more or less clearly in proportion to their greater or less degrees of information, it follows that the majority is not the most likely to be in the right. If twenty persons of ordinary capacity are to decide on a question by a mere majority, is it a certain rule that the majority will be right? By no means. If to these twenty as many more are added, will the certainty be greater? It will be *less*: for as the number is augmented, the deficiency of deliberative judgment, the most essential quality, will be greater. If therefore the plan of these reformers who say that nothing but a mere majority ought to govern are to be carried, the nation will be undone.

(Mr Windham, 1793)

Although Parliament is in many cases induced to follow the opinion of the public, it not infrequently corrects their errors. The public are greatly led by the press which mixes up with many facts and much sound argument so much fallacy and misrepresentation as to impose upon the public to an extent from which the better information and good sense of Parliament alone can relieve them.

(Mr Vansittart, Chancellor of the Exchequer, 1821)

I would contend that it is reasonable to doubt whether [the House of Commons] has ever been meant to express. ... opinions in their extreme popular sense. In my opinion, it is not only excusable in, but incumbent upon, Parliament to vote sometimes on the unpopular side of a question; we are not here so much as to represent the opinions of the people as to watch over the welfare of the country and it is no crime in any

Member of Parliament to believe that his constituents are sometimes more prone to change and vacillation than he is bound to be.

(Mr Twiss, 1830)

This was the greatest objection to reform – the prospect of the House being converted from a judicious, delicately poised and cool-headed instrument of sound policy to a raucous, polarized and hot-blooded dog-pit of a chamber which merely acted as a channel for agitation on behalf of the shallow and transient popular nostrums of the day. Widening representation would be little short of the end of civilized government as we knew it.

It is impossible that an assembly, purely democratic, could exist with safety to [the] country. Its measures would vacillate at every variation of popular opinion, however ill-founded; ... it would soon become the base pander of the basest passions of the people.

... If assemblies of this description did exist, it must be at a distance from the metropolis surrounded and strictly guarded by an armed force, for they will most likely be apt to indulge opinions that the King was [of no value].

(Mr Giddy, 1812)

Less apocalyptic but just as damning:

We ought not to place ourselves in a situation in which we might be governed by temporary opinions, the result of temporary delusions or temporary distress; ... we ought to cling more closely than ever to this fortunate and admirable system which enables us to distinguish betwixt the transitory feelings and the real permanent sense of the people. ... Popular representation will produce parliaments every [member] of which must tremble for his political existence whenever he does not anticipate [electors'] follies and outrun their madness; [they] would be affected by the popular feeling as the most delicate thermometer is by the surrounding air. It would be formidable enough in its ordinary operation and its natural temperature but when raised to blood-heat in the storm of enthusiasm, there is no cruelty, no violence, no absurdity to which it might not be transported.

(Mr Ward, 1817)

The shape of elections to come was clear even so very early on in the battle against reform.

It is melancholy to know the serious truth ... that the only result of yielding to the desire of conciliating popular favour ... [will be] that many will be ready to outbid for applause by still more extravagant concessions and the highest bidder will not be the most honest and most enlightened but the most servile and submissive, the most mad or dishonest....

(Mr Brougham, 1818)

The impact on the House of Commons, and government in general, would be fatal.

The sentiments, the desires of the people deserve every degree of respectful attention from their representatives; but the legislature must exercise its own judgment; and to abandon this is a great folly, a greater breach of duty than even the most entire disregard of the public voice. This abdication of our proper functions is however incomparably more criminal if done also with a view to court popular favour at the expense of sincere and deliberate conviction; it is also beyond all question a still more short-sighted delusion to fancy that such a base stratagem can succeed. The adoption of universal suffrage might for a moment lift one unworthy or obscure individual to popularity; another less scrupulous or more consistent would soon rise over his head; ... the only rule in the competition would be to go beyond the last man who had offered, and as the degrees of human folly are infinite in all directions, this unworthy rivalry in pandering for the vices or the craziness of the multitudes [will have] no limits....

... when popularity is thus sought after, it loses all the lustre which makes it so precious a possession to honourable minds. When it is to be bid for not in the sterling coin of pure conduct, enlightened views, statesmanlike accomplishments which few men hold a large stock of – but in the base dross of subserviency and compliance and pretence and cant which everyone might have without stint and the most unprincipled alone will use, then the people are degraded by being so courted and their favour becomes a worthless, nay a debasing, enjoyment, a boon as fleeting as it is vile.

(Mr Brougham, 1818)

I must confess that there is no evil that I should more dread than that state of morbid agitation which would be produced ... by teaching every man that the first, and the last and in fact the only material step towards political reputation and power is popularity and consequently by raising the art of flattering and bribing the people above all other arts.

(Mr Ward, 1812)

Who in our modern world would not find themselves in a certain degree of sympathy with this dark prophecy of the shape of politics to come? All the certainties of the old system were to be swept away in favour of the turbulent, unpredictable, uncontrollable lottery of the popular will. It was clear to many that the quality of those who would come into the House would be much reduced. In the unreformed Commons, discussion was informed by:

persons who bestow all their time and their very best abilities on this object and who under the present system are nearly certain of always obtaining a seat in this House. That certainty is in a manner essential to the formation of such characters; for what person – at least what person of that description – will throw away his time and his talents in qualifying himself for a situation from which mere accident [i.e. an election] might exclude him through all the best part of his life? And yet one of the objects of any such reform ... is to put an end to everything like permanence and stability in the situation of a Member of this House.

(Mr Ward, 1812)

Submission to periodic, and unpredictable, elections would persuade the very best of the country's minds to turn to other more reliable pursuits leaving the task of government in the hands of uncultured, fly-by-night tenants whose only claim to public preferment was their ability better to flatter. The proper discharge of the responsibilities of being an MP could not survive the popularizing of politics.

It is a task that requires abilities of the first order, exercised and cultivated by continual attention and care. And how are we to expect that labour and that devotion if the system is not such as will afford a reasonable certainty of a permanent political existence to the persons that engage in it? Men of the highest character and talent may become unpopular ... and is it fit that on that account they should be completely expelled from political life? or what is still worse for the public, that they should be obliged in order to avoid becoming odious, and in order to preserve to themselves the means of exertion and display, to court the people in opposition to their own opinions and to the interests of the people itself? In this view, the ['pocket' and 'rotten'] borough system has a salutary effect [enabling members to be] rescued from that state of vile dependence upon the temporary will of the people in which they would be placed if there were no such refuges.

(Mr Ward, 1817)

Politics was the serene cultivation of wise ideas, sound policy and virtuous service. That was all to be discarded in favour of plain and perpetual appealing to the people.

Do gentlemen really think that electioneering is the pursuit that is most calculated to enlarge or elevate the mind? ... I cannot help thinking that the youth of many of these I see around me [in the House] was much better spent in acquiring those accomplishments and treasuring up those vast stores of knowledge which now adorn and enlighten this House than in the obscure and vexatious labours of a canvass and in devising means to recommend themselves to this or that body of electors in any of the six hundred and fifty districts into which the country would be parcelled under the new system.

(Mr Ward, 1817)

In short, only two types of person would benefit from the reform of parliament.

... persons standing upon their local interests and those to whom from whatever cause, some share of popularity was attended – proprietors and demagogues.

(Mr Ward, 1817)

Great evils would attend a change to popular elections.

While members returned for burgage tenure seats or through other obscure and noiseless modes of election pass into the House of Commons unnoticed and uncriticised, their talents unquestioned and their reputations unassailed, the successful candidate of a popular election often comes here loaded with the imputation of every vice and crime that could unfit a man.

... The first effect of a reform which should convert all elections into popular ones would probably be to ensure a congregation of individuals against every one of whom a respectable minority of his constituents would have pronounced sentence of condemnation. And if it be so very hard that there are now a great number of persons who do not directly exercise the elective franchise and who are therefore represented by persons whom others have chosen for them, will this ... be much mended when two-fifths of the people of England should be represented not only without their choice but against their will? not only by individuals whom they have not selected but by those whom they have declared utterly unworthy of their confidence?

(Mr Canning, 1822)

Canning's euphemism for jobbery and corruption – 'obscure and noiseless modes of election' – is probably the most delightful of any of the colourful phrases offered in defence of the old regime. The line of argument Canning employs encapsulates the ease with which opponents of reform were able to heap reproach upon the advocates of change. The logic, as seen from the standpoint of the time, was far from easily refutable. Not only was it not self-evident that reform would bestow advantages, there were demonstrable disadvantages, not the least of which was the oft-stated fear that any, even the smallest, breach would open the way to an endless and uncontrollable clamour for change which would lead who knew where. As the skirmishing continued into the years leading up to the first Reform Act, and as it became accepted that some reform was necessary, if only to seek to stave off the worst till later, the two sides cagily circled each other, the one trying to see what was the maximum degree of reform that could be won, the other what minimum degree of reform could be got away with. Both tacitly accepted that once the genie had been let out of the bottle, it could not be returned. The struggle for the old guard turned to damage limitation. The real bogey of the affair was that ultimate fantasy – universal suffrage, which sent many into near apoplexy.

It is a system which would manifestly destroy the whole balance of the constitution, produce a revolution and carry the nation through the whole circle of revolutionary calamities, beginning with anarchy and ending in military despotism.

(Sir John Nicholls, 1817)

Would this uniformity of representation improve [Parliament's] character or extend its universality? Just the reverse. The representatives would for the most part be of one description – the demagogues of each district: those who could flatter and could best cajole the worst passions of the multitudes. [Would it] tend to render elections more free from corruption, riot and expense? How far a representation so constructed or any ways approaching towards it would be an improvement upon the present constitution seems unworthy of refutation by argument. It is sufficient just to have stated it.

(Sir John Nicholls, 1817)

I have always deprecated universal suffrage not so much on account of the confusion to which it would lead as because I think we should in reality lose the very object which we desire to obtain because I think it would, in its nature, embarrass and prevent the deliberative voice of the country from being heard. I do not think that you augment the deliberative body of the people by counting all the heads but that in truth you confer on [candidates] by this means the power of drawing forth numbers who without deliberation would implicitly act upon their will. My opinion is that the best plan of representation is that which shall bring into activity the greatest number of independent voters and that which is defective which would bring forth those whose situation and condition take from them the power of deliberation. I can have no conception of that being a good plan of election which should enable individuals to bring regiments to the poll. ... It would be a defective system that should bring regiments of soldiers, of servants and of persons whose low condition necessarily curbed the independence of their minds.

(Mr Fox, 1797)

Prime Minister Pitt was in no doubt as to the damage it would wreak.

If this principle of individual suffrage be granted and be carried to its utmost extent, it goes to subvert the peerage, to depose the king and, [finally] to extinguish every hereditary distinction and every privileged order and to establish that system of equalising anarchy announced in the French legislation and attested in the blood of the massacres at Paris. ... The question then is whether you will abide by your constitution or hazard a change with all that dreadful train of consequences.

(Mr Pitt, 1793)

Others chipped in with their pithier, but no less baleful, forecasts.

I am decidedly for opposing the beginning of a system which must end in national destruction. [It is] pregnant with the most fatal consequences.

(Mr Canning, 1817)

[Reform was] founded ... upon the destruction of social order and of all that was wise, permanent and useful in our invaluable system of law and government.

(Mr Lambton, 1817)

[Universal suffrage] is the wildest fancy that could possibly enter into the conception of any human being.

(Lord Holland, 1817)

Reform ... is a lever or instrument by means of which the whole force of the lower and more turbulent classes of the community can be applied to the overthrow of all that is stable and salutary in the state.

(Mr Wilmot, 1819)

That corruption now exists cannot be denied ... [but] the extension of the elective franchise, if carried too far, might tend rather to aggravate it ... for the more indigent the voter, the more inclined will he be to sell his vote.

(Mr Dundas, 1830)

Such presentiments of catastrophe ensured that there was no prospect of the country going anywhere near embracing universal suffrage when it came to consider the content of the first Reform Bill. Indeed for a full year it seemed touch and go whether any measure of reform would be enacted at all. It was to take two abortive attempts, the first bill thrown out by the Commons, the second by the Lords, and a state of upheaval in the country which was the closest we have come to the outbreak of civil war this side of Cromwell before the third edition of the Bill was successfully routed through onto the statute book; that was only achieved by the Government persuading the King to announce publicly a threat to the obstructive Lords that he would create sufficient new peers to vote the passage of the Bill if they did not relent. In the event, opponents in the Lords boycotted the final stages, and Pandora's box was finally opened.

The 1832 Act was at the same time both modest and momentous. In its modesty, it enfranchised a mere handful of individuals; but these amounted to an increase in the electorate of fifty per cent, the most startling and fundamental shift in the superstructure of the State ever before managed by peaceful means. Both sides were fully aware of the magnitude of the reforms and the arguments of those opposed to them took on, during those feverish twelve months of debate, a subtler air turning from the catch-all, slogan type denunciations to more ingenious, specific complaints. The battle lines were principally drawn on three fronts: condemning the overall system that would be created by more open and direct representation; castigating the type of new elector that would be introduced to the serious art of politics; and cursing the new brand of MP likely to emerge from it all. Others ploughed more solitary furrows, some hinging their case on the advantages of the old system about to be lost for ever, others simply contesting that any reform was, in principle, a bad thing.

For many, the new arrangements threw up as many questions as they purported to solve. One had a new-found sympathy for the ordinary man in the street.

> What becomes of the minority in a contested election? If the principle [that those who pay taxes should enjoy representation is accepted] the minority are not only excluded from the practical benefit of voting but are taxed by laws made by a man whom they specifically have rejected and are governed not only without their choice but against their will.
>
> (Sir Robert Inglis, 1831)

On this basis, it was facile to maintain the argument, in seeking to extend the franchise, that there was any link between paying taxes and the right to vote.

> ... can you ever secure, except to a bare majority of the people, that right, the exercise of which is said to be so indispensable

as the condition precedent to any obedience on their part?

> (Sir Robert Inglis, 1831)

But this line of argument portraying a concern for the voter was a rare – and specious – one. The more consistent theme was that representation of the people had to be considered a delicate, indirect almost ethereal concept. Paradoxically, the more directly MPs reflected their constituents' views, the worse, not better, things would become. By far the greatest disadvantage was that prudence would give way to passion.

> ... is the good sense [of the country] or are the passions of the people to be represented? On the good sense of the country, I have great reliance – on the passions none. And if there is a moment when the passions of the people are more liable to excitement than another, that moment is the period of an election. If upon such an occasion the passions are moved in behalf of a particular candidate, whatever might be the character of his pretensions, up he goes to the top of the poll. A person so returned is not at liberty to exercise his own judgment. He is necessarily but the echo of the passions of those who have sent him here.
>
> (Mr Ward, 1831)

The practice of government would be dealt a fatal blow.

> In cases of excitement, either pledges must be given or the Minister will not be returned to Parliament. Really, under such circumstances, it seems difficult to say how a member of the government is to retain office. ... the state of thraldom in which the Ministers will be kept by the [new] voters in the House, the instability of any government, will be the necessary result and such an instability in the government must have the worst effect on the public funds and on all the international

relations of the country.

(Mr Mackinnon, 1832)

A fundamental change in the way parliament worked would come about. From its present position as a community of the great and the good serving together for the interests of the nation as a whole, the House, if it was subjected to election by mere numbers of ordinary people, would become simply a mirror of the outside world, factioned into majority and minority and taking decisions by sheer weight of might rather than deliberation of the merits of each issue which came before it. (And how true it turned out!)

I believe the greatest peril to be apprehended ... is ... the representation of the large towns, the members for which will be not only formidable from their numbers but still more formidable in a moral point of view. ... [They will be] animated by the same views – acting systematically together ... [and be] exposed to the feelings, the interests, the prejudices of their constituents. [They] will be the men to whom the government will have to look up. These will be the iron men who will hereafter govern the Government and direct the destinies of the empire.

... Ministers deceive themselves in anticipating the effects of the Bill and when they see the ruin which will ensue they will regret the madness of their misguided zeal. It appears to me that so far from adding strengths to our counsels, it will produce the most shallow and fluctuating policy that ever enfeebled the energies of a people.

(Lord Porchester, 1832)

Worse would follow.

Members will be continually harassed by the demand of pledges at the hustings and an inquisition into all the details of their parliamentary conduct on the ground of responsibility. ... This constitution great and glorious as it is, splendid and renowned as it is in the history of the world is now about to be madly, rashly and unsparingly destroyed.

(Lord Porchester, 1832)

Concession to popular clamour [will] never answer the end for which [Parliament] is designed. ... I feel assured that it must give rise to a continual war of beggary against property, of ignorance against intelligence, of numbers against respectability and to a perpetual change of established institutions for untried novelties. Under such a system, all who have the real and permanent good of their country at heart must tremble for its future state ... [the Bill] being a measure calculated to lead on to a state of anarchy, confusion and ruin and to inflict the most serious evils upon all classes of society from the peasant in his cottage to the king on his throne.

(Mr Trevor, 1832)

Whenever any popular excitement takes place at the time of a general election, will not nearly the whole House represent only the temporary opinion and passions of a majority in the country leaving the minority, however respectable in intelligence, property or numbers, almost without an organ? With such an assembly, fluctuating as it must do with every variation of a breeze which may blow by turns from every point of the compass, what will become of stability, the great element of social and political happiness?

(Earl of Harrowby, 1831)

How can security for any consistent line of policy in the Government be obtained when in the event of a dissolution of Parliament each Minister must depend upon the caprice of popular opinion ... for his return to Parliament?

(Marquis of Salisbury, 1832)

Let this Bill pass and there will be such a House of Commons
as will render it impossible for any Government to be conducted on any regular principle of action.

(Lord Ellenborough, 1832)

One of the more reactionary of the band of anti-reformers
sought to foretell the state of affairs by comparing present
difficulties the House already faced with what would
follow.

It is with some difficulty that we now refuse to entertain
propositions ... that are occasionally urged upon us. How then
will a House of Commons formed not to deliberate but to
follow the impulse of petitioners, be able to resist them?

(Sir James Scarlett, 1831)

No respecter of fashionable whims, Sir James left no-one in
doubt about which side he stood on.

With respect to the theoretical right [of representation] for
which some persons contend, it appears to me [to be] so
perfectly void of all reason and principle that I shall not waste
a word upon it being satisfied that all attempts to support a
measure of Reform upon the fanciful theories of [the rights of]
individuals, however ingenious, must be treated in the House
with scorn and contempt.

(Sir James Scarlett, 1831)

Others were equally perturbed at the prospects.

It is my belief that every general election under such circumstances must be attended with serious riots in all parts of the
metropolis.

(Sir Richard Vyvyan, 1832)

One Member of the House of Lords offered a cutting, and refreshingly acute, observation on the motives for reform which, in his view, seemed to be based essentially on a self-contradictory logic.

> It is somewhat extraordinary ... that the House of Commons has passed a Bill of Reform in compliance with the wishes of its constituents whilst in the same breath it is asserted that Reform is necessary because under the present system it is impossible that the sense of the people can be represented in Parliament.
>
> (Earl of Mansfield, 1832)

Touché. Most of the time, though, the debating points were not a tenth as good as that. At times they plumbed the depths of arrogance and condescension. If the system was going to be bad, opponents maintained, it would have as much as anything to do with the quality – or rather its lack – amongst the influx of the uncultured and uneducated who would join the privileged electoral fraternity.

> One of my greatest objections ... is the extremely extensive way in which [the proposals] admit the lower orders to the elective franchise. ... [It] will probably lead to consequences of the most fatal kind.
>
> (Colonel Conolly, 1831)

> [The] result must be popular tumult and national calamity.
>
> (Mr Fane, 1831)

> It will not purify the election[s] to descend to a lower class of voters.
>
> (Mr Baring, 1831)

Keeping in mind that the Bill proposed still to exclude from the franchise ninety-six per cent of the population of the country, the calumny heaped upon those about to join up must be considered mild compared with what they must have thought about the rest of their countrymen (and women).

> It is proposed to enlarge [the electorate with] men of limited information, of strong prejudices, of narrow and contracted views such as shopkeepers and small [businessmen]. ... Persons of narrow minds and bigotted views ... were now to be called in to counsel the nation. [They] were not fit to execute that important trust. ... I know that among the classes are many men of intelligence, but as a class they are shallow and dogmatical, the supporters of those political principles which make light of public faith and think nothing of public credit – who regard reduction of taxation as everything.
>
> (Mr Twiss, 1831)

> [They] are precisely the description of persons who, from their being condensed in populous places and from their being employed in manufacturing towns in similar occupations are most likely to be improperly excited. They are persons on whom agitators and itinerant orators are most likely to exercise an improper influence.
>
> (Earl of Carnarvon, 1831)

There was of course no possible expectation that such people could hope to exercise independence of mind.

> So far from being fit to elect Members of Parliament, [they] are the very persons who, if the elective franchise is given to them, will be the most likely to sell it.
>
> (Lord Wynford, 1831)

By bringing into the electoral fold those who did not enjoy aristocratic rank by birth or had not reached the higher echelons by dint of their own industry, those new recruits would be vulnerable to manipulation, in particular:

> ... most liable to the influence of Government from the desire to rise above their station in society.
>
> (Mr Cumming Bruce, 1831)

It was, in short, a dangerous principle to give the vote to people who might exercise their choice in a manner based on a calculation other than that of the national interest. It was also necessary to make an informed choice, which the lower orders could not hope to fulfil.

> It is useful ... to have ... elections by persons who, from their station in society are acquainted with the characters of the men of talent of the day.
>
> (Lord Wharncliffe, 1831)

None were as succinct, or as disparaging, as Sir John Brydges.

> Set a beggar on horseback and we know what will be his career.
>
> (1832)

If the newly enfranchised voter was held in low regard, the likely new MP produced by the system was rounded upon with equal venom.

> The members elected under the proposed system will be too much under popular influence, and however right they might be in principle they will carry their principles too far and will never adopt the system of compromise which is productive of so much benefit when applied to questions which have long divided public opinion.
>
> (Lord Ellenborough, 1832)

A whole different breed of Parliamentarian was about to be born, far removed from the current paragons of virtue.

The only thing which can render office desirable to any man who is worthy of having it is that it gives him the power to carry into effect measures which will benefit his country. [Could the 'popular' member] carry any measure which was opposed to the public feeling of the moment? ... All measures to be proposed must ... be submitted to the consideration of influential individuals out doors and framed so as to flatter their opinions. Thus will be removed the great practical advantage which the country now enjoys of having Ministers selected for their ability, who weigh all measures maturely before they bring them forward.

(Lord Ellenborough, 1832)

Though [Reform] might increase the quantity of talent in the House, [it] will diminish its stock of honesty. [A 'popular' member] will [arrive in] this House without any fixed principles of action, without any stake in the country, without any means of livelihood perhaps but his patient industry and he will be debarred from the exercise of that industry by his attendence on his Parliamentary duties. What then must he do? Why he must either redeem his pledges by entering into a most unjust and most mischievous opposition or else break them and sell himself to any Ministry which thinks it worth while to buy him – either bluster forth a noisy agitator or dwindle down into a venal voter.

(Lord Mahon, 1831)

This was a crucial point, as we shall see later in the fractious debates over whether MPs should be paid – they were not to receive salaries until 1911; without a private income, a 'popular' member had either to inveigle himself,

if he was on the ruling side, into a government office or
position (and hence compromise his independence)
or rely on external organizations for support; these
were likely to be narrowly-based, partisan and, it almost
went without saying, trouble-making. It thus was self-
evident to opponents of reform that introducing to the
House men without secure independent wealth would
be the downfall of Parliament – and ultimately the
country.

> [Theirs] will not be the talents which will benefit the country
> – they will destroy its institutions. The talents will be those of
> men who have nothing to lose and everything to gain and who
> will make themselves the willing instrument of terror. They will
> be demagogues and their talents will be employed to the worst
> purposes.
>
> (Lord Wynford, 1831)

It would be the end of the 'decent' member.

> No man but one possessed of great landed interest or powerful
> family connection can hope to enter [Parliament] unless he
> consents to pander to popular prejudices and would advance as
> his own the most exaggerated popular opinions.
>
> (Lord Porchester, 1831)

Equally, those who traditionally had been able to combine
a profession with membership of the House would be
excluded because of the onerous obligations of soliciting
popular votes.

> No-one but those having a local interest, none but persons
> having means and opportunity and time to cultivate an inti-
> macy with the voters in some district of the country can ever
> hope to obtain a seat in the House. The lawyer and the banker

and the merchant therefore, must bid farewell to these walls for ever.

(Mr Shelley, 1831)

Misplaced though such fears turned out to be, the vision presented by the impending reform was ruinous in itself but also sinister in its wider implications.

As the democratic contagion spreads, pre-eminence of every sort becomes suspect – whether it be that of birth, of fortune, or of talent, education or professional rank; and moreover, the pursuit of popular favour will be so eager and joined in by so many that no man will have a chance of either acquiring or maintaining it ... unless he cultivates and watches it on the spot with a degree of assiduity incompatible with the calls of a profession.

(Sir George Ross, 1832)

In other words the MP to come would be too busy preserving and cultivating his popular support actually to do very much practical service to his constituents. Does the image seem familiar? All would crumble before the onslaught of popularism.

The tendency on the part of the [reformed] House will be to gratify ... constituents by popular measures and to increase [MPs'] own power; and the countervailing influence of any of the authorities in the State will become gradually weaker and ultimately owe its bare existence to its practical disuse.

(Sir Robert Peel, 1831)

That is, the Monarchy and the House of Lords.

The effect of the whole system under the Bill will be to exclude a useful and practical body of men from the House ... [to be replaced by] men who will flatter and delude – who will excite the people by violent addresses and declamations – who will promise what they know they cannot perform. [These] would take the place of sober, intelligent and practical men who however useful they might make themselves to the public if returned will never condescend to obtain a seat by those arts.

(Mr Courtenay, 1831)

There was much to be said for the old system. Consider, opponents told reformers, what valuable advantages were about to be lost for good. The much maligned structure of closed boroughs and nominated returns had produced bounteous good.

In this manner the greater part of our distinguished statesmen have entered Parliament and some of them perhaps would never have found admittance by any other way. The use of such members to the House itself and to the country is incalculable. Their knowledge and talent give a weight to the deliberations and inspire a respect for parliamentary discussion which in these times it is difficult for any assembly to obtain. The speeches of able and eloquent men produce an effect in the country which is reflected back again on Parliament and thus the speech of one member for a close borough is often of more benefit to the cause of truth and justice than the votes of twenty silent [elected members]. . If these close boroughs are abolished, young men of talents will be compelled to become demagogues in order to make themselves sufficiently known to the people. ... Can such a system be accompanied with good? ... I should be sorry to see the day come when a candidate must go about the country making inflammatory speeches, exciting the passions of the people as the only means of obtaining a seat in Parliament.

(Lord Wharncliffe, 1831)

The House of Commons has become an assembly which

requires a mixture of every different species of talent. That being the case, we must have by some expedient or other the means of bringing into the House that multi-form knowledge, that diversified experience, that variegated familiarity with all the different and complicated interests in the state which are necessary to arrive at safe conclusions when any of these different and complicated interests come under discussion. ... How can this be done [with the abolition of closed boroughs?] [We] are destroying the means of getting at those lights which are necessary to elucidate the questions in which these great interests are materially concerned. ... You will prevent an opportunity from being opened to talent, and ... also prevent talent from expanding.

(Mr North, 1831)

They were essential to the good order of society – you could not always trust the people to make the right choice.

They afford a refuge for the holders of unpopular opinions. If all popular opinion were just, if what pleased the multitude also pleased the wise, there would be no weight in this argument ... but [could] any Minister carry on the government honestly to the people ... for any length of time without rendering himself occasionally unpopular?

(Mr North, 1831)

And in such cases, the people needed protection from themselves. It was the view of many anti-reformers that too much faith was invested in the general population.

[Reformers] take it for granted that all populous places would form such steady opinions respecting integrity and talent that no man of integrity and talent would meet with a refusal of their suffrages.

(Mr North, 1831)

Which was, of course, a hopelessly naive presumption. For sceptics, the changes heralded the collapse of all that was good without any prospect of advantage.

> What, Sir, are the practical advantages which we are now promised as the consequence of the change we are invited to make – as the compensation for the risk we must incur? Positively not one. Up to this hour no-one has pretended that we shall gain anything by the change, excepting indeed that we shall conciliate the public favour. Why, no doubt you cannot propose to share your power with half a million of men without gaining some popularity, without popularizing by such a bribe some portion of good will. But these are vulgar arts of government.
>
> (Sir Robert Peel, 1831)

> I consider it a measure of revolution, calculated to destroy those institutions under which the country has flourished and to substitute a system the consequences of which no man can predict with certainty but which must excite the most anxious fears in the mind of every man who considers it. ... The measure is more than dangerous, it is actually destructive.
>
> (Mr Freshfield, 1831)

> It will let loose in society a spirit of the bitterest kind.
>
> (Sir John Walsh, 1831)

The foundations of society would inevitably be swept away.

> The steps by which we must descend to the catastrophe may not be precisely seen but termination is certain, nor can it be remote. ... With a House of Commons thus 'reformed', ... the fate of the peerage and the monarchy would be sealed.

... Can we suppose that such unwieldy and expensive parts of the system would be retained, their functions having become totally superseded and their very existence useless? That the monarchy itself, expensive as it must necessarily be, would in these days of rigid frugality and retrenchment be retained ... it is folly and infatuation to suppose.

(Mr Sadler, 1831)

Let his Majesty's present advisers ... approach the Sovereign with this Bill and practising on his generous and unsuspecting nature, obtain his assent – at the moment his royal hand shall inscribe the fatal act it will require no peculiar strength of mental vision to perceive the image of another hand, shadowy indeed, but darkening into reality and inscribing in portentous characters upon the tablets of the history of this ancient monarchy, 'Thy Kingdom is departed from thee!'

(Mr Sadler, 1831)

It was all so unnecessary, too.

[The reformers] appeal to the momentary excitement which has been suddenly and intentionally raised and which is as rapidly subsiding. The people of England like not sweeping changes nor dangerous experiments; their sober judgment is in favour of their ancient and happy institutions.

(Mr Sadler, 1831)

It was incumbent on the House to ensure that their 'proper' feelings were respected.

We are here to consult the interests, and not to obey the will, of the people if we honestly believe that that will conflict with those interests.

(Sir Robert Peel, 1831)

I doubt the existence of any [popular enthusiasm for Reform] and if you do find hereafter that you have been mistaken – if you do find that the people have only been acting under an excitement produced by temporary causes ... let the House remember that when the steady good sense and reason of the people of England shall return, they will be the first to reproach us with the baseness of having sacrificed the Constitution in the vain hope of conciliating the favour of a temporary burst of popular feeling; they will be the first to blame us for deferring this question to popular opinion instead of acting upon our own judgment.

(Sir Robert Peel, 1831)

The cause for resisting new fangled ideas gained support from the spiritual quarter, from one who was worried that change would all be too much for the ordinary people to handle.

The effect ... will be most prejudicial to the moral and religious interests of the people. ... It will be impossible to maintain tranquility without further innovation leading to the complete annihilation of all those institutions on which our forefathers ... prided themselves and which have for ages secured the prosperity of the country. ... I know that a considerable change has taken place in society. The so-styled march of intellect has done much but its good remains to be proved. 'Knowledge is power', unquestionably; but much of the knowledge now disseminated is superficial and injurious instead of beneficial. ... Unfortunately that species of knowledge when possessed by a person of inferior station too often gives him an evil influence over his associates.

(Bishop of Durham, 1832)

In the final straight, a scion of the Old Guard summed up the opponents' fears.

It is undoubtedly true that there is no real and lasting security against dangerous extortion but the wise and timely concession of what is just and reasonable; but the rash concession of what is unjust and unreasonable will have a directly opposite effect and can only increase our danger and accelerate ruin. ... I am convinced that it will be found impossible to make any considerable innovation in the principles of Representation which will not expose the country to dangers of the greatest magnitude whilst, on the other hand, it can at best confer upon us a very small and precarious advantage; and that is bad speculation in politics, as in commerce, where chances of gain bear no reasonable proportion to the risk of loss and ruin.

... I much fear that the new House of Commons will supply a ladder to ambitious demagogues by which a rapid succession of ephemeral tyrants, the favourites of the day, will rise to heights where they will be beyond the reach of all control and be enabled in the name of an injured and deluded people to trample into dust the laws, the liberties, the happiness and the institutions of the country.

(Marquis of Bristol, 1832)

So the Act came into force and, surprisingly for some, perhaps regrettably for others, the heavens did not fall and neither, as the years passed, did they seem likely to. Of course, as many critics had predicted – on this occasion correctly – as soon as that reform was under the belt, advocates of ever wider change started drumming their beat. It was never in fact to be completely off the agenda, not even after 1928 when the franchise by then extended to every adult in the country. There were many other battles to fight to reduce electoral anomalies and ensure the most level of playing fields. That battle would not be completed until 1958: by then, a long succession of privilege and hangovers from the past had finally been eradicated. We take a separate, detailed look at two monumentally contentious issues, the Secret Ballot and women voters, but for the remainder of this chapter we wrap up the other reforms, each of which were also landmarks in parliamentary history.

By 1958 then, centuries of inequality had been ironed out: MPs no longer needed, in order to take a seat in the House, a property qualification (abolished in 1858); they were no longer drawn only from the select section of society which had private means – they were now paid a salary from public funds (introduced in 1911); and they were now elected purely on a one person, one vote basis – archaic privileges of extra votes for business owners and university graduates were abolished (in 1949). Finally, the hereditary hold on the House of Lords was broken with the introduction of Life Peerages (in 1958). Only then – under forty years ago – could the journey started in the turmoil of the French Revolution be said to have reached its end. It had taken almost seven generations.

Each successive reform was fought as bitterly as the last, with equal measures of deep, genuine concern and crass, reactionary bloody-mindedness. Some arguments were logical; some were bizarre and far-fetched. At the time, though, it was invariably impossible to tell which was which. Only history and hindsight could do that.

The rest of the story of the extension of the franchise after 1832 is one of more of the same: it will be recalled that the 1832 Act brought the national electorate to four per cent of the population. Having breached the dam, the issue of extension was to be essentially a matter of degree – how far down the social scale was it safe to go in according the right to have a say in electing Members of Parliament? Two major electoral reform acts signpost the journey down to 1918 when all adult males and women over thirty were finally deemed responsible enough. After 1832 it was to be 1867 before Government felt it was wise to change again.

Then, the so-called 'Leap in the Dark' added a million
voters to the electorate bringing the total to some two
million voters in a population of 20 million – or ten per
cent. The next leap came twice as quickly and was twice as
big. Just seventeen years later, in 1884, the Third Reform
Act added two million more. The total electorate was now
about five million in a national population of 35 million
(or fifteen per cent). For the critics, each increase nar-
rowed what they regarded as the cushion of safety, that
margin of security which protected those who enjoyed and
exercised power from the great uncultured masses which
did not. The arguments of these years were essentially
aimed at illuminating the point that some degree of intelligence was required to exercise responsibly the privilege of
a vote.

One early contribution to the debate set the critics' stall
out on the theme.

The education fitting a man to decide on the important
interests and mighty questions involved in the government of
a great nation can never be acquired by those who, because
they are earning their daily bread by daily toil, can never
possess the leisure for study or for thought: therefore I altogether deny that the education of the masses can ever be so
raised as to fit them for becoming practically the sole posses-
sors of the suffrage. ... I am in this saying nothing offensive or
derogatory to the class. I do not doubt the goodness of the
intentions of such persons in the views they take of national
affairs ... [but] because they are without the leisure, they are
without the habits of mind qualifying them for the consideration of difficult and complicated questions, especially when their
importance is rather remote than immediate. Moreover, however qualified, they will have their class views, class feelings, class
interests; in every community they will compose the great majority and the result of a system of representation resting on no other

basis than that of the most populous communities will be that one class only will be represented, namely the most numerous – all the best educated will be practically and effectively disenfranchised.

(Earl of Harrowby, 1852)

Mere weight of numbers could never be a sound basis for wise government.

The general feeling [now] is simply that in representation all that has to be done is to collect the opinions of the majority of the people; and this view seems to be almost growing into an admitted axiom. But this view, if allowed to prevail, will lead to dangerous consequences. There is nothing in ancient or modern experience to encourage its adoption. The government of numbers gives no security for liberty. ... A majority has no natural right to govern a minority: it is purely a matter of convention. In itself, it is merely the domination of the strong over the weak: only one form of tyranny; and the object of all government is to protect the weak against the strong. There is, therefore, neither right nor experience in favour of the domination of mere numbers.

(Earl of Harrowby, 1852)

The effect on the nature of politics of 'popular' participation was seriously negative.

Candidates for election recommend themselves to one or other section of ... constituencies by topics specially interesting them to the neglect of the general interest ... and by professing what are termed extreme opinions on these topics one way or the other. Hence men of temperate natures, matured thought and moderate opinions – precisely that class of men who would constitute some of the noblest, the most valuable, elements of a representative body – are practically excluded from public life. When a gentleman goes down to present himself to a constituency, he insensibly, and as it were instinctively, adopts the tone requisite to recommend him to the crowd he is about to canvass. ... He is a furious Protectionist or he is as furious a Free Trader. Moderation finds no place; every conviction is passionately expressed and to this or that policy in its extremest form every man comes into the House of Commons pledged. This is the undoubted character of the present system, and the result is the creation of a House of Commons which has less the character of a deliberative assembly than it is desirable that it should have.

(Earl of Harrowby, 1852)

Few more cogent, logical and demonstrably true analyses of the politicians of the future as this would ever be voiced. The Earl would have no sympathy for the modern citizen complaining at the antics of MPs unable to agree on anything. The very system, he would say, which we like to hold up as the paragon of virtue practically requires extremism for success. Even enlightened minds, like that of Lord John Russell who had been largely responsible for steering the 1832 Act through Parliament, had a clear view that the line had to be drawn considerably further up the social scale than other reformers wanted.

My deliberate opinion is – and I have always expressed it – that in all the relations of life, the working classes of this country are, as to their general conduct, worthy of the highest commendation. But does it from that fairly follow that if the suffrage is rendered universal, that if every adult male in the country possesses the power of voting for the Members returned to this House, their choice would always be the wisest? Does it follow that because they desire, and perhaps in a certain sense deserve, to enjoy the privilege of sending Members to this House, they must therefore be competent to form sound opinions on all the great questions which come before us relating to the empire, to the preservation of the Constitution, the important subjects relating to colonies and commerce and the various other difficult matters which come before this House? So far from thinking them competent to such a task, I do believe that many of them would be misled – that most of them would be deceived by the people who would tell them they are unjustly paying [taxes].

(Lord John Russell, 1850)

The Prime Minister himself supported earlier doubts about the effects further reform would have on the type of politics it would produce. The modest changes of 1832 had already shown the way.

Now, generally speaking, it is necessary that the men becoming candidates for popular elections ... should ... recommend themselves to the electors by adopting the intemperate and usually the impracticable views of extreme parties on one side or the other; and thus moderate men of good sense and sound judgment and not holding extreme opinions may find it more difficult than it used to be or than it should be to find a way into the House of Commons.

(Earl of Derby, 1852)

A vicious circle was forming. The 'popular' competitive system required appeals to the ever more extreme and extravagant political platform and that, in itself, meant that politics would in future attract, and indeed reward, the more extreme-minded individual at the expense of the moderate public servant; and their involvement would increase the extremist content of politics, and so on to who knew where.

Universal suffrage, by bringing every class to the level of the lowest and most numerous, will not arrive at liberty; but by opening a path to vulgar wealth or strong ambition will only serve to break down the power of the middle classes and destroy by direct process of degradation what I would call the beneficent power [of Parliament].

(Mr Adderley, 1859)

'Vulgar wealth or strong ambition' were to be the implicit catchwords behind every opponent's argument. It was the threat of domination by characters who neither deserved power nor acquired it by gentlemanly means.

The knowledge of the working man deals with impressions – with pictures formed upon the mind, with information that comes at first hand, rather than with ideas based on reflection; it is essentially a hero worship – a few political men of whom he has particularly heard or read are, in his mind, the foundation of the system. That the working classes would exercise the franchise with the intention of subverting order and pulling down established institutions, I do not say; but with their dwarfed and political views they will be the tools, the instruments and the ladders by which dangerous and degrading men will rise into power.

(Mr Beresford Hope, 1859)

Some could express their doubts in vituperative terms. This contribution to the debate mixes a sweeping condemnation of an entire class with an apparent discerning concern for the better parts of it. Despite the muddle, the point is clear: there was a level below which it was not safe to go in awarding the vote.

[All thoughtful men agree that] by lowering the franchise as is proposed in this indiscriminate way, while you will get a certain number of good, prudent and intelligent men, yet inasmuch as the mass of men are improvident and ignorant, in spite of mechanics' institutes, and perhaps will be so till the end of time, the thoughtful and provident working people will be swamped as entirely as any other class of the community. ... This measure is one which strikes at those of the working classes who are thoughtful and provident and places the political power of the country in the hands of the thoughtless and improvident.

(Lord Elcho, 1865)

The nub of the issue was the fallacy of the superficially attractive principle on which the French Revolution was founded, that all men were born equal. Every experience of life told any thinking person that that was patently absurd. To base a political system on that principle was the height of folly.

The principle of numbers involves the principle of equality; leading to the conclusion that every man is equally fit to choose a Member of Parliament – the ploughman as fit as a Prime Minister, the spinner as fit as the master manufacturer. Is this what you now mean to say? Do you really think that a hundred artisans ought to have more political power than ninety-nine employers? Ought a hundred labourers and ploughmen to have more political power than ninety-nine squires?

(Mr Horsman, 1865)

Another employed the equally familiar argument that there should be no taxation without representation to its other, equally logical, conclusion.

It seems to me that a man so poor that he is excused on the grounds of poverty from bearing any burdens due to the State ... is not in a condition to impose burdens upon others.

(Mr Lowe, 1867)

One man, one vote was by no means a self-evident, natural

state of affairs and as the last excerpt shows, the arguments against it were never based solely on blind prejudice. It would be a brave person who would predict with confidence which was the 'right' answer. A frequent participant in the debate provides one of the more plausible expositions of the argument that the lower one went and the more of 'them' one involved, paradoxically the less truly representative the electorate would become.

In the upper and middle classes persons can choose their own occupations, their own amusements, their own pursuits and this produces that healthy and wide diversity of mind which really gives these classes their preponderating influence in the administration of the land. But [working classes] from the very nature of their occupations and circumstances are more subject to the influence of class feelings and more accustomed to surrender themselves to the guidance of the stronger minds of local leaders. The very nature of their employment involves their working in continuous grooves and in constant association with their fellow workmen ... From these influences there is a more powerful effect produced upon the weak, the ignorant, the dissipated among them by the stronger minds out of their order. ... Thus a class feeling is necessarily created in the minds of the working men and so with equal talent, equal desire for knowledge and equal goodness, each single working man is a less unit in the composition of the great national mind and character than each individual of any other portion of the community. Enfranchising a number of working men will not therefore be enfranchising that great number of minds all independently turned upon the same question from different points of view which the widening of the franchise would be in other portions of the social polity but merely performing a multiplication sum.

(Mr Beresford Hope, 1866)

He concluded with the timeless, and unanswerable, question which bedevilled reformers.

> How are we to enfranchise the intelligent, well-conducted man and not enfranchise the drunken, worthless fellow who would pull him back and more than neutralize his vote?

What another critic called 'this continual appeal to the simplicity of numbers' sparked a vein of argument which believed that legislators were being pushed down the wrong road. Far from lowering the standards for qualification for the vote, ought not they be looking at ways to raise the level of the people to the high privilege the vote represented? In this sideshow of the campaign the basics of the case was that the vote was more a reward to the honest citizen than a God-given right. Mr Beresford Hope again:

> I wish to see the working classes possessed of more political power than at present. But I would give the franchise not as a right but as a reward. ... I hope the whole of the Members of this House regard their seats here as rewards for honest and conscientious discharge of duty; and why should not the working man regard his vote in the same honourable light ...?
> (1859)

> What I want is a test by which to ascertain the character of the man. Instead of bringing the qualification down to the man, I would hold it up as something which a man is to rise to and to attain.
> (Mr Macaulay, 1860)

Surely, the argument went, the successive dilution of the qualification for a vote only sent the wrong message to the country.

> I consider the course proposed by this Bill to be exceedingly

dangerous, that it is only the first step in a downward progress towards revolution. ... It does not stimulate the working man who is anxious for a vote to increased industry, economy and prudence in order that he may obtain the object of his ambition ... but it in effect says, 'You need not exert yourself to rise for we will come down to you.'

(Mr Black, 1865)

There seemed to him to be a carefree attitude towards the long-term consequences of what reformers invariably called piecemeal changes.

No prudent man would step into a railway carriage without first ascertaining where it was going to stop; it will be too late to inquire after the train has begun to move.

He was clear in his own mind what lay in store.

If in the electoral franchise we agree to a downward movement, we must be prepared for an accelerated descent, and that by geometrical progression till we reach the bottom.

(Mr Black, 1865)

Even Disraeli, then Leader of the Conservative Opposition in the Commons and soon to be navigator there of the 1867 Act, voiced doubts about going the whole distance.

The suffrage should remain a privilege and not a right – a privilege to be gained by virtue, by intelligence, by industry, by integrity and to be exercised for the common good. And I think if you quit that ground – if you once admit that every man has a right to vote whom you cannot prove to be disqualified for it you will change the character of the Constitution and you will change it in a manner which will tend to lower the importance of this country. ... I doubt very much whether a

democracy is a Government that would suit this country.
                                                   (Mr Disraeli, 1865)

On the Bill itself, there was as ever the reminder that the vote was a possession of responsibility, not a token of birth, indistinguishable from mere existence.

> Once [accept] the franchise to be a right ... limit it as you might it lands you in universal suffrage ... but hold it as a trust ... and it follows that it is a trust to be exercised by that portion of the community which has reached a certain standing and acquired a certain stake in the country and whose ability to act upon solid sense and reflection rather than from inconsiderate impulse might be presumed upon.
>
>   (Mr Laing, 1866)

On a number of occasions, a more pro-active approach to the question was adopted. Instead of simply trying to draw the bottom line higher up the human scale in a negative way, some imaginative ideas came forth to achieve the same result in a positive way – the creation and application of educational tests for qualification for the vote, the first time anyone had proposed a non-property or non-financial basis for the vote. It would still be a privilege, but one which, theoretically, anyone could acquire.

> Let a man pay in some shape for this privilege [of voting]. If he cannot pay in money let him pay in mind. Under our present system we do not require property to be intelligent. I shall not ask intelligence to be rich.
>
>   (Mr Clay, 1866)

Surely the principle could not be contested?

The franchise gives persons power over the property of others to a certain extent – is it not then perfectly reasonable to require that those who have power over the property of others should be qualified to administer their own affairs; that they should have learnt at least sufficient to perform their duties to their families? [Opponents] say, 'No: give them the franchise; give them power over others though they may be totally unable to look after their own affairs and though they cannot even give the lowest grades of education to their children.

... I maintain ... that the franchise should be a stimulus to self-culture; and not only so but that the possession of it should be the result of a certain amount of self-restraint and study. ... I contend that the only claim to the franchise consists in intelligence and that it must not be held as a right. If it is a right, a man [can] dispose of it for his own advantage; he [can] accept a bribe; he [can] sell it and no-one could interfere.

(Lord Robert Montagu, 1866)

On the Third Reform Act of 1884 there was a similar but unsuccessful attempt to introduce a subjective test of competence. An amendment tried to require voters to be able to write the name of the candidate for whom he intended to vote.

At present there are the disqualifications of pauperism, criminality and lunacy; and I only ask the [House] to add the disqualification of palpable and demonstrable ignorance.

(Mr Stanley Leighton, 1884)

As late as 1934, after all the confrontation over who should and who should not have the vote had been settled, one critic tried to turn back the tide with a personal Bill to eradicate from the electoral register the 'negligent' voter, by which he meant those whose failure to vote in elections clearly demonstrated a lack of interest in the democratic process.

I think if people found it a little more difficult to get the vote they would think a great deal more of it. ... These people occasionally become terribly excited and may cast a vote which, in a fit of emotion, ... puts the wrong party into power. You have, because of this great mass of negligent voters, a much greater instability of public opinion as expressed at the polls than would otherwise be the case.

(Mr Williams, 1934)

Each elector would be removed from the register: 'unless they could show that their failure to vote had been due to sickness or absence or any other good, sound and reasonable cause or, failing such a good reason, that they must pay a fee of five shillings in lieu thereof'. The House actually voted in favour of the Bill on its introduction, but as with many private measures it suffered the usual fate of not being given debating time for the rest of its passage.

THE PROPERTY QUALIFICATION

One of the earliest anomalies to be completely abolished was the ancient rule that MPs had to possess a certain value of property (£300 for a borough member; £600 for a county member) before they could stand for, and take, a seat in Parliament. This was supposed to guarantee that Members had a physical stake in the affairs of the country, were affluent enough to devote their time exclusively to the business of the House without prejudicing their personal affairs or be susceptible to bribery and, doubtless too, that they had passed the most basic tests in financial responsibility. In practice, the rule was notoriously ignored. Many famous figures sat with only paper qualifications to their names, if any at all. In the closed society of Westminster there were few to rock the boat or expose the laxity. As the franchise widened though, and more non-aristocratic citizens sought election, the rule could be used as an effective device to exclude those likely to disturb the comfortable Commons life – the Radicals and the working-class members. As early as 1837 one Member objected to abolishing the time-dishonoured rule by contending that:

> a more obnoxious or objectionable measure ... has never been suggested in this House.
>
> (Mr Trevor)

He gave his reasons.

> Those who aspire to the honour of a seat in this House should have something like a stake in the country instead of men without property being elected the representatives of the people ... At the present time, when novelty is the order of the day, it might appear to be impolitic to endeavour to oppose what is called the tide of improvement, but which, in my opinion, is nothing more or less than the tide of innovation and mischievous interference. By getting rid of the qualification we would open the door for men to get into the House who would have to legislate on property in which they have not the least interest. ... The security of property will be best upheld by those who have some interest in it.
>
> (Mr Trevor, 1837)

The consequences would be destructive of Parliament's integrity.

> I can not see and never been able to see what good reform has done the country. ... I only wish the property qualification was ten times greater and then the House would be more respectable than it is. ... For the House of Commons as a body I entertain a high respect but there are those among us whom I can only look upon as belonging to the tagrag and bobtail of society. I have been a Member of the House of Commons for twenty-six years and am sorry to say that I find it going down

and sinking lower in respectability every session. Keep up the respectability of the House of Commons by property men and the people at large will be more satisfied that their true interests are protected.

(Colonel Sibthorp, 1855)

Is the House prepared to sanction the principle that a large number of Members might be admitted whose property was of such a reduced character that it would be impossible for them to devote the whole of their time to the business of the country without ruin to themselves and whether it is fair to place them in such a position as to render them liable to temptations which few men [would be] able to resist? It is clear that if men of such limited means are to be admitted it will be impossible to maintain the principle of freedom from arrest ... otherwise the House will become neither more nor less than a refuge for bankrupt and disreputable characters.

(Mr Bentinck, 1858)

The future was summed up on the eve of the abolition.

There can be no greater peril to the country than the having in Parliament a body of men who have nothing to lose and everything to gain by a scramble.

(Colonel North, 1858)

PAYMENT OF MPs

The same essential logic lay behind the opposition to one of the most bitterly contested of all the reforms to sweep Parliament after electoral reform itself – paying Members. Hitherto only those with private incomes could afford to sit in Parliament. Those without such means and who would have to earn a living simultaneously with Parliamentary commitments found that, with the possible exception of the legal profession, it was a practical impossibility.

Like property qualifications, absence of payment was an effective exclusion clause preventing members of the lower classes of society from ever having the chance to pursue a Parliamentary career. Those safely on the inside defended the status quo with the traditional argument that service in Parliament was exactly that – service, a public duty, not a profession from which to draw profit. Turning it into a job like any other would attract the wrong type of character into the House.

Curiously, the notion of paying Members of Parliament was not an entirely novel one. It had in fact been the established practice from the earliest days of Parliament for representatives to receive expenses and wages. In Edward III's time, in the early fourteenth century, it had been four shillings a day for a knight and two shillings a day for a burgess. The system had survived until about 1620, just before the Civil War. Prime Minister Gladstone, responding to the first attempt to revive payment, deftly used the past evidence to support his own view that the practice should *not* be reinstituted. His curiously logical argument was that the system died out precisely because it must have been concluded that no good reason could be advanced for perpetuating it.

Whenever there is a public service to be done you do not pay for it unless you find it necessary to do so. ... The public has no difficulty whatever in finding competent and qualified persons ... to discharge all these offices without pay.

   ... I contend that the public enjoys the fortunate advantage of having plenty of persons who are ready to serve it for nothing and that the public is entitled to the benefit. When there are numbers of well-qualified men ready to give their labour without being paid, why should we go out of our way and insist upon adding to the taxation of the country for the purpose of giving them a payment? I think we are only doing the public fair justice in taking advantage of circumstances which happen to be in our favour.

(Mr Gladstone, 1870)

It was, though, far more than a matter of finance. Long-standing traditions of character, service and responsibility would be jeopardized.

There is no other country in the world where there is anything like the amount of gratuitous unpaid labour that there is here. Not only have we unpaid work in Parliament but in the innumerable [councils, school boards, boards of guardians and magistracy] scattered all over the country; our voluntary system has become a habit and tradition of the country; and I think this public spirit is the very salt of our social and political life. It keeps the administration of our affairs free from corruption, it maintains a high level and standard of duty such as I think you will find in no other country in the world. I do not think you can change the constitution of Parliament without affecting public life at its very roots. To introduce the system of paid Members of Parliament will be to supplant the voluntary with the professional politician. ... I believe the introduction of paid Members will sooner or later lower the character of this House.

(Mr Smith, 1889)

The leader of the Conservative Government in the Commons maintained that all the voluntary spirit in the country would evaporate.

If you adopt this proposal you will kill at the root the spirit that has produced this gratuitous work; you will give it a blow from which it will never recover; you will put the Parliamentary stamp upon the theory that a man who gives his services for nothing is a fool.

(Mr Balfour, 1892)

Others worried about the diluting effect payment would have on the quality of the Member attracted into politics. In countries where politicians were paid at public expense:

> ... politics are degraded into a trade and there is nothing like that public spirit which induces men in England to give their services to the State without reward or hope of reward. ... I maintain that if the proposal under consideration is carried out the social distinction of this House will be destroyed and a class of representative will be introduced who will not be drawn from the highest best-educated and best-cultivated class of the community but from the ranks below that class ... the new representatives ... will not be so cultivated and politics in England will be reduced to the level of what they are in some other countries.
>
> (Viscount Bury, 1870)

Twenty years later the same worries were more forcibly put.

> When you attach payment to membership, you place it on a like footing with the other professions and you make it an object that may be sought by the poor and deserving and by working class representatives but that will equally be the object of the idle, the necessitous and the unscrupulous.
>
> (Mr Curzon, 1889)

Human nature would ensure that nothing good could come of it.

> I believe that one absolutely universal failing of mankind is vanity; and when we have vanity and a chance of £300 a year, I think we will find plenty of candidates at the elections.
>
> (Sir E. Clarke, 1906)

It would not achieve the objective set for it either.

> I say that payment of Members of Parliament will tend to bring
> in not a larger number of working men but a large number of
> place-hunters, men whom I must call self-seeking demagogues.
>
> (Mr Smith, 1889)

Home Secretary Henry Matthews hit on a novel argument.
Not only did the people need to be protected from the
unscrupulous Member. Payment would also put the Member at the mercy of the people – and that was an unthink-
able position to be in.

> I do not say that from the fact of being paid a man necessarily
> receives less respect and social consideration but at any rate
> the fact of there being no payment saves a Member from the
> suspicion of one more inducement added to those so elo-
> quently enumerated [such as bribery, fraud and corruption]. ...
> I do not say payment degrades a man ... but I do say that the
> position of Members will be more open to suspicion, more
> open to the reproach that they were not earning their salary.
> This will be thrown in their teeth by the constituencies and
> they will be called to account and reminded that they are
> expected to speak not because they have something to say but
> because they are paid to speak.
>
> (1889)

Another imaginative argument came from one who foresaw that the new breed of paid Member would have different motives, the effect of which on Parliament would be
calamitous.

> Has there been any great want of progress in legislating for the
> social and material progress of the people because Members of
> Parliament are unpaid, and will it be quickened in the least if
> you have paid Members of Parliament? In that case, you may
> make very much slower progress than at present with the

business of the nation. It will be the earnest desire of these
Members of Parliament to stand well with their constituents
and there will be a great many more men in this House who
will desire to take part in the proceedings and so the business
will be greatly delayed.

(Mr Hayes Fisher, 1892)

And, another maintained, the willingness of Members to
have General Elections would be reduced.

I am quite certain that one effect will be a very much greater
length to Parliament than at present. Members are often
telling us that we ought to face the country. There will be no
threat so terrible as a dissolution if it means that every man is
to lose his salary.

(Mr A. Graham Murray, 1904)

As late as 1893 the whole idea was still preposterous.

There is an abundance of men with first-class education, men
of culture, men of accumulation of wealth who are proud to
serve the country for nothing. As long as the nation has men
of this kind it seems to me a startling proposition that we
should insult them by offering to pay them. ... The proposition
has only to be described for its absurdity to be apparent and it
is a proposition which I am sure Parliament and the country
will never endorse.

(Admiral Field, 1893)

To say that such observers were missing the point would
not be the colossal understatement it might at first appear.
Non-aristocratic Members *were* entering Parliament in
increasing numbers. That was quite incontestable. But
they did so only at great sacrifice by hundreds of others;
working-class MPs usually had their expenses paid by count-

less collections of small donations from the faithful determined to ensure a different voice in the House than hitherto. It was only by such time-consuming and logistically
nightmarish arrangements that those without private means
managed to scrape an existence in the Commons. In the
eyes of the critics of payment such a situation was no bad
thing. The requirement for self-support was, for them, the
guarantee of integrity and probity in public life. The great
reformer of the civil service – who should know a bit about
public service and motivation – fully endorsed this point of
view. It was essential to protect both the Member and the
public from those:

> ... temptations from which the rich are free from the very fact
> of their wealth but to which poor men are particularly exposed.
>
> (Sir Stafford Northcote, 1895)

Of course, the same kind of argument could be used to
support payment – that where Members were down on their
luck the absence of payment opened up the risk of corruption. Payment would resolve any such risks. The argument
was contested bluntly.

> How can a man be made more free and independent by
> accepting a dole out of State funds. ... The effect of the whole
> proposal is to make a Member dependent on the State.
>
> (Sir H.Kimber, 1906)

What would payment do other than to compromise the
free spirit?

> When a man knows that by taking a line in antagonism to a
> large section or to a majority of his constituency he might lose
> not merely his seat but his salary, if a poor man he could be
> placed in a position which he would find, in some cases at

least, considerable difficulty in resisting.

(Mr Curzon, 1895)

This argument was not without some weight. Without his own means of income, a paid Member would be acutely vulnerable to pressures from Party influences. Many saw the fatal hand of the party manager and a future in which Members would find themselves forced to consolidate within firm party boundaries, killing the indepenence of mind and ossifying policy into huge lumbering dinosaurs of Parliamentary machines.

If you introduce a system of paid Members they will be considered more as delegates and less as representatives. ... I honestly believe that the status of a Member will lowered by payment.
(Mr Goschen, Opposition spokesman, 1895)

Examples elsewhere in the public service told the same story.

I can not agree [with] men looking upon membership of the House as a means of living and promoting interests other than those of the State. We have never found that a soldier fights better in the field because his pay is higher or that the State is better served in any Department by men whose sole idea is remuneration.

(Mr Randles, 1904)

After a tussle lasting forty years, the issue was resolved with surprising abruptness and simplicity. On a summer day in 1911, in what looks like a heady piece of bullet biting, the Liberal Government, doubtlessly still emboldened by the envigorating effects of having just two days earlier passed the Parliament Act emasculating the House of Lords, swept aside all misgivings and proposed a simple motion granting MPs a salary of £400 a year. There was to be no further examination of the principle, no follow-up legislation. The simple resolution of the House has been the legal basis for payment ever since. The final debate prompted ever more extreme visions of the effect the move would have on the nature of Parliament.

> The payment of Members will be money thrown away. The work of the House has been done very well up to the present by the voluntary services of the Members. Now we are going to have introduced into this chamber glib-tongued, loose-lipped, street-corner orators instead of having our affairs conducted as they have been conducted in the past.
>
> (Mr Kebty-Fletcher, 1911)

> [I] think the effect will be evil. ... In my view the disadvantages of this proposal are both cumulative and overwhelming. In the first place I think this proposal must lead to the loss of the moral authority of the House of Commons in the public mind.
>
> ...It will lead to the extinction of the class of Member who is active and distinguished in other walks of life and who, in spite of having other work, does as a matter of fact attend to the business of this House because he believes it an honour and a duty to do so but who in future will have neither time nor inclination to compete with the vast number of candidates that will come forward when the reward is not merely election to the House of Commons but [payment] for his work as a Member of Parliament.
>
> ... I believe we will get a different type of Member in this house from that which we have been used to. We will get a type of Member and a much larger proportion of men resembling the paid professional speakers of political parties. ... Above all, I object to it because I believe it will sound the death-knell of that system of voluntary service which has been the chief and unique glory of British public life.
>
> (Mr Lee, 1911)

From the good old days of landed squires, successful businessmen and cultured minds, the House would now have a different, unedifying, complexion.

> Who is this new system going to attract? It is highly probable that it will attract the class from whom the professional politicians are usually recruited in other countries, namely unsuccessful barristers, needy journalists and the jack-of-all-trades and masters of none.
>
> (Mr Sandys, 1911)

He probably had a point! The fear was genuine – and perhaps history has borne the critics out on this one – that the individual nature of membership of the House would be sacrificed to the overbearing power of the Party machine.

> [It will] create a class of professional politician upon whom [the Party] can absolutely rely. Men of this character will be able to draw their salary from the National Exchequer but they can only ensure their re-election and they can only guarantee a continuance of their means of livelihood by the most complete and absolute surrender of their independence and by the most complete obedience to party discipline and organisation. I say not only will this tend to enormously increase [sic] the despotic power of party organisation but in the end it must, I greatly fear, tend to lower the standard of public life in this country.
>
> (Mr Sandys, 1911)

As night follows day, the takeover by the Party bosses was inevitable, and MPs would become pack donkeys for the Party rather than individual, thinking, spirits.

Look at the position of the man who is entirely dependent

upon his £400 a year. He has given up the best years of his
life to political service and is consequently entirely unfitted for
any other form of lucrative employment. Is a man like that
going to risk his seat and salary by giving an unpopular vote?
Surely the temptation to vote for safety will be very much
stronger than it is at the present time.

(Mr Sandys, 1911)

For the Conservative Opposition spokesman, the salary on
offer was: 'too much for a fool, not enough for a sage'. It
would therefore attract the worse kind of people – those
who would end up totally reliant on continued membership for personal security.

The payment of this money to men who have given up
everything else in order to come to the House and who have
nothing to depend on but this money lays us open to a serious
danger. ... How far greater will the terror of a Dissolution be if
it means not merely the loss of a seat in the House but the loss
of a livelihood and perhaps the only livelihood that a man at
the time of life he has reached can draw?

... [It will attract] not ... the man who comes here because
he is a genuinely earnest politician, interested in these affairs
and anxious to accomplish a work but ... men who, having
failed in other departments, whether as workmen with their
hands or as workmen with their heads, being gifted with glib
tongues and easy manners, find this the easiest and simplest
way of procuring a living.

(Mr Austen Chamberlain, 1911)

Perhaps the last prophetic words should go to one who
envisaged a future which may seem uncomfortably familiar
to us now.

I believe that this policy if ever adopted is much more likely to increase the ranks of the talkers than the thinkers. Everyone of those gentlemen, relying as he will have to do to a very large extent on that £400 a year, will naturally cast his eye more upon the reporters' gallery than upon the Chair. He will be almost bound to advertise himself in order that his salary of £400 a year may be something in the nature of a permanent salary.

... I think that a loss of independence will ensue. ... We are supposing that owing to our voting a salary of £400 a year a great number of men who could not otherwise exist in this House are induced to come into it. Then what is their position? A year or so before an election they want to use their independence. ... They want to vote against the majority of [their party] for the time being. ... The party whip has them in the hollow of his hand. He would be able to say to that man: 'You are just beginning to get a foothold on this Parliamentary ladder; you are an ambitious man; I shall not run you at the next election and that £400 a year on which you are relying will no longer be yours.' I believe that would make the country less and not more independent.

(Mr Hayes Fisher, 1911)

PLURAL VOTING

The last anomaly might come as a surprise to many, but until as late as 1949 the concept of 'one person, one vote' notionally sanctified in 1928 was, in fact, less pure and conclusive than on the face of it it appeared. It was true that every adult had the vote – one vote, at the very least – but for 250,000 others, remnants of past practices allowed them to have more than one. The legacy of the days when votes were awarded essentially as rewards for property acquisition, the nation's electoral laws still granted a vote wherever a person maintained a property of a certain rateable value. The possession of two houses was rewarded with two votes (so long as they were in different constituencies). Similarly, a businessman with factories strewn across the country got a vote for each of them.

The property basis for a vote was anchored in the ancient assumption that electing Members of Parliament was a responsibility to be calibrated by one's stake in society, the presumption being that the greater one's stake the better sense one would use when casting one's ballot – or ballots. (Hence the antipathy towards giving the vote to those who owned nothing in society and who it was presumed, thereby stood to lose nothing by making ill-considered decisions at election time.)

Justification for plural voting, as it was termed, was based on the fairly incontestable premise that if one had a home in one constituency and a factory in another on both of which one paid rates to separate authorities, natural justice and the 'no taxation without representation' principle commanded that one got a vote for both. In an 1891 debate on the subject it was revealed that one entrepreneurial elector had managed to amass an entitlement to twenty-three votes! Clearly, however, their value which was significant in the days of patrician influence and tiny electorates had consistently declined over time as electorates became unimaginably larger. By the twentieth century they were an anachronism, but nonetheless avidly protected by opponents of the sterile numbers game which politics in their eyes had become. There was also a rich element in the debates that this was the last refuge, the final bunker, for those wishing to preserve some recognition in the electoral system that in reality people were *not* all the same, and that the 'all men are equal' premise which underlay 'one person, one vote' was a folly of the greatest order. The early debates started on pragmatic arguments.

I do not see why I should not have a vote for my office in the Strand and also for my house in the country since I pay taxes and rates for both. If there is any reliance in the axiom that representation should accompany taxation, I see every reason why a man paying double ... should have two votes.

(Colonel Hughes, 1891)

Another pointed out that there would be a grave injustice without some acknowledgement of their case.

If you take away the electoral right based upon property ... are you also going to relieve him from the obligation of paying rates [on the property concerned]? Otherwise you will have representation dissociated entirely from taxation.

(Mr Russell, 1892)

I would like to know why it is considered so unreasonable that a man, having two interests in two places, should not be allowed two votes. I think the great bulk of those who have two votes are people of some position and property who have a largish stake in the country and who are possibly more intelligent.

(Mr Webster, 1895)

Surely too it showed that such people took their civic duties seriously.

Men, who by the very exercise of their vote, prove their interest. ... A freeholder living in one place who takes the trouble to vote in another constituency must be genuinely interested.

(Mr Whitmore, 1892)

But money provided the apparently insurmountable constitutional argument.

'No taxation without representation' has been the cry throughout all the ages and now observe that in this Bill you are proposing to institute a system which provides that in certain cases it shall be possible to have taxation without the corresponding opportunity of representation.

(Mr Mitchell-Thomson, 1906)

I have always thought that the constitutional theory was that each locality should be represented in Parliament and that therefore it was not only right that each man who has an interest in that locality, with a proper qualification, should, independently of any interest elsewhere, be entitled to vote in the choice of the Member for that locality. If you take away his right to vote because he has a qualification elsewhere, you do not only an injustice to the individual but to the locality in which he has a considerable interest and in which he has a perfect right to express his preference for one candidate over another.

(Mr Akers-Douglas, 1906)

Thus:

If the principle of local representation be sound and if the principle that taxation and representation should go together be sound, then the position of the plural voter is logical and unassailable. ... If you sweep away plural voting it may be true to say that you do not disfranchise a man in regard to his national interest but you do disfranchise him in regard to his local interests which the law now secures to him.

(Mr Salter, 1906)

The purpose of electing representatives was, after all, to reflect the locality's interests in the national Parliament.

I believe that the proposal to abolish the plural vote is vicious in principle. ... My reason for holding that view is that our electoral system is based upon the representation of the communities in particular localities. ... If you have a system based upon that principle, it must be obvious to every one that you ought to make a return of the representative as truly typical of the character of the constituency as may be and that you ought not to prevent from voting anyone who is really and genuinely a member of that constituency. ... It is a complete mistake to say that because he is also a representative constituent in another district he is to be deprived of the right of voting in each of the districts in regard to each of which he has substantial and vital interests. ... The most common case is that of a merchant who has his offices in a great town or city but who has his residence some way out in the country. ... That merchant is a member, it may be a very important member, of the city constituency. As a resident in the country he takes an active part in all the life of the countryside and why is it to be said that he is only to vote in one of these two constituencies?

(Sir R. Finlay, 1913)

That view was echoed by many others.

Surely as long as you leave untouched the system of representation by constituencies, it is but elementary fairness that those who bear the burden of expense in a constituency should have the right to choose its representative? If that is so, by what system of logic or justice can you justify depriving a man of his vote in a constituency where he contributes to the common expenses for the sole reason that he makes a similar contribution in another constituency? If he pays twice why should he not vote twice? If he is exercising the rights and bearing the burdens of citizenship in two areas, each of which Parliament has defined as a constituency, why should he not have a voice in both in choosing the man who is to represent his interests?

(Mr Hume-Williams, 1914)

Put like that, it is certainly difficult to contend with. Increasingly, though, a more sociological strain to the argument developed. The unhealthy odour of 'levelling down' was detected.

> Why should you level down to those voters who happen to be interested only in one constituency? What sense is there in saying that because there is a number of voters who have interests in only one constituency therefore those voters who have interests in more than one should only be allowed to vote in one constituency? Surely there is no reason in that. It is merely proceeding on the principle that because one man has only got one vote because he has only one set of interests, therefore no man is to have more than one vote although he has more than one set of interests. There is no justice in that and there is no reason in it.
>
> (Sir R. Finlay, 1912)

The insistence on wholesale equality could only be destructive in its effect on society.

> We consider that there ought to be a difference between the improvident man and the thrifty man and we think it unfair that those who take the trouble to make themselves worthy members of society should be treated just on the same footing as the careless and improvident.
>
> (Mr Tomlinson, 1895)

This early view had its supporters amongst those who believed that acquiring the plural vote was a spur to social advancement rather than a negation of civic rights.

> There are many members of the working classes who have saved a little money and have got a little freehold of their own and so obtain a double vote; that is an inducement to them and we ought to foster in every possible way the desire of the

people to possess small properties.

(Mr Webster, 1895)

Even in 1914 some deplored any move to equalize the unequal.

> [Proponents of abolition] talk a good deal about anomalies but what strikes me as the greatest anomaly of all is that we should have ... a Bill to take away what little recognition is given in this country to what I may describe as education and progress. In Belgium an extra vote is given to a man who passes a certain standard in education. [Our] plural voters too, we find, are educated and progressive people and not the idle rich. ... They are men who initiate and start works and businesses in various parts of the country and I say that a man who starts a business in any town or village is a benefactor because he gives employment and wages. To men of this class we ought to give increased votes; we ought not to seek to deprive them of the vote they have.
>
> ... [The Bill] is purely destructive. It tries to bring everything down to the lowest possible level.

(Colonel Yate, 1914)

After this pre-First World War agitation, the issue was not broached again until the 1930s and the second Labour Government. It had now become a party issue – the multiple voters were well-off, Conservative electors. With a Commons majority in favour of abolition, the plural vote was saved on this occasion by the House of Lords, which threw out the measure. The Labour majority evaporated before it could be forced through under the Parliament Act. The antagonisms had, by now, become even more bitter.

If a man is more intelligent than others then, other things

being equal, his opinion is more worth having than that of the man who is less intelligent; however much [we] may say his opinion is of equal value [nothing] can make it so.

(Mr Ramsbotham, 1931)

No two men are equal and it is clear that a good citizen should have more power to advise the nation and more power to settle the government of the realm than the poorest brain which just keeps its owner out of the lunatic asylum. We must give everybody a vote, but why should not some people have more than one vote? I would not base it on the value of money in the slightest. ... I would put vote-power upon deserts and ... value.

(Sir Charles Oman, 1931)

He elaborated further.

'One man, one vote' is an absurdity. It is based on the theory that all men are equal and it is obvious that no two men are equal. ... I have been acquainted with three people all of whom have a single vote. – One has governed 15 million people successfully for many years and has been honoured with every honour short of a peerage that the Crown can offer. The second is intermittently in a lunatic asylum and the third is a skilled artisan who chooses to lose every position which is offered to him through an unfortunate addiction to betting. These three men have the same amount of voting value. It is absurd that the lunatic and the wastrel living on the dole should have a power of voting equal [to the first]. ... The simple fact is that the ideal of democracy is not 'one man, one vote,' not that the semi-idiot and the genius should have the same amount of vote power.

(Sir Charles Oman, 1931)

I feel that democracy has gone a great deal too far when it carries us to 'one man, one vote.' That is not a business slogan for the country. I would prefer another maxim – 'The man who pays the piper calls the tune.' ... [Businessmen] pay a very large portion of their income in Income Tax and a great deal of the capital is taken from them for the benefit of the State when they die. It has come about that out of 29 million electors, fewer than two million are direct taxpayers. I consider that those direct taxpayers who are funding one half of the whole income of the State are entitled to some protection and should at least be given a business vote.

(Colonel Sir James Reynolds, 1931)

The pluralists held out only until another Government, even more securely in command of Parliament, passed the Representation of the People Act in 1949, which made residence the only qualification for a vote.

A second odd electoral privilege marking a further section of society apart from the rest in terms of equality was also abolished by the same Act – the unique phenomenon of the University seats. They were unique because they were the only example in British Parliamentary history of Members being returned by what might be termed 'functional' rather than geographical constituencies. Since James I initiated the practice in 1603 allowing Oxford and Cambridge to return two Members each, they had been a small, practically insignificant, element. They were voted for not only by staff and current postgraduates of the institutions but all past graduates of the University. The University Member acquired a special place in the Parliamentary constellation as being independent of party politics, returned by the cream of the educated elite. They might have been expected to wither, but ironically, as electoral reform widened opportunities as the nineteenth century progressed, so did the University seats increase.

As new universities sprang up, so did Parliament

acknowledge their right too to return Members. The four
Scottish universities between them sent two Members
from 1868 and from as recently as 1918 institutions in
Northern Ireland, Wales and the 'Combined English Universities' also gained the privilege. In all, for the twelve
seats, over 200,000 university educated people across the
country enjoyed a second vote care of their alma mater. It
was, of all the privileges, the most explicit appeal to the
principle that different levels of society should have influence in proportion to their culture, breeding or intelligence. As one of the select band of University Members
told the House when the first attempt was made to deprive
him and his colleagues of their seats.

> I say it is for the good of the nation at large that there should
> be some variety in the representation of the people.
>
> (Mr Stormonth Darling, 1889)

Other sections of society were, after all, represented. Whereas
industrial seats returned working class Members and country
seats returned those with the landed classes uppermost in
their interests, only the educated as a stratum in society
missed out.

> It is impossible to apply that principle of locality to the great profes-
> sional classes. They are scattered all over the country; they are always
> and everywhere in the minority and if you want to arrive at their mind
> on a particular question, it is impossible to group them as you group
> merchants of the City of London or the artisans of the East End or the
> agriculturalists of Wiltshire and therefore the only way to get at their
> real mind on public questions is by some such expedient as University
> representation.
>
> (Mr Stormonth Darling, 1889)

As late as 1936 the point was argued with equal vigour.

Trade unions, for example, managed to get their representation by direct sponsorship of MPs. Why not the professions then?

> Because the members of the professional occupations are so scattered they cannot secure even a single direct representative of their own except through the University vote.
>
> (Miss Rathbone, 1936)

In the same Bill of 1931 which had sought to abolish other plural voting, the universities were in the sights of the abolitionists. The resistance was just as strong.

> I feel that those who have had the advantage of a university training are entitled to some special representation in the House. I do not believe in the principle that one must merely count noses in order to determine representation.
>
> (Major Church, 1931)

The different character of an election for a university seat added an estimable quality to the Member thereby elected. Unlike the rabble of the hustings, it was conducted through correspondence.

> The whole business of a [normal] electoral campaign is to create excitement, to blackguard your opponent. The atmosphere has a certain warmth, you endeavour as far as possible to raise the temperature of your audiences, you have a meeting and you are not satisfied unless the audience go away in a high state of excitement. You wish to have them roar applause, to have them change from a number of people exercising their private judgment into an excited crowd. ... All the members of a crowd become excited with emotion and lose all the use of their brain. ... Instead of selecting a representative by their intelligence, by quiet thought, they are rushed, in the passion

of the election, into expressing not their judgment but their passion, not their intelligence but their emotions. The result is that all those hon Members I see around me with the exception of a few returned unopposed and my University colleagues have emerged from a passion of excitement. Not a single supporter of theirs has ever had put before them any rational reason why he should vote one way or another, whereas we who are University Members are elected by our constituents all over the world after they have received our election addresses and considered them. They send in their paper and do not hide behind any anonymity, but sign them in the quiet of their own studies so that we are returned by their intelligence. For better or worse, it is the intelligence of our constituents that chooses us and not their emotions. We do not represent the emotions or the passions but we represent the wisdom, the thought and the sober judgment of our constituents. Therefore, I say, that so far from being an anomaly, all the other Members except us are the anomaly. We are the only representatives; we are chosen by intelligent people using their intelligence, and not by howling crowds.

(Sir W.M. Conway, 1931)

Later, in 1944, the same measure came up; the same arguments came out.

[University elections] are in a way, I think, the most civilized form of election we have got. There are no speeches, no spellbinding, no canvassing, hardly any expenses.

(Petty Officer Herbert, 1944)

The modern bull-dog, Mr Hogg, the would-be Lord Hailsham, put it in his own inimitable style.

The way I see it is that it is a compliment to the things of the mind paid by democracy – a compliment which democracy can well afford to pay – a compliment which should come willingly from every political party which believes in the development of the mind. I make no bones about asking for privilege for things of this kind because it is not based on class, money or party. It is based on the one form of aristocracy which can be justified – the aristocracy of the intellect, and I should deplore a departure from the tradition of this House which has allowed universities to be separately represented.

(Mr Hogg, 1944)

The curtain came down after the Second World War in the face of the landslide Labour majority government determined to strike out the anomalies of privilege. If anything, it prompted the sternest opposition ever mounted.

I would venture to put forward the view that as a matter of theory and principle there cannot be anything undemocratic in classifying voters according to their personal and individual quality. That is absolutely impractical as a general plan but if it can be done, as it can in regard to the section of the community whose education has been carried further than the general average, my submission is that there is nothing undemocratic in that.

... The case for maintaining the University franchise is stronger today than it has ever been. ... The universities count for more today in our national life than they have ever done. ... University elections present certain features which they do not share with ordinary territorial elections. There is no canvassing, there are no meetings and there is no emotional appeal. The electors decide upon consideration of a single, balanced statement of the candidate's views.

(Sir J. Anderson, 1948)

Far from being the culmination of a great movement to an ideal end:

The case for abolition of University seats is weaker today than at any time in its long history. For a long time past, university education has not been the privilege of a well-to-do minority. It is open to all who have talent and in the future ninety per cent at least of graduates will be drawn from the ranks of the elementary schools. Nor is there anything undemocratic about giving extra representation to the best educated section of the people.

(Mr Peake, 1948)

In modern politics some diversity was essential for the health of the body politic.

Too much tidiness, too much symmetry and the application of too many rule-of-thumb methods in securing the election of Members can only have one result: it will lead to an increase of the robot-type of MP who is completely subservient to the all-powerful party machine. ... Entrance to Parliament through University representation is about the only channel left which affords an opportunity of avoiding this undesirable development.

(Mr Skeffington Lodge, 1948)

The pressures on normal Members made it even more important, rather than less, that there be some MPs immune from the day-to-day hassles, and could see the woods instead of only the trees. An 'ordinary Member' offered his support to his University colleagues.

All conscientious Members of Parliament returned by ordinary constituencies are, in my judgment, hopelessly overdriven in these days of stress and strain. ... We are afflicted, everyone of us, by a quite bewildering multiplicity of cares and calls and as a result we can rarely collect our thoughts and ideas in a way which is fully desirable. This, I suggest, makes it more than ever necessary to maintain this small section of people here

who are comparatively free from the burdens which afflict the
bulk of us.

> (Mr Skeffington Lodge, 1948)

It was ironic indeed that with more and more people from
different walks of life going to university, the Government
was choosing now to disfranchise them.

> An immense change has been made in the constitution of the
> universities [with 6,000 going there supported from public
> funds] and ultimately the university electorate. Yet it is at this
> time that the Government choose to abolish University repre-
> sentation. The more democratic is the University electorate,
> the less the Government think it right to give them the power
> of using the vote.
>
> (Mr Butler, 1948)

The final words go to the Conservative spokseman wind-
ing up the final debate.

> The first test I wish to apply to University representation is
> whether we as a House ... are more representative of the
> commons of the Realm with University representatives or
> without [them]. I claim ... that we are far more representative
> ... with University representatives among us than we are
> without them. ... We have managed by the territorial method
> to get into this House interests which it is important should be
> represented here but I do not think that we entirely manage to
> represent every section of the community through the territo-
> rial method alone. [While agriculturalists, businessmen and
> trade union interests are directly represented] lawyers, scien-
> tists and medical men [are] not represented as such in the
> House of Commons. I claim that it is precisely that type of
> men, representative of the professional classes, who should
> have representation and self expression through being able to

vote in a University constituency. I maintain that it is that type of interest which it is most important to have represented in our midst today.

(Mr Butler, 1948)

It was not to be and, along with plural voting for business-men, the University vote was despatched into history by the 1949 Reform Act.

LIFE PEERAGES

Arguably the last bastion of unfettered privilege, the House of Lords, was to remain unbreached until 1958, with the intro-duction of Life Peerages (although, of course, the Chamber's powers had been severely constrained by the two great Parlia-ment Acts of 1911 and 1949 which meant that it could no longer block completely the Commons' wishes). Life Peerages removed from the Upper House the exclusive hereditary principle it had enjoyed since the foundation of Parliament. Like other notions we have surveyed, the idea of Life Peerages was, surprisingly, not a new idea. The first proposal had come as early as 1869 – by the House of Lords itself, worried by the prospect of a diminution in its natural stock of able peers. The idea set out by Earl Russell, the former Lord John Russell and still the indefatigable reformer, was to create just twenty-eight life peers: four a year over the next seven years to keep the House topped up. The idea failed, though more through scepticism than outright opposition.

I very much doubt whether many persons will be found to seek for the honour of a life peerage, for it seems to me that it would amount I will not say to an insult but to a very humiliating slight to offer a gentleman a peerage and at the same time to tell him that the title and dignity conferred upon him shall not descend to his son....

(Earl of Malmesbury, 1869)

I do not believe that ... representatives of the [commercial or industrial] interests would be willing in any large number to accept seats in this House for they would come in upon a different footing from those among whom they sat and accordingly would feel the position more or less a position of degradation.

(Earl of Harrowby, 1869)

The same noble Lord also foresaw the danger of vulgarity encroaching on his House.

Those alone who could be admitted with advantage as the holders of life peerages are those whose intellectual superiority places them, in spite of moderate means, upon complete equality with others enjoying the highest social advantages. But it would be quite another thing if men from the industrial classes, having attained no celebrity in any branch of the public service and with only their wealth and successful industry to recommend them are chosen for admission as Life Peers. Wealth and industry have merits of their own but not such as should claim for them the distinction of such a peerage.

(Earl of Harrowby, 1869)

There were more doubts about whether anyone would be interested in accepting.

[Earl Russell] says he can get every year two very useful men as life peers. ... But I am convinced that he will not find eligible men to accept. ... The recipient of it would be in a nondescript position – in the position of a man elected, if we can conceive such a thing, at a club without the privileges and status of other members.

(Earl of Malmesbury, 1869)

Quality would always be the chief obstacle.

> It is supposed that there are men who would accept life
> peerages: but I very much doubt whether any such men as your
> Lordships would wish to enter the House would do so. Of
> course there are persons ready to accept anything that is
> offered them; but these are not the men whose admission the
> noble Earl contemplates. It appears to me that they would
> stand in such a false position that no men with the usual
> amount of pride and self-respect would accept these peerages.
> They would not be your Lordships' Peers according to the true
> sense of the expression because they would not be your equals
> in respect of privileges. They would not transmit the title to
> their descendants; and they would therefore be on a different
> and lower footing from the rest of the House. They would not
> be nobles because the very essence of nobility is the succession
> of the title to posterity. They would thus be in a false position
> to say nothing of the equivocal position of their families. ... I
> do not think therefore the noble Earl will easily get such
> recruits as he wishes and such as your Lordships would like to
> see added to this assembly.
>
> (Earl Malmesbury, 1869)

Despite the doubts, Russell's Bill establishing Life Peerages
reached Third Reading, its last legislative stage, in the
Lords before being defeated. Twenty years later the Government of the day tried again. To address the problem of
quality, it proposed to look for candidates from amongst
the retinue of distinguished statesmen, diplomats and public officials, those already, as it were, tried and tested (and
trusted). But this too had its problems, so memorably
described in 1888.

> These servants of the Crown [in every part of the globe] will
> not come here in the first flush and bloom of their youth; they

will be by no means likely to take a vivid or important part in our debates and what I fear is this, that you will not strengthen the House of Lords as a legislative body but that you will turn it into a sort of legislative Bath or Cheltenham or perhaps, if it is not disrespectful to say so, into a sort of legislative hydropathic establishment where these noble persons will take more care of their constitutions than of the constitution of this House.

> (Earl of Rosebery, Leader of the Opposition)

The House was spared the indignity of becoming a 'legislative Bath or Cheltenham' – until the late 1950s. By then a far more insidious threat had come to stare their Lordships in the face. It was increasingly being asked whether the House of Lords was simply dying of atrophy. Attendance had dwindled alarmingly, mainly through 'natural wastage' but also through plain lack of interest. In the sessions of 1953-54 and 1954-55, the average voting strength of the governing Conservatives was forty-four; that of the Labour Opposition, just seventeen. Of the Conservatives, a staggering twenty-one – virtually half their regular presence – were either retained as Ministers or had appointments in the Royal Household. More years of similar decline and the House would disappear of its own accord. Life Peerages injected vital fresh blood into the system. The new, modern breed of working peers gradually took over supremacy of the day-to-day life of the Lords from the hereditary clans. As essentially pragmatic as the rationale was, so were the objections.

> I have no idea of the kind of persons we are going to get as Life Peers. I am sceptical about whether we are going to get anybody worth while at all.
> ... I hope that nobody over the age of fifty-five at any rate will be appointed as a Life Peer. ... I hope that this will not be used as a reward for past services.
>
> (Lord Silkin, 1957)

I think this Bill is an exercise in unreality. It is quite impossible to contemplate the House of Lords ever being given more powers than it exercises today; it will more likely have its existing powers reduced. Yet it is my firm belief that without more powers you will not get an influx of men in the shape of Life Peers who will devote themselves to its work. ... They will sink into the apathy which already characterises some Peers. ... Probably it is the hereditary principle which stimulates some Peers to give of their best out of a sense of duty. ... A hybrid assembly such as is proposed ... may not do the work half so well.

(Lord Winster, 1957)

There were still some crusty old diehards who frowned on reform and saw evils and sinister motives behind every move.

I do not believe it is universally accepted that the introduction of women in [the House of Commons] has been a roaring success and I suggest that we should profit by our failures. Members of [the Commons] are, of course, delighted at the thought [of Life Peerages] because they can elevate their more rumbustious female elements to this House. I hate the idea of your Lordships' House becoming a repository for over-exuberant female politicians and unfortunately we are unable to elevate them further, for that prerogative rests with the Almighty.

(Earl Ferrers, 1957)

The Opposition spokesman in the Commons identified perhaps a more real objection – the increase in patronage it gave Prime Ministers of the day.

If [the Government] try to operate the Bill and make any use of it they will be embarking upon a most dangerous precedent.

They will be placing any Prime Minister in future under the disagreeable and invidious necessity of having to distribute largesse ... on an immense scale. ... I would ask whether it is desirable as a necessity of our government life that the Prime Minister should have at his command [such] a distribution of largesse. ... It is a Bill of evil presage. If we start doing that sort of thing we are embarking on an extremely undesirable course and I think that it would be extremely invidious for any Prime Minister in the future to contemplate the discharge of the new duty which would be put upon him.

(Sir F. Soskice, 1958)

Perhaps unsurprisingly, Prime Ministers have shown admirable fortitude in bearing up to the new burdens thrust upon them. They have valiantly shouldered this extra task – uncomplainingly: all in the course of duty, naturally.

'A System Injurious To The Morals …
Of A Free People'
The Secret Ballot

The second major strand of the agitation for parliamentary reform in the early years was the long struggle for the Secret Ballot. This, the reformers argued, was essential if the right to vote was to have any practical meaning. When the battle got under way in earnest, the practice had been for ages past, and it turned out would remain so for some time to come, for elections to be conducted 'openly' – that is, an elector presented himself in front of the polling clerks and declared orally and publicly his choice and the clerks entered the vote in the polling book. (Heaps of these polling books survive in archives today, a formal record of individual voters' decisions in countless elections down the years.) Anyone was entitled to be in the polling station at the same time to witness the casting of each and every elector's decision.

The consequences are not difficult to see. With small electorates, mostly tenants of powerful landlords, the scope for both bribery and intimidation was both self-evident and enormous. Candidates or their representatives could be ensured of the effectiveness of bribery by making promises before the poll and redeem them once the voter had publicly done his 'duty'. Even more pernicious, landlords were able to deliver block votes of their tenants by the simple expedient of intimidation: vote for the landlord's choice of candidate or lose one's cottage, land and livelihood. For the majority of elections, the decision was made not by the free, independent choice of many diverse opinions but sewn up behind the scenes by controlling forces – candidates flush with bribe money, and landlords organizing more brutally on their behalf. In these circumstances, getting the vote was likely to be rather more an unwelcome burden in life than the aspiration of a good citizen. As the momentum for reform increased generally, the Secret Ballot became the touchstone for real, as opposed to cosmetic, change. It was the essential ingredient if all the progress of widening the franchise was not to be a hollow victory.

Clearly such efforts challenged the entrenched power of those who had up till now been able to manage elections to their own desired ends, and it guaranteed that the Ballot would be keenly opposed – as it turned out, for forty years until it finally came to pass in 1872. The resistance to the reform was to be expected, but it was no sterile act of simply massing numbers in the House to vote it down. Opponents ventured forth on a much more imaginative, ingenious and plausible campaign of argument, professing that far from being worried about their own interests, their main concern, without any hint of irony attached, was the distinct moral blight that would descend upon Britain if the Ballot ever came to be used. This mainstay of our modern conception of democracy would, in fact, be the most evil and degrading innovation ever known. It was, no less:

> a system injurious to the morals and contrary to the feelings of a free people.
>
> (Mr Dundas, 1830)

It was:

> incompatible with the constitution of this country.
>
> (Lord John Russell, 1830)

(That statement came from the architect of the 1832 Reform Bill). Two decades later, the Ballot remained 'exotic' (Mr Howard, 1848), and:

It would be the fertile and certain source of violation of all law and order – of anarchy – of destruction of life and property – and lead most decidedly and directly to bloodshed and plunder.

(Mr Richards, 1835)

Why? How could such an approach to voting, one which on the face of it seemed likely to rectify so many abuses be in the least objectionable to any fair-minded person? Simple – the main plank in the argument against the Ballot was that it offered men a chance they had never had before: of making a promise and then reneging on it with impunity and without fear of discovery. An early opponent set the hare running on this theme and it ran and ran right to the bitter end.

[Will it not] accomplish one of the blackest and foulest purposes of any that could debase and destroy the character of man.? ... [Will it not] make a hypocrite of a man throughout the whole period of his existence? [Will it not] make him exist as a person whose 'whole life is one contrived lie'? Such a person must be perpetually on the watch against his warmest friends and closest connections, always tremblingly afraid to betray a secret, the discovery of which would be equally fatal to his interests and character. This [will be] nothing more or less than to lead a life of deception and fraud to the last moment of human existence.

(Mr Brougham, 1830)

And where might it all end? If one could be faithless in one part of one's life:

The man who could for months conceal the manner in which he had voted ... who could keep his secret from his friend and his wife ... would be false to his country ... and could neither be true nor faithful in any of the relations of life.

(Mr Brougham, 1830)

There were many more of similar opinion:

> What is the promised benefit ... which the Ballot will confer
> on the elector? ... the only possible privilege which I can
> conceive it capable of bestowing upon electors would be the
> privilege of lying with impunity – of taking bribes with less fear
> of detection – of becoming greater masters and adepts in
> casuistry and deceit. ... I believe it will not be denied that the
> characters of nations, no less than of individuals, are to a great
> degree dependent on moral causes, on examples, on circum-
> stances, on institutions. Everything therefore that tends to
> awaken the loftier qualities of our nature, everything that
> tends to call forth a manly avowal and exertion of principle, is
> productive of benefit to society. ... But does the Ballot hold out
> any such incentives? Does a system which enables a man to
> promise one thing and to do another with impunity and
> perhaps reward – does such a system tend to elevate the
> characters of nations? Can it teach duty? Can it inspire virtue?
> Or is it not rather calculated to impair both?
>
> (Mr Peter, 1833)

> With the feelings of an Englishman, I protest against this
> secret and unmanly mode of voting ... I do not think that any
> public benefit can arise from this change ... Is it desirable that
> men should make a promise with one hand and break it with
> the other? Will not such a system demoralise the lower orders?
> It will tend to destroy the honourable confidence between
> man and man and will make all men look with jealousy upon
> each other. ... The Ballot will change the frankness of charac-
> ter by which the English voter is now distinguished for guile,
> hypocrisy and fraud.
>
> (Earl of Darlington, 1833)

[In the language of the day, 'demoralizing' had a different
connotation to that with which we are now used. In its

original usage, as in this and other excerpts, it meant destroying morals (as in 'de-moralize') rather than the tamer tag we use today.]

> Surely it cannot be supposed that Parliament will deliberately take a measure calculated to familiarise men's minds with falsehood?
>
> (Mr Herbert, 1838)

> [The practice would have] a material influence on the character of the people for the opportunity of concealment will give the opportunity for fraud and for the indulgence of malicious and revengeful feelings which cannot be attended with advantage to the country.
>
> (Mr Walpole, 1852)

One of the most eminent, and sternest, critics of the Ballot was Lord Palmerston, Foreign Secretary for fifteen years and Prime Minister for nine. He it was who phrased perhaps the most evocative critique, in his address to his electors in 1852.

> I object to it because I think it at variance with the national character ... I think a true Englishman hates doing a thing in secret or in the dark. I do not believe that a majority of Englishmen would consent to give their votes in secret even if the law permitted them to do so. ... I say that for men who are charged with the high and important duty of choosing the best men to represent the country in Parliament to go sneaking to the ballot-box, and, poking in a piece of paper, looking round to see that no one could read it, is a course which is unconstitutional and unworthy of the character of straight-forward and honest Englishmen.

Inside the House he was no less strident. The Ballot was

either totally unnecessary or damningly de-moralizing.

> [A] promise [of a vote to a candidate] will either be given or withheld. If it is given, and if the man votes according to his promise, of what use is your ballot? If the promise is given and broken, what becomes of the improvement in the morality of your electoral system? The ballot will then exercise a degrading and demoralising instead of a beneficial influence. You will be lowering the people instead of raising them in the scale as social and civilized men.
>
> (Lord Palmerston, 1854)

Its pernicious influence would be perpetual.

> This measure will not, if passed, confer any advantage upon the public generally but will simply act as a cloak to the mean, the cowardly and the dishonest among the electoral body because unless a man is consistent in his lying the Ballot can be of no use to him.
>
> (Mr Gathorne Hardy, 1871)

No man's life would be the same again. This from the Earl of Shaftesbury, in other fields one of the century's greatest social reformers, but on this topic, unconvinced.

> Many men will pass their lives under suspicion for the honestest can never prove that he has acted up to his declaration and you will thus keep back from the poll the best of the electors who will rather lose their vote than be subject to doubt and misrepresentation.
>
> (Earl of Shaftesbury, 1872)

The running theme throughout the four decades in which the issue was aired almost annually in debate was that the whole character of the nation would be subverted and the fabric of society would be irrevocably deranged.

I feel persuaded that election by ballot would not give the necessary security for the concealment of the vote unless by incurring much greater evils than those which this measure professes to remedy. ... In all probability [a voter's] landlord, on applying to [the voter] would obtain a promise from him in these convincing terms: 'I'll vote for you and you alone; you are my landlord, my benefactor; I fairly and honestly tell you that no power on earth shall ever make me vote against you,' still meaning all the while to vote for his landlord's opponent. ... Who then can tell me that such a person ... can be so much on his guard as not to excite the slightest suspicion as to the manner in which he has given his vote? To observe such profound secrecy he must say nothing whatever to his wife; nothing whatever to his children; nothing whatever to his dearest friend; nothing to his [drinking] companion; no, he must be as dumb as the tankard which they have just emptied between them. This is the situation in which election by ballot will place this worthy and independent freeholder for [all the] years till the next opportunity presents itself for him to exhibit his rare qualities.

(Mr Brougham, 1830)

As for the landlord, should he get fewer votes than his pre-election canvassing had led him to expect, he would undoubtedly wish to investigate who had deceived him.

Both [landlord and tenant] would separate with much suspicion ... and no good feeling. Election by ballot will give rise to a continual system of vexatious watching and annoyance.

(Mr Brougham, 1830)

The voter might conceal the actual fact of his vote at the time of delivering it but of what avail is this secrecy unless it is to be followed by security afterwards; for I can hardly call that a state of security in which a man lives, as it were, by a perpetual

falsehood, and in continual fear lest by a breach of confidence
in some friend to whom in an unguarded moment he may have
disclosed the truth, or by some other chance, the whole should
come to the ear of the landlord and his total ruin should ensue.
... The landlord will use every endeavour to obtain the promises of the votes of their tenants for themselves or their friends
... [and] will make every exertion to discover ... defaulters. [As
I] conceive it to be more difficult for a man to adhere continually to a falsehood than to avoid ... letting out the truth, I have
little doubt of their success. ... At all events, the system of
chicanery, trick and perjury and the total destruction of all
confidence between landlord and tenant which will arise from
this measure are, in my opinion, serious objections to its
introduction.

(Lord Acheson, 1830)

A voter who wishes to be screened by the ballot can never dare
to state his political sentiments at any time or in any place.
Should he state them at home, in his own house, he might be
betrayed – unintentionally no doubt, yet he might be betrayed
even by the members of his own family. At the tavern ... he will
have a still greater risk to encounter. At no political meeting
... will he dare to show his face; to no petition to Parliament
will he dare to put his signature. To this condition then will
the free-born Englishman be reduced.

(Mr Brodie, 1836)

The theme that politics itself would be irrevocably inhib-
ited was pressed with plausible but extreme warnings.

Suppose the voter can conceal his vote; how is he to conceal
his opinions? He may do it by two methods, and none other –
by systematical falsehood or by total political apathy: a fair
choice for a free man! He must take in no newspaper, he must
belong to no club, ... he must be silent ... before his wife – she

may be a gossip before his children; they may tell tales before
his friend....

    ... Suppose this man to have been the victim of intimida-
tion and to be now resolved to foil it by use of the ballot. ...
Surely the second state of this man is worse than the first. If the
evil of intimidation be, as is asserted, so deeply ingrained in our
political system, then must the remedy be deeply and severely
applied. No more political demonstrations ... no public meetings, no public requisitions to candidates, no more open conflict of public opinion. [Proponents of the ballot] will reduce
the high and responsible duty of a citizen to the exercise of the
small conventionalities of polite life; they will readily establish
the victory of the ballot on the ruins of the public spirit of the
people of England.

(Mr Milne, 1839)

If it was impossible to maintain one's political confidences,
the ballot would be useless; if one *could*, things would be
even worse.

Suppose the secret [is] inviolably kept – that never, in any
moment of conviviality or friendship, of confidential intercourse
with a friend or relative, did [one] divulge the vote [given]; what
an abominable system must that be, under which persons can not
discuss with their nearest connections how they had fulfilled or
meant to fulfil a public trust. Can it be expected that men in their
private societies, in their familiarities, in their clubs, at the
market, are not to mention that which is probably uppermost in
the minds of all? If strict silence is to be observed, vote by ballot
will ... stop public discussion.

(Sir Robert Peel, 1833)

The impracticalities of the ballot were insuperable.

How [is] a person entitled to the franchise ... to form his

opinions upon great questions – opinions which alone make
his vote valuable – but by attending public meetings and
discussions. [Do the proponents] imagine that the ... agents of
the landlords of the district will not follow the tenants to such
meetings and watch every act of theirs so that before they
come to the ballot box they know perfectly well from the
previous actions and movements of the party the bias and
tenor of his political views, opinions and sentiments? That
being so, they will be as much the objects for intimidation and
temptation as at the present moment. ... In order to make the
Ballot useful as a protection, the expression of public opinion
must be wholly suffocated.

(Mr Vernon Smith, 1837)

One of the measure's most tireless and implacable foes
could see little moral uplift for the masses in the idea.

The thing is ridiculously absurd – it is an insult to common
sense. One of two things [the voter] must do. To be sure a ...
man may hold his tongue, but that is what such a man will not
do. The mass of men are not gifted with silence. He must either
speak the truth or tell a lie. If he speak the truth what have you
gained by your [Ballot]? If he tell a lie then your Ballot Bill is
only an expedient to demoralise the people. It is true he may
fence with questions that are put to him. But to put a man on
the wrong scent is not a very elevating process; it has a taint of
immorality about it.

... Have you considered what a purgatory it must be for
such a man to keep a secret? The only person in history to
whom he will bear any resemblance is Samson when the
Philistines tried to worm his secret out of his Delilah, only that
our imaginary voter will be no Samson but only a weak-kneed
and rather stupid working man. You will only convert him into
a mean sneak if not into a liar. He may under our present
system have voted openly and yet voted from one motive or

another all of them mean and ignoble – but at least the poor
fellow will have done one good thing in his life: he will have
voted openly and the truth of the vote will stand on the record.
But if he votes in secret and then persistently lies about it he
will have made himself a worse man than if he had been
brought dead-drunk to the poll: that would be evil, but the evil
would be patent and have its limit; the life-long falsehood has
no limit to its mischievous influence.

(Mr Beresford Hope, 1871)

The upshot of this attempt to reduce malpractice at the
polls would, the argument went, result in a greater not
lesser atmosphere of suspicion between fellow men.

One of the worst results of the system [will be] ... the destruction of all confidence between man and man. Canvassing can
never be prevented ... weak people can never be prevented
from promising [their vote] especially when they were not to
be called to account. The result of the election will be,
therefore, more disappointing than ever to the beaten candidate and whereas now in many instances hands are shaken and
a frank admission made that a fair fight had been fought, the
unsuccessful man will henceforward retire with the conviction
that his neighbours and familiar friends have played him false.

(Mr Cave, 1871)

To illustrate his point, he quoted an anecdote about a
candidate who, having obtained twenty promises from
among the thirty members of a social club for an election of
officers, still lost.

When the time came [the candidate recalled] I got ten votes
and lost. But that was not the worst of it, for in the course of the
day the whole twenty came in, one after the other, and said,
'My dear fellow, I am so sorry you did not win; you know, I

voted for you'.

... [The Ballot will take away] the boldness to discuss public questions ... and what do we get in return? We get the character who cringes to our face and strikes us behind our backs. [The Ballot] makes it impossible to distinguish an honest man from a knave and therefore [it] destroys at least one of the inducements to honesty. Public spirit will be gone. Public meetings will pass resolutions one way and vote another. There will be no more faith in politics than in horse-dealing.

(Mr Cave, 1871)

Of course, these moral arbiters pronouncing on the turpitude into which their countrymen were about to be plunged rarely troubled themselves with the other side of the coin – to ponder whether the voter under the open system forced by circumstance to cast his vote against his conscience was possessed of any better moral condition. For those one-eyed antagonists of reform, there was only despair on the horizon. The arch-representative Lord Palmerston encapsulated the shape of things to come.

You must make a general election to be like a Quakers' meeting. No man must utter what his opinions are – there must be no converse, no mutual confidence. There must be no canvassing, no committees, no friends urging the merits of this candidate against the demerits of the other. The whole must be a dumb proceeding. No man must give utterance to his political feelings however deeply they may engross his mind ... all must be done in silent sadness; no human being must be aware of what another is going to do. Is it not ridiculous to suppose that such a process can by Act of Parliament be carried into effect? I say again, Sir, it is absolutely absurd.

(Lord Palmerston, 1859)

There was, for him, no way out of the moral dilemmas

voting in itself posed. The Ballot would not solve them.

> The same coercion which it is now asserted is used ... to make
> men go openly to the poll will be used for the purpose of
> extorting from them a promise to give a secret vote in the sense
> which [their] employer or landlord wishes. Suppose the man
> refuses and says, 'I will make no promise'. Is it not plain that
> the same penalty which it is said attaches to the man voting
> against his landlord or employer now will be inflicted then?
> Suppose the man gives his promise and breaks it? I say a man is
> deeply degraded who makes a promise knowing he will not
> fulfil it and if he votes as he promises and that promise is
> extorted from him, he is in the same condition as if he votes
> openly under coercion without any promise at all. You do not
> relieve him from the difficulty the least in the world by
> enabling or compelling him to vote secretly instead of going
> openly to the poll.

>   (1859)

In sum, there was more to lose than gain.

> If you begin by withdrawing political functions from publicity
> in their exercise you aim a fatal blow against that which I
> maintain to be the foundation of our liberties.

>   (1859)

One of the most comprehensive clarion calls against the
iniquities of the Ballot wages battle on several fronts which
in their combination spell the end of English tradition as
we know it.

> It is not in the nature of the English character to skulk behind
> a mask, in doing that of which, far from being ashamed, he is
> justly proud because it is his duty. ... How in practice can you
> secure any secrecy ...? A man must do more than conceal his

vote. He must conceal his opinion. He must hurrah at the wrong speech, eat [at] the wrong dinner, break the wrong heads, do everything to convince the public that he is acting in the interests of the opposite candidate ... But even if ... a man were to obtain that degree of perfection in the concealment of his opinions to enable him to become a model voter, I think he would become so confirmed a hypocrite that it is very doubtful if a man so trained and successfully trained would be fit to exercise the franchise at all.

... In viewing the question, we cannot keep out of sight this consideration − supposing it possible to gain in this way the perfect secrecy which you anticipate; what effect will that perfect secrecy have on our national character and our national institutions? Men diffident of their own judgment and mistrusting their own powers frequently form their opinions upon the opinions of those in whose character and ability they place confidence; but how, if everything is to be secret and concealed, can a man have this advantage? How is the man who has not a great confidence in his own opinion to be guided? Why it goes to the very root of our whole system, the tendency and the intention of which are to develop individual opinion, to give free action to every mind and give free expression to every thought. ... I say that if you introduce this system, you introduce a retrograde system − you are introducing a system contrary to the real spirit of free institutions ... if ever you succeed in adapting the English character to this measure, so that the English people really avail themselves of it and consent to exercise their rights or their duties under the veil of secrecy, you will have demoralised the English character and done a great deal to sap the foundations on which our liberty stands.

... I think by it, instead of educating the lower class for political duties, you will be destroying their self-respect, their manliness and even their willingness, if need be, to suffer for conscience' sake; you will be striking a blow at one of the best

qualities in the national character which has been created by
a long course of habit and opinion – by the exercise of public
functions, whether in humble or lofty station, in a manner
requiring honesty and independence. You will be striking at a
quality which has given to the national character a stability
that could not have been created by any system such as that
now proposed, which gives to every person acting in a public
capacity the means of concealing not only his vote but his
opinions.

(Mr Herbert, 1853)

Sir Robert Peel pursued the more practical questions, in
similar vein to Lord Palmerston just gone.

The landlord and his stewards with a long train of friends will
canvass the tenants. ... The doubtful voter will be asked to stay
away, to pair off with the certain enemy. What remedy does
the ballot-box give? ... Is it possible [when] the ... election
occupies the thoughts and is the theme of conversation for
weeks before and weeks after it takes place, a man can so
regulate his language, his company, his very looks that there
shall be no guess as to his inclinations and intentions, that the
cunning agent shall have no means of discovering from his
intimate associates, from his family, from his servants, from his
wife or at least of vehemently suspecting, what is the tenant
that has kept and that has failed to keep, his word?

(1838)

His doubts were widely shared.

If [voting] is to be secret, it will have the effect of very greatly
diminishing, if not entirely doing away with, what I consider
one of the greatest blessings and privileges the people of
England can enjoy – I mean the free canvass of public men and
free discussion of public measures; for it appears to me that if

we are to continue publicly to canvass men and discuss their deeds, as I hope we long might, a man's vote will be equally well known whether it is given by ballot or whether it is taken [openly].

(Lord Alexander Lennox, 1853)

More, not less, suspicion of foul play would accompany the ballot.

Suppose there is a canvass in which all the promised voters are taken down on each side; and suppose that the result of the voting differs altogether from the canvass. Each man would believe that his neighbour had deceived him, and [even] if they had the best possible administrator of the ballot-box presiding, it would be difficult to persuade men that some foul play had not been practised. ... The whole principle of secret voting is repugnant ... to the institutions of a free country. ... We will never advance the interests of a nation by calling upon men to exercise the most important function with which a citizen of a civilized state can be charged in impenetrable darkness; and we might be assured that we can never turn a knave into an honest man by making it impossible to distinguish between an honest man and a knave.

(Mr Moncrieff, Lord Advocate, 1853)

Intimidation would by no means be prevented. If anything, it would become even more invidious for being based only on suspicion rather than evidence of crossing one's landlord.

A tenant will then be whispered out of his holding and while at present he only runs the risk of losing his farm if he votes against the wishes of his [landlord], he will, under the uncertainty engendered by the proposed measure, be equally exposed to that risk if he votes with him. Harrassed by the spy and maligned by the informer, he will then sigh for the time when every vote was recorded in open day and he could point to the vote-book in his favour.

(Mr Peacocke, 1856)

[The Ballot's] first effect will infallibly be an organised system of spies to ascertain whether persons voted according to their promises which will create heart-burnings and jealousies among the lower classes that must put an end to all social peace and comfort.

(Viscount Howick, 1835)

In the long run, it would all be to no avail.

Where people's sentiments are known as they are in the country by the conversation which takes place so much in public houses and in market places with respect to politics, where the general character and political sentiments of every man are so generally known, can it be supposed that the stewards of the landlords ... will not take care before a few years are over that all the tenants are all of them of the same political sentiments as their own? Where then is the remedy? I contend that this measure instead of being a benefit to the voter will only be an injury to all the tenants in the country.

(Lord John Russell, 1838)

How will the Ballot remedy [a] grievance? Take first the case of [a] poor tradesman. It seems that he is known by his habitual acts and language to be a [Liberal] and is grieved to be compelled, by the fear of ruin in his business, to vote at the election for a Tory. Now if his vote had been cloaked by the ballot, no-one would doubt that he would have given it according to his professed sentiments whatever protestations he might make to the contrary in order to save his custom. The result would be that the custom would be withdrawn by anticipation and transferred to some tradesman of recognised Tory principles and thus this tradesman would actually be ruined. ... He clearly prefers at present the privilege of uttering freely his political opinions and giving his vote for a Member of Parliament contrary to those opinions. Whatever may be urged as to the political result, at least to the elector himself this state of things is much more agreeable than the alternative of ruin.

(Mr Vernon, 1842)

So with spectacular adroitness, it was thus plausibly demonstrated that more harm would be inflicted by guaranteeing the confidentiality of one's vote than by leaving the system, bribery intimidation and all, as it was. The ingenuity of the opponents knew few limits. A secret vote, they maintained, could only encourage voters to exercise it in an unthinking way. The only kind to benefit would be the demagogue or 'popular declaimer', who:

... might excite [voters] against the legitimate influence of intelligence and property [into voting] under the shelter of ballot ... in a way which, without that protection, they would probably hesitate to do ... in opposition to the more enlightened and dispassionate of those with whom, by a community of personal and commercial interests, they were naturally associated.

(Major Fancourt, 1833)

This was the closest opponents ever came to acknowledging the essential bottom line – that the powers that be risked losing that control which they had hitherto quite satisfactorily enjoyed. Another tack was to question whether the system could, in practice, be made absolutely secret. Lord Palmerston was convinced that Englishmen would refuse to a man to conceal their votes and would continue publicly to declare their votes before popping the ballot paper into the box. Others, pursuing an equally quixotic line, argued, on the face of it rather cogently, that corruption would be made all the easier.

> I would ask – *Quis custodiet ipsos custodes*? [Who guards the guards?] How is it proposed to prevent fraud on the part of those who received the votes, guarded the ballot-boxes and declared the result of the election? ... The ballot will, in one way, check corruption among the constituencies because it will then be cheaper and far more certain to bribe the officials and returning officers.
>
> (Mr Peacocke, 1856)

Pre-emptive of many a latter-day controversy in other parts of the world, he identified the perennial hurdle.

> ... even in the most improbable contingency that you would have a pure election under a system of secret voting – would the losing side ever be brought to think so, much more to acknowledge it? ... Would not the losing side always say that the victory had been gained by fraud or achieved by corruption and do you think that public opinion would be uninfluenced by such clamour? Would the public be disposed to place confidence in hon Gentlemen as being the real exponents of the opinions of their constituents? Would the public even place confidence in this House itself when composed of members elected under such a system? I do not believe any system can be devised which is so calculated to bring representative government into general odium and contempt.
>
> (Mr Peacocke, 1856)

Even if the mechanism could be made to function as intended, detractors argued that it would go against the entire spirit and sense of decency of the ordinary Englishman. It was the 'un-Englishness' of the process which agitated a steady stream of opponents.

The ballot is not the way in which Englishmen would wish to exercise their political privileges. Secret voting ... is not only un-English but will afford protection to none but the skulking coward who blushes for his own weakness. If a man promises to give me a vote and, because his violation of faith is screened by the ballot he breaks his word and votes against me, what can such conduct be called but moral delinquency?

(Mr Fector, 1835)

The ballot ... will be accompanied with much evil – it will spread fraud and deception throughout the country [and] tend to destroy the love of truth and that spirit of manly and open conduct which is the peculiar characteristic of Englishmen.

(Mr Poulter, 1835)

As we have already seen, even those on the side of general reform were loath to go this far. Lord John Russell, basking in the glory of the Great Reform Act of 1832, still cautioned on this front.

I believe that a change of voting secretly instead of openly would be a change most abhorrent to [the people of England's] feelings and their desire to act with openness, fairness and manliness ... I think that this question will gain strength and if it does ... I cannot but perceive that very great evils are impending over the country.

(1838)

The Englishness theme was a favourite one because it contrasted us with the revolutionary French and Americans, both of whom had adopted the Ballot. Some flattering self-portraits were painted of the upright nation outraged at the prospect of this foreign practice.

Nine-tenths of the constituencies of the whole [country] do

not ... want the ballot either for protection or secrecy. [They were not] prepared at once to abandon all their long established tastes and usages. They ... feel that it would be a reflection on their integrity, on their honesty, not to avow by the public record of their vote what were their ... feelings on great political questions and I honour that principle. I am not disposed to part with any essential feature of our English national character. I am not ashamed myself of any vote I have ever given and I know this, that having to meet a popular constituency on the hustings and being examined as a candidate for [electors'] suffrages on such occasions and having my political views publicly canvassed, I have a right on the other hand to be dealt with openly [by the electors.]

(Mr Heald, 1850)

In my opinion the ballot, instead of being a liberal was a very illiberal measure, for the result will be to narrow men's minds and preclude all discussion upon subjects which ought to animate men in the discharge of a political duty. ... The Bill will introduce a sneaking and a selfish suffrage instead of that open and manly expression of opinion which has given us free institutions and an indomitable people.

(Lord Romilly, 1871)

'Character' was a potent image; intangible, capable of many definitions, employable (or exploitable) for many ends, it conveyed the impression of deep-seated attributes, which had made the country great but which were fragile enough that, once tampered with, would be lost forever. It was a favourite tack of anti-reformers in many other fields besides this.

The English character has hitherto mainly been a manly, upright and straightforward character – a character, in my opinion, well-suited and adapted to the dignity of Liberty.

Then, I think, it well to consider whether it is wise or whether it is politic to introduce a law like the ballot, the very essence of which is meanness and servility; and I cannot but think that the habit of opinions concealed, equivocation substituted, private judgment destroyed, wholesale hypocrisy legalised – the natural effects of the ballot will give the people a disregard for the value of truth and, at least, a regard only for the outward semblance of integrity.

(Lord Alexander Lennox, 1853)

For Lord Palmerston, no law could change the habits of a nation.

It will be degrading to the national character and I say no Englishman will submit to it. I say that no law you can pass will compel the majority of electors of England to vote in secret, no law can compel the people to suppress the political opinions they entertain. Sir, the majority of the electors will evade the law and give their votes in public; and it will be only the few who will go sneaking to the poll for the sake of screening themselves, from some personal inconvenience, but who will thereby become objects of obloquy and degradation in the eyes of their fellow-countrymen.

(1855)

The simple truth was that the Ballot, termed on the eve of its introduction, 'a secret, silent and insidious system', ran counter to the spirit not only of England's changeless character but of the times as well. The age was moving in the opposite direction, towards more, not less, openness in every other walk of life. The scion of reform, Lord John Russell again:

When I consider ... that our public functionaries, whether judges, or ministers, or Members of Parliament, all act in the face of day – and

I believe we all make better in the exercise of our duties by the publicity of our proceedings – I do say that I see no reason for exempting from that responsibility to popular opinion the great body of those in whom the elective franchise is vested. I see no reason why they alone should be removed from the eyes of the public.

(1838)

The ballot was nothing less than a scheme:

... to dispense with the responsibility of all electors by enabling them to give their votes at elections in privacy and darkness! And this in the nineteenth century! This at a time when the universal feelings of mankind call aloud for publicity – increased publicity – in all affairs of government, in all debates and votes of Parliament, in all tribunals of law and justice, in all county and local proceedings ... in all departments of Church and State and when public opinion may be said to have been constituted, with consent of all, [the] supreme arbitress of human conduct and affairs. ... This is the time at which it has been deemed expedient to propose a law for exempting all electors from responsibility and control and for allowing one of the most solemn trusts, one of the most sacred and important duties than can devolve upon the citizens of a free state and on the faithful discharge of which the peace, the liberty and the happiness of the whole community so vitally depend, to be performed under the shroud of darkness and in the mask of night!

(Mr Peter, 1833)

Deeply then should I be concerned at the introduction of a system into this country which will convey the impression that any one enjoying the right [of voting] is afraid to come forward and avow publicly the notions and opinions which he entertains.

(Duke of Wellington, 1838)

Other critics were just plain indignant.

I maintain I have a right to know how my neighbour voted and I hope this country never will be so dead in reference to political matters that one man should be indifferent as to the side on which another voted.

(Viscount Sandon, 1838)

And unforgiving:

Of all the political crotchets ever invented, I think the secret vote is the least calculated to increase the stock of public virtue in any country or to stimulate the intelligence of the people. If there is [as was claimed] a body of persons in this country who cannot exercise the right to vote which they possess without injury to their pocket, that only proves that the franchise has gone too low. The franchise is given to a man because he is supposed to possess a free will; and it should not be given to him if he does not.

(Mr Whiteside, 1854)

Neither the Member of Parliament or the elector would emerge with credit from the system.

[The MP] is to be hatched in the dark; nobody is to know how he is produced and everything connected with his production is to be conducted with secrecy until he makes his appearance from the ballot-box. Coming in as one of the people, he will come out a Member of Parliament and that will be all that anybody will know of the matter. ... Now, what is the position in which the adoption of the principle of secret voting will place the honest and independent voter? Under the existing system a man of character and consistency carries with him great weight and his vote is of considerable value in an election; but [with secret voting] that man will be reduced to the same level of degradation as the corrupt and dishonest voter.

(Lord Seymour, 1855)

Influences which in every other walk of life men of eminence and culture provided to the lesser bred of the population, such as being exemplars of good taste, decorum, civil manners, industrious habits, public probity or learning, would be denied in the one area which was arguably the most important connection the ordinary person had with society as a whole: the choice of their government. This was surely not the way to ensure national progress. A rich vein of argument centred on the contention that the Ballot, in addition to all the retrograde influences it would give rise to would not in fact redress the shortcomings it was supposed to counter; in practice, there would be no redeeming features at all.

In the USA, the Ballot has proved to be a deception – a cloak – and an encouragement to corruption. By the privacy it secures, it induces men to sell their votes.

(Sir R Wilson, 1830)

I do not see that the ballot will prevent bribery; it will be likely to double bribery for voters [may now] delude both sides.

(Sir George Phillips, 1833)

I cannot but think that it will be far more easy when there can be no scrutiny into votes and when you will have no right to inquire how this man voted or how that man voted, to practise bribery wholesale; and a man who would be inclined to take a bribe now but will be restrained by the fear of doing so, will not feel the same fear when he has an opportunity of receiving a bribe with impunity.

(Lord John Russell, 1835)

The notion that secret voting would usher in an era of calm to elections in place of the raucous skulduggery that went on at present was also misplaced. Indeed, the reverse.

Many moderate men would [have to] conceal their opinions ...
[T]he worst possible state of things that could exist [would be
created.] By making moderate men hold aloof from delivering
their opinions, we will discourage the open avowal of independent sentiment and leave the whole dispute to be carried
on by the most violent partisans.

(Viscount Howick, 1837)

Nothing but an air of malevolence would spread over the
nation.

[It is] a proposition for legalising falsehood, for rendering
honesty the worst policy.

(Mr Herbert, 1838)

I am persuaded that the ballot will make voting secret in those
cases in which it ought to be public while it will leave voting
public in those cases in which it is sought to render it secret. It
will secure secrecy in those cases in which it is the interest of
the community at large to know whether or not bribery and
intimidation had been practised; but it will never prevent the
agents of corruption from learning through wives or children
or apprentices or other persons whether the parties they had
bribed had voted according to their promise.

(Mr Denman, 1860)

The argument that the Ballot's secrecy denied the certainty anymore of bribes being effective was dismissed by
Lord Shaftesbury, whose reforming zeal, as we have already
seen, did not extend to the Ballot.

It is said that you take away the certainty of any briber
receiving a return for his bribe and that no man will give away
his money unless he is sure of getting an equivalent for it. Is
this so, however? Is it not the case that in commercial transac-

tions, men risk large sums of money in speculations and that in gambling men hazard great stakes without any certainty of winning? You will simply increase the gambling spirit and reduce elections to the level of dice-playing or horse-racing.

(1872)

To the last, some were convinced that it simply wouldn't work, given the sort of people who now voted.

> Do you believe that an ignorant or moderately-educated man in the excitement and agitation of an election when put into one of these secret booths armed with a pencil or pen and one of these unintelligible forms – do you believe that the chances will be equal in favour or against his filling it up correctly?
>
> (Lord Cairns, 1872)

A noble colleague, in one of the last debates, reassured himself that the country would soon see the error of its ways.

> It will soon become so repugnant to the feelings of the community, it will give rise to so much hypocrisy and fraud that before long the tide of opposition will set strongly against it and the House of Commons will be petitioned for its repeal.
>
> (Lord Ravensworth, 1872)

The opponents gained one small victory at the last ditch. The 1872 Act was made temporary, to expire after eight years. When the time came for a renewal of the whole campaign all over again, the extension in perpetuity was carried with virtually no opposition at all.

It is evident then that the fight against the Ballot was many sided, sometimes ingenious, sometimes plain crude. Parliament debated the issues for hundreds if not thousands of hours. Of all the orations, perhaps the best all-encompass-

ing speech came early on, in 1835. It is worth citing
extensively to illustrate how, at times, opponents were able
cogently to assemble a vast array of convincing arguments
and deliver them, machine-gun like, against the tireless
but increasing band of balloteers. Against a fusillade such
as what follows, one can only marvel that they did not give
up the fight.

> If there is any one principle which more than another pervades
> every branch of our national institutions and operates as the
> purest check upon public men and public measures, it is
> publicity. Whatever temptations men might encounter to
> betray their trust, I am satisfied they are far more likely to be
> deterred from doing so by the ill opinions of their neighbours
> than by any artificial check which ingenuity can devise. Once
> allow men to act in secret and the House will invite them to
> act in fraud.
>
> ... [A] promise once given, if the voter is an honest man
> he will keep it, whether he gives his vote by Ballot or openly,
> and concealment will be of no use save to the knave for whom
> assuredly an upright legislature will not increase his facilities of
> disgracing himself and of deceiving his neighbour. ... If it
> operates at all, it will step in, not between solicitation and
> promise but between promise and performance, and instead of
> protecting a voter from persuasion to pledge his word it would
> only absolve him from the necessity of keeping it. It will make
> him a freer man only at the expense of his integrity and will
> vitiate his moral character under the pretext of preserving his
> political independence. Whether or not it will release him
> from the influence of superior wealth or superior power, it will
> at all events absolve him from the obligations of fidelity and it
> will debase even the corruption of receiving a bribe by the
> turpitude of violating a promise.
>
> ... But assuming that ... secrecy was obtained at the poll,
> what chance is there that it will be preserved afterwards? It is

for voters in the humble walks of life that this secrecy is devised and when the House considers what are the habits of such persons, is it probable that on an occasion of such general interest and excitement as an election a man should not tell for whom he had voted and thus expose himself, if not to constraint before the election, to what will be equally annoying to him – vengeance and resentment – afterwards?

... What universal suspicion and mistrust will be the almost inevitable consequence of the Ballot. Suppose a man to have received 600 promises and only 400 votes; he will feel that 200 of the electors have betrayed him and in his uncertainty on whom to fix the stigma, he will spread the blame over the whole and impute turpitude to many who had not deserved it.

... [I acknowledge that] it enables a man to prefer the obligations of public duty to those of personal pledge ... but at the same time you must be prepared to take with it this consequence – you must be prepared to uphold the most odious doctrine which the world was ever deluged by, a false and corrupt philosophy, that private vice might prove public benefit. ... In short, there is no end to the difficulties and inconveniences that will result from the secret practice of the ballot.

... My firm conviction is that instead of mitigating [present deficiencies] it will aggravate many of the evils that are at present experienced and also introduce many new evils. We who object to these inroads upon the institutions of our country are not called upon to show they ought not to be made: it is not for those who are in possession to prove a good title but it is for those who impugn that title to make out theirs is better.

... The Ballot will be an innovation of our National Institutions and a violation of our national feelings to which I trust the House of Commons will not readily be brought to submit. Publicity has hitherto proved the life and soul of English Institutions, English character and English habits. We never have done, and God forbid we ever should do, things as if we were ashamed of them and obliged to perform them in a corner. The character of the nation is at stake. As long as voting continues open, as it is at present, we have at least some security in the value which every man places in the good opinion of his neighbour and in the maintenance of his own character for consistency and truth. Let the House of Commons take away the great sanction of safety and publicity and it takes away one of the strongest ties by which men are bound to the discharge of their public duties. I dread as a national calamity and deprecate as a national disgrace underhanded, clandestine proceedings and I shall not be frightened from the propriety of that by the un-English prejudice and what to some persons might seem the charm of novelty.

(Mr Charles Russell, 1835)

'Freaks Of Nature'
Votes For Women

Of all the battles recalled here, none was so filled with invective, myopia and immovable prejudice than the struggle for the enfranchisement of women. Perhaps the greatest and most far-reaching of the social reforms of the last 150 years, it became to some of its detractors far more than a mere alteration in the national political mechanism. For them it was not just political wisdom that was about to be contravened; it was no practical question of organizational expediency. For them it meant nothing less than the overturning of the natural, primeval order of things granted by Providence and the insurance of the human race since it won supremacy over the beasts.

The victory of the reformers came piecemeal; ironically, for all the popular images of rampaging suffragettes chaining and window-smashing themselves across London, it came essentially in spite of, rather than because of, the militancy of the decade before the First World War. Events before and after this outburst were to have the clinching effect. Beforehand, the crucial breaches in the dam had been made quietly, almost unnoticed nearly fifty years earlier when in 1870 women were accorded the right on the same terms as men to vote and stand in elections for school boards. It was no great scheme of emancipation – nor was it intended to be the start of one. It was conceded by the Government simply because it did not view such local administration as particularly important politically. In dealing with educational charities and good works, schools and the welfare of children, the concerns were very much the domestic matters for which women were deemed to be primarily suitable. They were largely an extension of

the home, vastly different from the public, high profile
concerns of the national parliament. So, with heavy irony,
women were allowed the local vote because it fitted in with
men's conception of what woman's role was really all
about.

The same air of indifference – and ultimately self-
defeating arrogance – allowed for further advances. In
1894 women were permitted to vote for and be elected as
parish and district councillors and in 1907 they could be
elected as borough and county councillors (and even become mayor – the first took office the very next year). As
local government began to spread its concerns throughout
a wider and wider range of social activities, and with its
women members playing a full part, it became increasingly
difficult to continue to bar them from the national political
forum. The old arguments about women's incapacity for
political life were becoming less and less tenable. It was
ironic then that the suffragette militancy ensued, providing last-gasp ammunition for the detractors, who pointed
to it as evidence that women remained unready for rational
political activity.

It is too simplistic to say that the First World War gave
women the vote. There was no explicit – or implicit – quid
pro quo in response to the role played by women during the
conflict. It was rather that, for Britain, the time had come.
It no longer seemed such a huge leap in the dark. The
arguments foretelling of cataclysmic doom appeared to
pale into insignificance compared with the actual cata-
clysms which had unfolded on the Western Front. As cliché
ridden as it may sound, as the Great War drew to its close
in 1918 a sense of a new beginning emboldened legislators.
The old rotten order had been cleansed, purged, eradicated
forever. Empires had fallen on the Continent. In Britain
too, an empire fell – the empire of gender. It was consigned
to history in true British fashion: tentatively. The 1918

reform gave the Parliamentary vote to women thirty and over. It was to be 1928 before the vote was granted on the same terms as men.

The journey had been a tortuous and infuriating one. The grounds of the arguments against women's suffrage shifted with a frequency of staggering proportions over the years. New arguments were developed; few old ones were ever discarded, so that by the end there had accumulated a formidable weight of 'evidence' standing in the way of reform. To begin with, the opposition was premised on what might be called the objective view – simply that the natural order of things had it that the social roles of the sexes were irredeemably different, and that to tamper with what God had ordained was a recipe for catastrophe. Whatever good folk felt about it, the brutal reality was that nothing could be done. This theme spawned two parallel lines of argument to reject attempts to change – a 'positive' strand that held that women possessed certain admirable qualities which should not be sacrificed by the descent into the murky world of politics and then, more viciously, a 'negative' strand that had it that there were other qualities which were necessary for the onerous responsibilities of political life which women demonstrably lacked and had no chance on earth of acquiring.

Another simultaneous theme was one of unabashed patronizing, which reached nauseating heights, the argument that women were too precious and fragile to be exposed to the rigours of politics, that men did not like politics either but, gallant as ever, they would take on the job with great modesty and under severe sufferance in order to protect the ladies (the classic 'it's-for-your-own-good' argument).

Two other central lines of attack were opened up – that such an upheaval would destroy the ties which currently held the family as we knew it together and break down all manner of social bonds; and, as the vehemence and violence of the suffragette campaign outside Parliament increased, a distinctly caustic view developed suggesting that those campaigning on behalf of women were not 'real' women, a deflective tactic of quite mischievous spitefulness.

There were other tacks too with rather greater grounding in logic (at least to the impartial observer). These homed in on the sense of inequality which would result from giving women the controlling voice in deciding policies from the consequences of which, by the nature of their sex, they were relatively immune. The burden of military defence of the country was the main arena for debate here.

When the contest commenced, the lines were clearly – and in the minds of the antagonists, simply – drawn.

It is not a question whether the male or the female intellect is the superior one. I simply say that they are different and that the difference makes man more capable of direct government and woman more fitted for private influence. ... Reason predominates in the man, emotion and sympathy in the woman and if the female vote makes any noticeable difference in the character of our constituencies the risk is that we will have in this House an excess of the emotional and sentimental element over the logical and reasoning faculty. Though emotion and sentiment are admirable qualities in their way, I maintain distinctly that reason ought to govern emotion and not emotion govern reason.

... The character of the legislation of a woman-chosen Parliament will be the increased importance which would be given to questions of a quasi-social or philanthropic character, viewed with regard to the supported interests or the partisan bias of special classes rather than to the broader considerations of the public weal. ... We shall have more wars for an idea or hasty alliances with scheming neighbours, more class cries, permissive legislation, domestic perplexities and sentimental grievances. Our legislation will develop hysterical and spasmodic features, partaking more of the French and American system rather than reproducing the tradition of the English Parliament.

(Mr Beresford Hope, 1871)

The long experience of history told a convincing story.

How did it ever happen that men stand in their present position in the government of public affairs and the transaction of the political duties of the world? Did the two sexes start upon equal terms at the beginning of the world? – equal in strength, equal in the character of their intellectual powers, alike fit for the discharge of the same social and political duties? Is it then by an unjust usurpation that from the very first man obtained the political status which to this day he occupies to the exclusion of woman?

   ... For if each sex by its nature, its constitution, its organisation, is equally fitted for the performance of the same functions and duties, then the justice of your Bill [for female franchise] is undeniable and our opposition is unfair and unreasonable. But if the natural difference between the sexes gives to and takes from each sex certain qualifications for certain duties, then that natural difference must be taken into account. ... Now can it possibly be denied that this natural difference exists and that, in consequence, there are many callings and occupations suited to one sex and not to the other – many duties for the performance of which one sex is unfit and incapable but for which the other is specially qualified? And taking this into account, when we are asked to reconsider and revise the apportionment of duties between the sexes, it behoves us to take especial care lest, misled by false sentiment and misplaced sympathy in the attempt to extend woman's rights we impose upon her duties and burdens which she will find intolerable.

... I think I need hardly point out the difficulties that would arise and how it would assuredly be discovered that the legislative duties which are discharged by men with tolerable facility would be burdensome beyond measure and beyond their strength in the case of women.

... We regard woman as something to admire, to reverence, to love; and while we will share with her the happiness of life we will shield her as far as possible from its harsher and sterner duties. ... We will not be parties to dragging her down into the arena of our every-day toil and strife.

(Mr Knatchbull-Hugesen, 1872)

This essentially set out the stall of the 'objectivists'. The argument was elaborated the following year.

To argue that ... women have a right to vote is simply to ignore the whole career which revelation and the experience of all ages and nations and the universal consent of mankind, no less than the peculiarities of their own constitution, organization and obligations have marked out for them – a career which runs parallel with that of man which is equally dignified with it but perfectly distinct from it.

(Mr Leatham, 1873)

He went on to quote a French commentator, the Comte de Gasparin, with whose views he clearly agreed.

'It is a question of the rights and duties of one sex claimed by the other – of an absolute change of vocation, ideas, occupation, individuality – and it will be difficult to persuade us that while men find it so hard to act as men, women can act as men and yet remain women, playing the double part, fulfilling the twofold mission, assuming the twofold character of humanity.

This is what will happen – we shall lose the woman without getting the man. What we shall get is that monstrous and repulsive creature which is already looming above the horizon, *la femme-homme*.'

It was not as if women did not possess influence in society even in the absence of a vote. A favourite argument was the 'silent power' line.

[Women] contribute through their own appropriate agencies quite as much as men do. They contribute ... imagination, insight, sympathy, a host of moral and intellectual qualities which are impossible to analyse and difficult to classify, but all of which have this common property – that they operate by personal influence and not by associated or representative action, and that is their natural sphere.

... Exactly to the extent to which the temptations offered by this measure will operate, in that degree they will tend to draw women from the sphere in which they are really powerful and transplant them to another where they will play a subordinate a secondary and an inappropriate part.

(Mr Asquith, 1892)

These 'appropriate agencies' through which women played their part in society were, in fact, in the eyes of such observers nothing more than being married to men of influence (and thereby able to affect them with a degree of intimacy never available to, say, the Leader of the Opposition in the House) or being able to impart good, sisterly advice to a brother in the supposedly unpolitical confines of the home. Women's influence was then real, self-evident – but conveniently rather indescribable, and hence irrefutable.

Women, it was asserted, stood somewhat better placed than men. In the age of limited male franchise, not to have the vote made a man feel stigmatized. No woman could ever feel stigmatized in relation to her sister citizens, so not having the vote proved a positive advantage!

No woman can feel a sense of inferiority as regards other women because she has not the vote for the simple reason that no woman has the vote. Nor can any woman feel justly a sense of inferiority as regards men because she has not the vote, for to vote and to rule have never been the prerogatives or the ambition of the sex and her relations with ours have always been of an entirely unpolitical character. ... They know that their kingdom is not a political kingdom and that they have no desire to exchange the vast influence which they exert over our conduct, aye, over our legislation too, on the ground that they are to be cherished and protected, for the flimsy and tawdry boast, without one particle of force to back it, that they have become our political equals and can protect themselves.

(Mr Leatham, 1876)

Surely if the enfranchisement of women was a natural affair, critics ventured, it would have come to pass before now.

Do [advocates] think that while mankind has been exploring now for thousands of years every nook and corner of political experiment, [the fact] that it has never occurred to anyone to suggest the promotion of women to equal political authority with ourselves is or is not an argument against the [idea]?

[It is] something ... so strange that it has never yet occurred to any member of the human family until we arrived at [this] enlightened generation.

(Mr Leatham, 1875)

The tongue-in-cheek sarcasm of the last retort was an all too common example of the tendency of some to treat the whole subject as less than serious. Others, however, displaced the full force of gravity when they entered the fray.

> [It is] a question of which, if it is carried out to its logical ends, the importance can scarcely be overrated and which will surely involve us all in an absolute and a complete revolution of all the social relations as well as political views by which not only we but the whole world has been governed since the earliest ages of History and the very creation of Man.
>
> [I am opposed] because in giving direct political power to women, we are embarking upon an experiment for which in History so far not one single precedent is to be found, which, however it may be regarded in the minds of dreaming philosophers or philanthropic professors, is unknown and untried and has no place at all in the world of practical politics.
>
> (Mr Chaplin, 1875)

He, too, confessed to disbelief that what was professed to be so natural had never before in all of history shown itself before now.

> [It is] a proposal which the collective wisdom of ages, the teaching of all religion in every form and under every guise and, as I believe, the instincts of the whole human race has ... never demanded. ... I find it exceedingly hard to believe that the united experience of the whole civilized world has been from the commencement erroneous and fundamentally wrong.
>
> (1875)

From the outset it was accepted that should women be allowed to vote there could be no logical reason why they could not be allowed to be voted for. Perhaps the original domino theory, it filled some not only with horror but undisguised contempt too. What would others think?

Does this country really want to see a mixed House of Commons composed of men and women? There is no denying that this must be the natural consequence of giving women the vote. ... and if they become Members they are bound to be Ministers. ... Is it really possible that we should contemplate making such a spectacle of ourselves to the Civilized World?
(Mr Burdett-Coutts, 1911)

It would place Britain in an unenviable position alongside her neighbours.

If we are going to have the franchise on a two-sex basis then we will have the policy of the country dictated and controlled by a majority which will not be a masculine majority. Our policy will be dictated by a feminine majority competing with the policy of Germany, France and Russia where the direction of affairs will be determined by a masculine virile male vote.
(Mr Bertram, 1907)

Unashamed running for cover animated some observers.

This is an experiment so large and bold that it ought to be tried by some other country first.
(Mr Bryce, 1892)

Others exhibited an equal strength of view and no less candour about where they stood.

Let me ... put one more argument – I am afraid that it is an entirely selfish one – the argument that men have the vote and the power at the present moment. I say for Heaven's sake let us keep it. We are controlled and worried enough by women at the present time and I have heard no reason given why we should alter the present state of affairs. A clever woman said to me the other day, 'If at the most critical period of a woman's life she has not got the sense to say no to the man who proposes to her, how can you expect her to have the sense to give a vote on a great Imperial question?' I would urge hon Members to consider seriously before you vote for this measure.

(Mr Grant, 1913)

Never far below the surface, though, was the ability to flatter and insult at the same time.

To men has been entrusted the responsibility of government and the defence of the Empire and whether we perform this great duty well or badly must depend upon our moral and mental fitness to carry them out and we can only look to the mothers of England to maintain this standard of moral and mental fitness in the coming generation. Are we justified then, seeing that the responsibilities of women to the country are already far greater than those of men, in imposing upon them the additional burden of Government and are we justified in running the risk that we shall tempt them to neglect those natural functions which are absolutely essential to our national existence in order that they may devote their efforts to those duties where they certainly are not indispensable and where many of us think they will be directly harmful.

(Mr Mills, 1910)

This assertion that there were specific roles for women in life which made other pursuits likely only to detract from them generated its most charitable side from those who argued that these positive attributes were too valuable to lose.

Women have a higher role in the organization of society. In matters connected with spiritual and moral affairs, in holding up ideals for the rest of the community they have a special function for which their intuition and refined minds render

their services of immense value to the community and my
opinion is that it is against the interests of the State that those
powers ... should be blunted and spoiled by being dragged
down into political and Party strife. It is highly desirable that
such powers as women possess should be kept keen in order that
they might contrive to guide and inspire other people irrespec-
tive of Party considerations.

(Mr Whitehead, 1907)

Such views were not always as graciously expressed.

[Women's] vocation is a high one. Their vocation is to make
life endurable.

(Mr Scourfield, 1870)

Her natural position [is] the helpmate and comforter of Man.

(Mr Scourfield, 1872)

It [is] the business of the man to do the hard work and of the
woman to make [the] home bright and cheerful for him.

(Mr Bouverie, 1872)

Those who pressed for more public roles for women failed
to appreciate the power women already had ... according to
some opponents of reform.

Nobody is more aware than I am of the enormous influence for
good of women in this world. It would be foolish to deny it; but
I think this influence, great as it is, is generally in proportion to
their unobtrusiveness. I think most of us, from our own personal experience, may well say that those women who have
gone to their graves having done most real good – having
exercised the best, the highest sort of influence and performed
best those purposes for which a human being is sent into the
world – are those women whose names have very often never

been heard of beyond their own immediate circle.

(Earl Cowper, 1890)

Clearly making a name for oneself was to be strictly a male affair. The notion that women possessed this immense but intangible power in society was turned with dextrous ingenuity by one opponent of reform to prove beyond doubt that women did not in fact want the vote.

> Women have at present such an influence over the actions of men that if they had been really united in the desire for the franchise they would have got it long ago. It is only a few women with masculine minds who take an interest in politics and desire to have votes.
>
> (Mr Labouchere, 1905)

Against arguments of this circularity there was no chance for the ladies. Even more infuriating would have been the following, one of many which started from the premise that in all things men knew women's interests better than they did themselves. Few, though, were able to surpass this for its mix of acclaim and denigration of the place of woman.

> I believe all men know and recognise ... on what an infinitely higher and purer and nobler plane the influence of woman over man rests than the influence of man over woman. ... Women's weakness is her real strength. It is because woman is weaker than man in respects which have always appealed to man ... that woman's moral influence over man, her formative, educative, guiding, influence over man is infinitely greater. I claim that in that matter Nature ... has given woman a full compensation in moral influence for what it has taken from her in physical strength. But when you destroy this fine balance of nature which indeed is always imperceptibly weighing down the scales in favour of woman, when you give her the

same physical right in the government of the country as man, when you arm her with the same weapons and say that she is to fight for herself independently of, and, if she likes, against man, then you bring her down to the level of man and you impair the very foundations of that moral and spiritual influence she has exercised over man to man's unspeakable benefit ... you are destroying the delicate equipoise which Nature herself has adjusted between the moral influence of woman and the physical strength of man.

(Mr Burdett-Coutts, 1917)

If all this pacific patronizing viewing of woman's role was not convincing enough, the artillery of abuse was not far behind. As well as being the greatest moral influence on the actions of men, women were also held to be bereft of every semblance of rationality in their powers of decision-making. Male opponents did not dwell too much on the internal inconsistency of this proposition – why did they hold woman's influence in such awe if it came from so manifestly irrational a source? – but swept on with a tide of chauvinism that rarely knew any bounds.

Between the two sexes it is abundantly evident that Nature has drawn clear lines of distinction. There are certain things which women can do better than men and others which they can not do so well. In all that requires rough, rude, practical force, stability of character and intellect, man is superior; whereas in all those relations of life that demand mildness, softness of character and amiability, women far excel.

(Mr Laing, 1867)

There is a broad and clear physiological difference between woman and man which amply justifies the present state of things. The male intellect is logical and judicial, the female instinctive and emotional. The instinctive and emotional has its own duty and its own functions in the progress of things; and that function is to guide, to influence, to moderate, to regulate, to suffer – not to govern. Any person who is of a liberal mind will at once see that the direct influence of the female mind on the progress of the human mind and on the progress of human affairs is immeasurable; but it is by her very weakness, her helplessness, her reliance upon man that she holds her power....

... Enfranchise women generally and make them a power in the country and you will find yourselves drifting on a sea of impulsive philanthropy and sentimentalism where you are now at anchor on the principles of political economy. With the highest respect for the female sex, I must say I doubt, if such a change as that which is now proposed takes place, whether we could discuss questions in this House or in the country with our present calmness or whether Parliament would retain the influence which it owes to its reputation for judicial wisdom.
(Mr Beresford Hope, 1870)

Do women possess the fitness and capacity to fulfil the duties of the suffrage they claim? ... I reply emphatically that they do not. The want of it proceeds from many causes but principally from that excess of sympathy in the mental constitution of women which shuts out from their mind logical power and judicial impartiality. Let a woman range herself on one side of a question or be identified with particular interests and it is nigh to impossibility to persuade her that there is any error on the side she advocates or any right in that she is opposed to.
(Mr James, 1871)

The implication was clear that women would not be able to think for themselves.

Surely it cannot be expected that women, if enjoying the franchise, will give an unbiased vote, the result of political conviction? Not depending on their own judgment, you are about to create a class upon which influence ... will ever be brought to bear.

(Mr James, 1871)

As potential voters, and legislators, it was a recipe for catastrophe.

Women undoubtedly are sentimental and there is no doubt that their keen sense of right and duty, added to their sentimentality, compels them to advocate any cause which they may take up, utterly regardless of any consequences that may follow. It is conceivable that if any project came before a body on which women were in the majority, a project against which nothing could be said except that this was not an ideal world and that to carry it out would cast a burden on the ratepayers which they would not be able to bear, such a body would be guided by the excellence of the project rather than by considerations of the finance.

(Mr Banbury, 1900)

Intellectually women have not the gifts which fit them for being elected. They have got a certain amount of what I might call instinct rather than reason [and] they are impulsive, emotional and have got absolutely no sense of proportion.

(Mr Labouchere, 1897)

The prospects for reasoned political debate were minimal.

You will have the whole gamut of the female nervous system varying from gross materialism on the one hand to absolutely altruistic interference on the other. Therefore if you involve the female element you make our whole voting system most complicated and difficult.

(Mr Kirkwood, 1910)

Everyone will recognise that women have great qualifications. They are extremely quick to catch a point and very quick judges of character, but they are not capable of looking at a case in all its bearings. I am sure we would never be able to convince a woman in this House if she did not wish to be convinced. I believe that there are very few instances of any Member having changed his vote by anything said in debate, but I am quite certain that if women are introduced into this House it would be useless to debate any point at all because the women will have made up their minds before the debate begins.

(Sir F.Banbury, 1905)

It is necessary to remind the House that women's passions are infinitely more violent when once called forth than men's.

(Earl Percy, 1873)

By their constitution, they are more liable to be affected by gusts and waves of sentiment ... Their very emotional nature makes women an easier prey to showy argument [and] to the influence of an attractive personality.

(Mr Bryce, 1910)

Former Chancellor, and future Foreign Secretary, Austen Chamberlain thought he had seen enough of the inside of government to voice an authoritative view in 1913.

For political functions it is not a question of the equality of men or women but it is the question of the suitability of the peculiar quality of the two sexes for the exercise of special and particular functions and, in my opinion, if I can put it without unnecessary offence, the qualities of women ... are not qualities by which we desire to be governed.

    ... the quality which women would bring to their political actions as to every other are not those which are most required

at any time in any country ... Women have great capacity for
self-sacrifice, sometimes too great a capacity for self-sacrifice.
They are, taken as a whole, more sentimental than men. They
are more rigid in decision and less willing to accept compromise. Half the wisdom of quality lies in judicial compromise ...
that kind of wisdom is more readily and widely found among
men than among women.

His conclusion was foreboding for women.

In my opinion, mentally, physiologically and physically there
is a real differentiation of function in these matters between
men and women which the law does not create, which the law
cannot remedy and which we have got to reckon with.

(Mr Chamberlain, 1913)

The more charitable found that it was not women's fault
entirely that they ended up ill-equipped to take part in the
choosing of their government.

[Men] by leaving their homes and moving among other men
have opportunities ... of picking up some knowledge on political affairs; but women, if they are not to leave their homes but
are still to remain, as I hope they will remain, as ornaments in
their homes, will have no chance of picking up that amount of
knowledge which would justify their giving a vote upon great
and complex questions.

(Mr Hanbury, 1877)

I think that every one will allow that Nature, speaking generally of the sex, has denied to woman the faculty of very close
reasoning. ... Under this natural and Providential arrangement, those duties which belong to the external world which
are rugged in their character and require the exercise of that
practical sagacity which it is not possible anyone can obtain

without mixing freely with his fellows, fall to the rougher and more rugged sex; while those which are best discharged in the privacy of home which appeal more to the heart have fallen to that sex of whose virtue shrinking modesty is an essential part and who in all matters relating to the heart are a higher and purer sex than ourselves.

... The questions which now come before Parliament are of the utmost importance and of a technical and complicated character. We have questions about the administration of the Army and the Navy, about finance and ecclesiastical policy, the judicature and procedure in the Law Courts. What information can women bring to us upon these points?

(Mr Leatham, 1875)

All was not lost for the woman desiring to play a role in life. The same commentator had earlier mapped out their path.

I think it argues strange poverty of resource in women to assert that there is no career open to them unless they have the career of men presented to their choice. In spite of the march of civilization there is still some human suffering left in the world. There is still pain enough to soothe and sorrow enough to solace. It is in this field that women in all ages have been able to satisfy the loftiest ambitions and in doing so have raised themselves and their whole sex along with them to a pinnacle of greatness which the best men have envied in vain.

(Mr Leatham, 1875)

Surely it was unrealistic to expect women to plunge into political matters?

Men as a rule gain a rough experience of the world; they mix in workshops and clubs and discuss the politics of the day and in a rough sort of way make up their minds on the current topics. Nearly all of them read newspapers and attend public meetings but how few women have either the taste or opportunity of doing so? It is doubtful whether even [a tenth] ... care the least about politics. What are the vast majority of these women? ... the great majority of them are wives of working men, struggling with families of small children from early morning till late at night, utterly unable to study the complicated questions which come before Parliament. What they do read is mostly ... the cheap novel and it is impossible for them to frequent clubs and public meetings without ruin to their children.

> ... Men as a class naturally take to politics when they get a chance but women will not because the bent of their minds is different. They live ... by the heart more than the head and the enfranchised servant girl will continue to prefer the novelette to *The Times*.

(Mr S. Smith, 1892)

All the experience of history told against this innovation.

From reasons deep-seated in physiology, woman has not the constructive mind that the male has. ... Women are less imaginative and more emotional and intuitional and if anybody doubts that I ask them to search the centuries of civilization for the women writers, scientists and artists and they will find only a few who are distinguished. There are exceptions which only prove the rule. ... You have only to look at the lists of writers and artists and if the women who had leisure and have been taken care of possessed those talents they would have displayed those powers had they possessed them.

(Sir J.Compton-Rickett, 1917)

If such an argument seems another circular one there were many more of far greater absurdity.

We are told ... that if women possess the right to vote and assist in the legislation of the House it will infuse into our legislation a humanitarian spirit. This is one of the reasons urged by those who advocate this claim. Some of us, however, have noted the remarkable headgear of women to adorn which millions of birds have been destroyed and although it has been pointed out to them that by this practice the most beautiful of the feathered tribe are disappearing, they still continue to wear feathers in their hats. Women have also been told over and over again by some nobler members of their own sex of the horrible sufferings undergone by the poor little seals ... yet nearly every woman who can afford to do so goes on wearing seal-skin jackets. And these are the people we are asked to admit to the franchise because they will infuse into our legislation a spirit of humanitarianism!

(Mr Cremer, 1904)

A later speaker rather uncharitably pointed out in response that certain other activities persisted in society such as game shooting and fox hunting which were indulged in 'by persons who certainly are not women'. The Cremers of the world were not to be daunted by such uncomfortable facts. Other examples were used to demonstrate that women were already privileged in significant degrees.

They are privileged all along the line. How many Members have been in an omnibus when it has been raining and the conductor has appealed to them to get out and let a lady get in? ... Men step off the kerb into the gutter to allow a lady to pass clean shod. Whatever view we take of the matter, no-one can deny that ladies, because they are ladies, are creatures of privilege.

(Mr Cremer, 1904)

And, therefore, the sentiment went, enjoying bus seats and clean shoes, how could they in all good conscience ask for the vote as well!

There was also the question of dress.

> There are obvious disadvantages about having women in
> Parliament. I do not know what is going to be done about their
> hats. Are they going to wear hats or not ...? If you order them
> not to wear hats you might be absolutely certain that they will
> insist on wearing them. How is a poor little man to get on with
> a couple of women wearing enormous hats in front of him?
>
> (Mr Hunt, 1913)

In 1871 (the first quotation cited from Mr Beresford-Hope)
the fear was that female impetuosity would lead to more
wars. By 1917, exactly the opposite view was advanced, in
response to a case in the United States where a woman
member of Congress had just refused to vote in favour of
America's entry into World War One because she was a
mother and did not want sons to have to fight.

> We do not want to put the power into the hands of women who
> naturally feel so very intensely and who will be averse from
> taking very strong action.
>
> (Sir F. Bunbury, 1917)

Women could well be forgiven for feeling that they simply could
not win. Perhaps they would be wiser to take the advice of an early
critic and be content with their present lot.

> [We have] recognised the fact that women are not as well fitted
> as men for the rough labours of life by prohibiting them from
> engaging in some of the coarser handiworks which men are
> obliged to perform. We do not allow women to go down into
> the sunless mines and yet the demand is now made that all
> women should be treated exactly like men....
>   ... Women should be satisfied with the great power
> they now possess indirectly which is far greater than anything

they can hope to attain directly.

(Mr Bouverie, 1870)

We move seamlessly into the theme which perhaps more than any dominated the debate: that it was really for woman's own good that man prevent her from acquiring this poisoned chalice of the vote.

> I fail to see how this measure can benefit the female sex in any way. ... Though unfitted by nature, habit or physical power for such a position, women will be placed in competition with men. What then will become of that refining and humanizing influence which is begotten of the respect and deference which now the stronger sex invariably pay to a woman? What, I ask, will become of that influence, strong though undefined, which women now so happily wield for good? For woman's sake, therefore, as well as for the general welfare of the country, I confidently appeal to the House to reject this measure.
>
> ... [If the measure is passed] instead of the present beneficient arrangement under which, according to the plan of an allwise Providence, men and women work side by side in their own sphere, each combining with the other to produce that harmony which promotes the well-being of the home and family and consequently of the nation, we shall inaugurate a new state of society where the two sexes no longer distinct in their occupations, aims and pursuits will enter on an unequal struggle in which be assured the weaker, the gentler and the frailer sex will inevitably be the victims and the conquered.

(Viscount Folkestone, 1876)

The greatest kindness we can do to the women themselves is to refuse them this vote and put them out of the turmoil and struggle of political life.

> ... it is not only a measure that would revolutionize

society but it would do worse than that for it would entirely
decompose it.

(Mr Hanbury, 1878)

I find [the Bill's] title to be that of 'A Bill to Remove the
Electoral Disabilities of Women'. I should rather describe it as
'A Bill to add to the Duties, the Burdens, the Responsibilities
of Women', ... I believe [it] would result in the infliction of a
grievous injury upon the weaker sex under the semblance –
and, no doubt, with the full intention – of conferring upon
them a benefit.

(Mr Knatchbull Hugessen, 1872)

Without any hint of disingenuity, the view could be held
that,

... it is not a disability that women should not have a vote but
it is rather a privilege that they should not be mixed up in
political strife.

(Mr Fowler, 1870)

If women were honest with themselves, they would realize
that they risked losing their present comfortable position.

The great bulk of the women of England have an instinctive
distaste for political privileges for they are aware of the evil
which would ultimately ensue to their sex if they entered into
competition with men in all the rough pursuits of life. Women
are weaker than men, at all events physically. If they have to
struggle in the world on equal terms with men they must
inevitably be oppressed. They are protected now by the habits
and ideas of society generally from oppression.

(Mr Bouverie, 1871)

While I believe that a man qualified to possess the franchise is
ennobled by its possession, woman is in my humble opinion

almost debased or degraded by it. She will be in danger of
losing those admirable attributes of her sex – namely her
gentleness, her affection and her domesticity.

(Mr Karslake, 1867)

I think they would lose much of that ... which is best that they
now possess and they would gain no good of any kind from
being mingled or mixed with Parliamentary contests and the
polling booth.

(Mr Bright, 1876)

The sentiments were not confined to maverick backbenchers.
Austen Chamberlain, whom we have already heard, had
already been Chancellor and would have a distinguished
career in Government ahead when he uttered his views in
1910.

No worse service can be done to the cause of the nation and
the women than to obliterate those attributes to which society
and the nation owe so much. It is not therefore because I think
woman inferior to men; it is not because I give way to any man
in my reverence or regard for them, but just because I place
their qualities so high, because I respect them so greatly,
because I think those qualities are so valuable an asset of the
national life and that they cannot be maintained unimpaired
in the turmoil of our political and party system that I am
reluctant to take this ... step.

Such suffering from men's kindness was nothing compared
to what was in store if women were inflicted with the vote.

We believe that the capacity of women lies in other directions
than in public life; we believe that their capacity is best and
most easily directed to the greatest advantage of the individual
and of the public when it is directed towards domestic and

local activities rather than to external and political considerations.

... The pains and sufferings which are entailed upon some of them are beyond the imagination of any man to understand and comprehend. ... They are subject to the strain of bearing children when men are devoting their years to the study and formation of character and ideals. It will put upon woman a physical and mental strain which is incapable of carrying.

(Sir C. Hobhouse, 1917)

How did men know? One early critic shows that the unashamed self-fulfilling prophecy was in full play.

It will inflict a calamity and a curse upon them; and what is more the great bulk of the women of this country have the good sense to know it. ... I can say that it has not been my lot to fall in with one *sensible* woman who is in favour of it. [Our italics.]

(Mr Bouverie, 1870)

The catch, of course, was that no-one who advocated women's suffrage would be thought 'sensible' in Bouverie's book. His contention was not capable of being objectively disproved. The following year he was again spouting forth, this time on the grounds that it was the retiring mass of womanhood whom they should be thinking about, not the rampaging minority.

Mixing up women in contested elections would be to contaminate the sex – that sex which we are bound to keep in respect and whose modesty and purity we are especially bound to hold in reverence.

... If we confer the Parliamentary franchise on women we should not be able to protect those who are unwilling to take part in politics – they will be driven to the poll whether they

like it or not; their lives will be made a burden to them during
a contested election; ... Therefore unless the great bulk of our
countrywomen ask for the franchise ... the House ought not to
impose such a *damnosa hereditas* upon them.

And, of course, 'sensible' women would not come forward
to ask: case proven.

Some arguments had a remarkable ability to deflect blame
for any likely ill effects of reform. Take the following,
which without a hint of self-reproach, casts women as their
own condemners.

> I candidly believe that the mere fact of women competing with
> men would deprive the former of many of the privileges which
> at present gallantry, courtesy and consideration always extend
> to them among all classes of the community. We all know from
> our own experience that the more women try to imitate men
> and to compete with them, the more does our respect for them
> gradually diminish.
>
> (Mr Hanbury, 1878)

Women would have been entitled to ask: 'Whose problem
is that?' As ever, the gallantry of men was there to woman's
good fortune.

> Although there may be some women masculine in all their
> ways, yet the majority of women – those loving and sympa-
> thetic women whom we all so much respect and admire – we
> have to protect and I, for one, will not place upon them a
> burden they are unfit and unable to bear.
>
> (Sir Walter Barttelot, 1892)

Women had reached their 'level' in society. To push them
any further would be counter-productive for all.

There are a few women who [have] obtained a great influence in society by their genius and their capacity for work and I honour them for it. ... The great majority of the self-dependent class are persons who by many sacrifices and ceaseless industry just succeeded in realizing competence sufficient with great thrift to support them in a moderate and quiet way. The extension of the franchise to such women would not only disturb the peaceful character of their lives but might seriously endanger that competence by forcing them into the arena of political excitement where they would be exposed to the animosities, the bickerings and the resentments which are so unhappily inherent in the rough work of electioneering. ... The very nature of women called for sympathy and protection and for the highest and most chivalrous treatment on the part of the men; but instead of this being accorded for the future, it is now proposed to thrust them into a position which they are by their sex, by their condition in life and by their previous training unqualified to grapple with.

(Mr Beresford Hope, 1871)

Perhaps the best, all-encompassing offering on the theme of protecting women from a hard life came from Earl Cowper in 1890. Lest it be thought there was any hint of chauvinism, he prefaced his speech with a disclaimer.

I am very desirous that those who take the line I do should not be accused of wishing to treat women as mere dolls. ... I would repudiate any suggestion of that sort.

If he did, it was difficult to tell it from what followed.

On the contrary, we take that line because we are so conscious of the present high position of women and because we are so anxious that they should not be contaminated by the deterio-rating influence of political life, the struggles and enmities and bitterness and ... the vulgarities of public life, that we wish to guard women from them.

Men had a hard time in politics, but after all it was their onerous duty to struggle through without any expectation of thanks for it.

> I am not quite sure whether the rough and tumble of political life always exercises the most enobling effect upon men. I am not sure that the violent Party animosities, the one-sidedness, the virulent personalities and the misrepresentations which often distinguish even the best people in political life ... do not sometimes exercise a rather deteriorating effect upon the men. Men must, of course, take part in the affairs of the country and in carrying on the public business must submit to these things ... but, for Heaven's sake, my Lords, let us shield women from this as long as we possibly can.

Even if women did enter the fray, it was unlikely to be with advantage to anyone.

> Some people say that women would exercise an elevating effect upon public life and would raise it and free it from many of those evils. I am by no means sure of that. On the contrary, I fear that women, with their more excitable natures and their tendency to look at things more from a personal and concrete than an abstract point of view, would be liable even more than men to the deteriorating effects of the platform.

The wider impact on society's organization was another important strand in the argument. The most fundamental relations of all – those of the family – would be utterly destroyed. It was in fact another of the classic 'can't-win' arguments where during the debate completely opposite arguments were advanced to prove the same point. The earliest reference traceable in Parliament's treatment of the women's suffrage issue, coming in 1797, maintained that giving the vote to women would serve absolutely no purpose because they would never act independently but follow the dictates of their husbands. As Charles James Fox put it:

> By the law of nations and perhaps also by the law of Nature, that sex is dependent on ours; ... therefore their voices will be governed by the relation in which they stand in society.

All it would do would be to give married men a second vote.

> We would give a dual power to the husband who in influencing her would exercise, in a manner, a double vote.
>
> (Mr Hanbury, 1877)

That was one view. The opposite became even more popular – that women would in fact exercise their own minds, with disastrous consequences for family unity. One Mr Karslake warned of:

> ... the difficulties that will exist in the way of woman exercising her right of voting in opposition to her husband.
>
> (1867)

Worse still, it could lead to who knew where.

> As to the question of expediency, [proponents] think that advantage will arise from giving the suffrage to women because among other things it will promote logical discussion between the man and his wife. ... I believe that the unerring instinct not only of the House of Commons but of men themselves will be utterly opposed to this innovation.
>
> (1867)

A future Prime Minister worried about the effect on the nation.

> I think many women will see that politics are not a very desirable field of exertion for them. One of the greatest evils we have to contend with is the bitter feeling that rises between friends and neighbours who take opposite sides on political questions.
>
> ... These bitter feelings would, if this Bill passes, be introduced into the home. Contests will not be not so much between neighbour and neighbour and between friend and friend as between husband and wife.
>
> (Mr Balfour, 1877)

Not to be outdone, the arch-enemy of women's suffrage predictably voiced his opinions in even more dramatic language. The point, though, was arguably incontestable – that either way, if women agreed or disagreed with their husbands, nothing good could derive from the situation.

> I must protest against such a system of domestic anarchy. Either the wife will vote with the husband, in which case he will virtually take two votes to the poll or she will vote in a contrary way and then there will be domestic discord. I think the House ought not to sanction either alternative.
>
> (Mr Bouverie, 1870)

Extreme and chauvinistic it all may seem to us now but who, at the time, could discount the logic of the vision of the future being portrayed? Early proponents of the women's suffrage movement sought to get round this problem of domestic harmony by proposing to give the vote just to unmarried women and widows. It was never really a tenable argument and opponents gleefully heaped ridicule on the idea. The population would fall catastrophically as women opted to vote rather than give birth to the nation's future (oddly at variance with the persistent theme that women did not really want the vote – but such inconsistencies were par for the course, as we have seen). The political future of the country would then, it followed, be in the hands of 'unnatural' women rather than the best of their breed who naturally wanted only to marry and have children, the normal role of womanhood. Even the proponents soon realized that it would have to be all or none, but when they reverted to the full blown case, even more bizarre obstacles were just waiting to be erected. Another die-hard opponent mounted the argument that women's suffrage would be a charter for philanderers since men caught with other men's wives could claim they were merely soliciting her vote.

> I saw an account the other day of a case in the North of England where a gentleman was found to be visiting a lady who was not his wife. ... His defence was that he visited the lady because he contemplated becoming a town councillor and that he went to see the lady in order to canvass for her support.
>
> ... I do not know how domestic bliss is to be continued if a man is perpetually leaving his own wife and visiting another man's wife on the plea that he wanted [her vote]. I think that [the House] will agree with me that that would be a very dangerous state of things.
>
> (Mr Labouchere, 1904)

If this was the most bizarre argument to be advanced, others were on hand which were not quite so capable of being dismissed for their sheer outlandishness. A rather more cogent theme came to the fore late in the debate which to the contemporary struggling to find a clinching argument either way only added to the doubts about the idea of women voting. This was the argument of unequal privilege, that in fact, giving votes to women would not be restoring equality to society but actually conferring privilege on women on the grounds that women would in future have a controlling say in formulating policies from the consequences of which they would be happily immune because of their gender. The approach was artfully explained in the following.

> A vote is a cross marked on a piece of paper; it is not an unladylike thing to make a cross on paper any more than it is an unladylike thing to sign a cheque, but the cheque is useless if you have no money in the bank. A vote is a cheque or draft on power and ultimately, on physical power.
>
> (Mr Mackinder, 1911)

The argument was simple. Unless women were able to back up their policy decisions by physical strength, which was after all the ultimate resort in life, they had no right to take part in the decision-making process at all. Their influence could not be responsibly based. At root, it was all a question of whether to go to war or not. How could policies which might affect the security of the country be contributed to, indeed controlled by, women who would not have to fight anyway?

> If we grant adult suffrage we run a serious risk of having legislation passed by a majority of women which, in my view, would be a very grave and unsatisfactory condition of things. Ultimately the government of the country depends on force and it would be a disastrous thing to give the technical and legal power to those who possess no real force and are not responsible for the ultimate control of the affairs of the country.
>
> (Mr Whitehead, 1907)

> It is upon men that the dangers of battle and the ordeal of service fall. ... Is it right that women should have the controlling voice in these things and that men should have so inde-

scribably greater a share of the suffering that is the consequence of the policy?

(Earl Loreburn, 1918)

It was a real problem because it was an uncontested fact that there were some 1.2 million more women in Britain than men by the start of the twentieth century. Amongst the all-male electorate there was an equally uncontested view that women would vote *en bloc* as a class in the same undiscriminating way they had always felt, for example, the working class voted. Thus women would hold an awesome power, a power without responsibility, in the nation's affairs.

If it is a question of war, surely a man who has to go on sea or land and take part in war is a better judge of a question of that kind than a woman can be, however skilful ... she might be.

(Sir F. Powell, 1907)

Surely this argument of all the arguments was beyond denial?

It is based upon the idea that the ultimate basis of political power and of stable government in a democracy is that the same hands that hold the balance of political power should hold the balance of physical force without which there can be no stable government. ... I would submit that the unit of physical force is the individual male citizen. ... Therefore when you count the heads of women as well as the heads of men you destroy the ballot box as an index of physical force in the country.

(Mr Scott, 1917)

I say therefore that you are asking for the first time for the introduction into the constitution of a new and a privileged class. You are asking the House to give women a vote and the power to count head for head with men in the making of laws, in the determining of policy, in the supervision of national administration; and yet, at the same time, you are not casting upon them − because nature does not allow it − the burden which is cast upon every male citizen.

(Mr Asquith, 1892)

All sorts of problems would result, opponents said, even in the ordinary run of national life. Still hooked on the notion of block voting by women against men, they foresaw constitutional crises ahead.

Supposing that a House consisting to a large extent of Members elected by the votes of women passed a law to which men as a whole object; do [you] suppose that it will be possible to enforce that law? They could not force men's obedience to laws passed by the influence of a majority of women contrary to the opinion of men on whose power the final sanction of the law rested. Something like revolution would result.

(Mr Robertson, 1905)

Fanciful though these thoughts might seem now, it should not be forgotten that at the time it was by no means clear how such a fundamental change to the electoral system would affect relations in society. Hindsight allows us to mock the fears as unfounded and extremist. Our ancestors had no such luxury. As seen from then, few could disagree with Home Secretary-to-be Mr Asquith:

It is not a democratic measure. The doctrine of democracy demands that we should equalise where inequality exists among things fundamentally alike but not that we should identify where things are fundamentally unlike. The inequalities which democracy requires that we should fight against and remove

are the unearned privileges and the artificial distinction which
man has made and which man can unmake. They are not those
indelible differences of faculty and function by which Nature
herself has given diversity and richness to human society.

(1892)

The first part of the sentiment was no nineteenth century
construction. The theme goes back to the very birth of the
democratic ideal, to none other than Aristotle himself, one
of whose lesser-known precepts admirably summed up the
dilemma facing Asquith and his contemporaries: 'Injustice
arises when equals are treated unequally and also when
unequals are treated equally.' (*Laws*, Book VI) We were
simply blinding ourselves to truth by such changes to the
natural order of things.

To impose upon two sexes so unequally constituted equal
burdens and equal rights, if you will to ignore the distinctions
set up by nature and to treat them as if they are artificial, to
regard as ephemeral those differences which are profound and
which have existed through all time and grow greater rather
than less with the progress of civilization, that is not to remove
inequality or to alleviate injustice. It is to perpetrate injustice
and create inequality.

(Mr Austen Chamberlain, 1910)

The sense of trying to equalize the unequal was argued out
on less profound levels too. How could women possibly be
treated the same as men in the rough and tumble of an
election?

I look with anxiety to women entering into these Party contests which are fought out with great heat. Political meetings
are held night after night and there is the greatest excitement.
Is the woman candidate when on the platform to be treated as

men are treated? Is she to be attacked and to bear the inevitable consequences of being placed in that position? I hope not; but if she is it is a destruction of the position she has hitherto held. But if courtesy is to be expected to be displayed towards her, what is to become of her unfortunate opponent? I can imagine an unfortunate middle-aged man who has done his duty and understands political economy being opposed by a lady who may be all that fancy may depict. She is to stand there safe from criticism while the unfortunate man is subjected to bitter personal attack.

(Lord James of Hereford, 1907)

With an inconsistency that has become familiar, this last excerpt conveys the opposite argument to that advanced in the final theme which dominated the contest. Far from portraying enfranchised women as paragons of womanhood as the last commentator does (and thereby ruling them out of political life because of their essential femininity), this theme maintained the opposite – that those agitating for the vote were not 'real' women but unwomanly misfits who were bringing the whole of the female sex into discredit. 'Real' women did not want the vote at all. Those who did began to be described in increasingly insulting terms, starting with restrained undertones as harmless as 'strong-minded', but growing relentlessly and with uncontrolled spite into some of the most unworthy of observations which ensured the debate descended into the gutter on more than one occasion. To begin with they were simply egotistical fanatics.

[It is] doctrinaire agitation on the part of people who live in the solitude of their own philosophic ideas and thought to recast society upon their private theories, forgetful of that great element of human nature which ought to predominate in the affairs of the world.

(Mr Beresford Hope, 1873)

These women ... do not represent their sex at all – women with more masculine minds than womanly sympathies.

(Mr Hanbury, 1879)

The 'real' women were the silent majority.

What evidence is there that women asked for the franchise? The evidence only of those ladies to whom I have alluded. There has been no demonstration on the other side simply because those who are opposed to the measure are those who consider it would be out of their sphere to demonstrate.

(Colonel Waring, 1897)

Colonel Waring had alluded to 'their fussy sisters' (by comparison to real women) as the agitators behind the campaign. All this was terribly gallant alongside the more vociferous objectors who unleashed a tidal wave of crude derision more in keeping with the school dormitory than the House of Commons. The mildest:

[The suffrage movement] is a sham and an unreal agitation manufactured to order and which may easily be traced to nothing but a bustling clique of masculine women and feminine men who have devoted their energies to the support of the cause.

(Mr Chaplin, 1876)

One Member had his own way of demonstrating the truth.

As a means of testing whether the women of England really wish for the power of voting, I would suggest ... that every person signing a petition in favour of the extension of the franchise to women should be instructed to accompany the signature with a photographic portrait; and that Mr Darwin or Professor Owen who can distinguish the sex of animals from very trifling signs should be retained to decide from an examination of the pictures as to the sex of the person represented – for I can not help suspecting that many of the signatories are not women but men in women's clothing.

(Mr Scourfield, 1871)

Some stinging sideswipes were to follow. Mr O'Donoghue referred to the agitation as the product of:

those who have been unfortunate as to have lost their wits or who have never been fortunate enough to have any.

(1877)

He thought that the reason for the campaign was that all the serious issues of life had now been settled.

I ... come to the conclusion ... that all questions affecting the happiness of the nation ... have been settled; and that, upon the principle that it is always necessary to be doing something, we are about to enter on a period of meddling legislation. I would anticipate, therefore, should this measure pass the introduction of Bills prescribing how we are to cook our food, how to bring up our children, how in certain circumstances we are even to blow our noses ...

(1877)

Humorous perhaps, but then things began to get nastier.

There are certain ladies of very great intellect, no doubt they are women by accident and they want to assume the position of men. Now I object to legislating for what, with all respect to the ladies, I may call freaks of nature. It might be said in favour of allowing women to enlist that some women have the muscular strength of the average man and there are such – but they are exceptions. Women are the exceptions who have the intellectual mind and nature to enable them to take a promi-

nent part in politics; would you legislate for such exceptions?
Each sex must accept the position nature has assigned to it. It
is as absurd for women to whimper because they cannot be
Members of Parliament as it would be for Members of Parliament to whimper because they cannot suckle children. Women,
by entering into politics, will lose the charm of their own sex
without acquiring the qualities of the other.

(Mr Labouchere, 1891)

Women were just not cut out for it.

What does one find when one gets into the company of women
and talk politics? We are soon asked to stop talking silly
politics and yet this is the type to whom [we] are invited to
hand over the destinies of the country.

(Mr Cremer, 1906)

A *tour de force* of the many dismal prophecies came relatively early on.

If the franchise is to be given to women, the legislative power
of this House will not be strengthened in any material degree
and women, as a class, will suffer by asserting their equality
with men and becoming their avowed antagonists in the race
of life. In that contest you may depend upon it that women will
get very much the worst of it.

    ... women can gain nothing but they will be likely to lose
a great deal. ... Will men be happier by the removal of that
diversity of tastes and training which now is the true cause of
concord? Fancy a Member returning home ... and finding there
a politician in petticoats ready to continue the debate!

    ... [It will result in] a system that will eventually destroy
the home and cover London with institutions of a sexless ...
character in which men and women, young and old alike, will
meet without any of the controlling influences, without any of

those checks and safeguards which at the present time tend to
soften and temper the relations between the two.

(Mr Raikes, 1879)

Why did things have to change at all? Deploying a logic of
seemingly unanswerable power, one of the last ditch efforts
attempted to counter the argument that the experience of
the First World War had seen women to be deserving of the
vote. Typically it mixed with gay abandon fulsome tributes
with barbed conclusions.

It is the War that has brought out more strongly than anything
else could the fundamental difference to which I have alluded
between man and woman. And whatever women have done in
this War – put it as high as you like and no-one living puts it
higher than I do – those women have been produced: their
character, their efficiency, their energy, their devotion and
self-sacrifice and patriotism, aye and the proud and splendid
courage with which they have borne themselves under heart-
breaking grief, all these things, all these noble characteristics
have been formed in English women without their having the
vote. Nothing could be better than what Englishwomen have
grown to be without the vote. Are you certain what effect the
vote will have upon them? ... Is it not better, is it not safer for
the purposes of the new Parliament and the great task it will
have to undertake and the great problems it will have to solve
... to keep it in form and kind the same as it has been in the
past; the same electorate that England has grown great under,
has won her name for justice and freedom, has made her
Empire and come to her present position? Has that position
ever [been] greater than it is now?

... And she has done these things under a male electorate.

(Mr Burdett-Coutts, 1917)

Of course, critics would have been quick to point out, there
was one obvious thing he had not mentioned which women

had manifestly *not* done in the Great War – started it! Somehow at the end of the greatest conflict in history, the threat of female suffrage never seemed again the apocalyptic vision it had for so long been painted. There was virtually no opposition to speak of against the Bill in 1918 which enfranchised women over thirty years old. Women were content to have had the principle accepted; men were relieved that they were still some way from being 'controlled' by a female majority. The classic compromise lasted for a decade. In 1928 voting on equal terms became a reality. There were still the die-hards, appearing as the courtiers of the French King in the Revolution had done, to have learned nothing and forgotten nothing.

> You find no women in the stokehold of a ship. ... You find no women down the coal mines today, and I thank God for it; you find no women in blast furnaces. Woman cannot physically perform these duties. Therefore it is a very dangerous thing for women to demand the vote on equal terms with men without realising what that might involve. Whatever happens, it must involve going into the rough and tumble of life. It must mean taking on grave responsibilities which would perhaps be too great a burden for women.
>
> (Colonel Applin, 1928)

Still the chauvinistic facetiousness was there as well.

> Suppose a woman sat on that bench as Chancellor of the Exchequer. Imagine her introducing her Budget and in the middle of her speech a message comes in, 'Your child is dangerously ill, come at once!' I should like to know how much of that Budget the House would get and what the figures would be like. It is obvious that with a thousand cases like that the whole system must break down and the women know it.
>
> (Colonel Applin, 1928)

Even now there were still some who doubted that most of the electorate were equipped for the job.

> We are not dealing with parochial questions. We have to deal with great questions of Empire and with international questions. If we were dealing with the question of a new handle for the parish pump, I quite agree that we should get very good advice and assistance from a larger electorate. But does the House realise that ... we are going by this measure to give to people who know absolutely nothing beyond the village pump ... the enormous power of regulating the foreign and colonial policy of this country?
>
> (Mr Samuel, 1928)

In the House of Lords, on the last leg of the historic campaign which first saw light almost 150 years earlier, echoes from the past continued to resound.

> I am against large extensions of the franchise on the ground that the aim and object of every Government is to represent the wisdom of the community. I know that the ladies are far cleverer than the men in certain relations of life; but the Government does not require cleverness; it requires wisdom and judgment and we do not so much expect wisdom and judgment from the ladies as enthusiasm in the pursuit of what they consider right.
>
> (Lord Clifford of Chudleigh, 1928)

> [Women] have warm hearts and quick emotions and they are anxious to do good without considering too long whether they are on the right track or not.
>
> (Viscount Sumner, 1928)

The Lord Chancellor said last night that a woman who had married, who had domestic work to do and perhaps a child or

two to look after could hardly be considered unfit to give a vote
for a Member of Parliament. I should have been inclined to
turn the question round and ask whether a young woman who
has just got married and is engaged entirely on domestic work
and cares will have much time in which to study the problems
upon which she has to vote for a Member of Parliament.

(Earl of Middleton, 1928)

To the very end, the spark of sarcasm was present. One of
the very last observations came from Lord Newton.

I would like your Lordships to realise that whereas men ... have
been endeavouring for over six hundred years to obtain the full
franchise, women have got it in less than ten years, and yet we
ironically speak of them as the weaker sex[!]

He did have a serious point to round off with.

What we are suffering from is not that the franchise is too small
but that it is too big. The more you increase the franchise, the
less value people will attach to the vote and the less value it
will have.

... When constituencies were of normal size, a man's
personality really counted for something. A man got in on his
merits. He got to be known and respected. But now how can
personality tell? ... Everybody admits that this great increase of
vast masses of ignorant voters will become the easy prey of the
political 'boss' and the political machine.

Perhaps, in the end, he was right. But as in all of life, other
checks and balances arrived. The untrammelled power of
the political machine turned out to be a short-lived one, if
it ever existed at all, for already the rise of the mass media
was apparent – radio was finding its feet and television
would not be far behind to begin to challenge the power of

the politician and give that vital ingredient – information – to those 'vast masses of ignorant voters'.

FOUR: MONEY

'This Fatal Measure'
Income Tax

Of all the innovations heralded here in this volume, one stands out as the subject of such dislike that antipathy towards it has continued unabated from the first day of its introduction right to the very present: the detested Income Tax. The irony is that compared with all the other new ideas we cover here which commentators said would never last (but which did) this was originally intended *not* to last but, save for two breaks, has also been with us ever since. Introduced by William Pitt as an emergency measure to meet the expense of the Napoleonic Wars, it proved too lucrative a device with politicians to give up. Like a sweet jar on the shelf, once opened it proved impossible not to keep going back to for more.

The introduction of the Income Tax was a formidable and passionately contested departure from the traditional method of raising money for government expenditure (which, in the period before the Victorian age of social reform, was almost entirely devoted to defence and military adventures abroad). Pitt has been described as one of the most ingenious tax gatherers ever to govern Britain. In his day, the orthodox approach to money-raising for public means was to levy taxes on goods. Some remain familiar to us today – beer, spirits, tobacco. But eighteenth century taxation spread itself over an extraordinarily wide area of national life – to the staples of daily living: tea, sugar, salt and grain to almost every item of purchase imaginable – horses, timber, cotton, bricks, paper, glass, candles, hats (and even ribbons), right down to the notorious chimney and window taxes. The burdens of the Napoleonic Wars were unprecedented and stretched this structure of public finance to breaking point. Its limitations were obvious and threefold. As a system based on actual goods, there was a physical limit to how much tea, sugar or salt etc the population could consume. This led to the second problem that the only way to increase income from any item was to increase the proportion of tax levied on the goods; there always existed a break point for each good at which the rate of tax imposed simply induced a lowering of consumption or even complete abstention. There was one alternative, and the third problem – put taxes on more and more different goods. The whole widening system of taxes on hundreds of different items made it a very complex, costly and inefficient way of raising money. The urgencies of war forced a change and the country took a new direction from which it only turned back for two brief moments – the road to our modern conception of public finance. The change can be dated precisely. On 3 December 1798, Pitt, Prime Minister and Chancellor of the Exchequer, introduced his Budget, which proposed for the first time the imposition of a tax on personal income – the potentially limitless crock of gold which was to become the basis for the ballooning growth of government expenditure in the Victorian age.

The objections were immediate, fervent and prophetic. Described by one critic as 'this fatal measure', it would, according to another:

> ... strike with peculiar force at industry and the fruits of industry while indolence is left untouched and encouraged. [It will] relax those springs which give life and activity to every branch of trade, commerce and agriculture.
>
> (Mr Hobhouse, 1798)

It will be a strange circumstance in finance to impose burdens upon those by whose ingenuity new arts are discovered or the old ones improved, who contribute so essentially to enrich the

nation and who are justly accounted the surest source of its
commercial prosperity. ... The man that is idle and profligate
will pay nothing; whereas the sober and industrious will be
burdened in proportion to their exertions.

... There is no circumstance so likely to be apprehended
from this measure as the emigration of the industrious classes
of the community. If in addition to all the usual taxes to which
the people of the country are subjected and which are in
general reckoned tolerably oppressive, persons are also made
liable to a compulsive disclosure of property, which has ever
been accounted so odious and vexatious a measure, and also to
have that property severely taxed, it must induce great multitudes of individuals to desert a country where they are subjected to such grievous oppression and to find out some quiet
asylum where they may escape such rapacity. If such a circumstance were to take place and it is evidently not impossible nor,
in my opinion, improbable, it would be the source of infinite
mischief to the country. ... The passing of such a law ... may
banish for ever from this country some of the most valuable
subjects it can at present boast of.

(Sir John Sinclair, 1798)

The merits of the existing system – which continued
unabated too – as far as taxpayers were concerned were
precisely the limitations which the tax gatherer suffered
under: the scope for rapacious and irresponsible expenditure was restricted. Income tax shattered this physical
restraint.

[Currently] the profusion of government is fortunately checked
by the conviction that if taxes are carried beyond a certain
length, the produce instead of increasing will diminish. But if
this Bill passes, the whole property of the country will in future
lie at the mercy of the minister; and though he now proposes to
exact but a tenth part, what is to hinder him next year from

demanding a fifth, or even a third of our respective incomes? Allow me to ask, how long it can be expected that either the wealth or the industry of the people can hold out under even the apprehension and terror of such exactions?

... [It is] a project which can only have ... originated in the harshest tyrannical principles and must either terminate in the disgrace and ruin of the bold projector or the destruction of the nation. ... It will be an event [which] posterity will have just cause to lament as one of the greatest calamities that could possibly have befallen the country.

(Sir John Sinclair, 1798)

The poor would suffer disproportionately. While the rich would simply tighten their belts, the poor would lose their shirts.

If this Bill is supposed chiefly to affect the rich, it is a mistake. It does not hurt the rich man, it only makes him curtail his expenses. And who suffers? The industrious poor who are employed by him.

(Mr Taylor, 1798)

From the outset, the intrusion into the private affairs of a man was the aspect which rankled most bitterly with opponents. Such an imposition was more than unwelcome; it was ungentlemanly.

[At present] an excise man comes to a man's dwelling to see whether he has taken into or sent out of his house some particular articles without previously paying a given sum to the Revenue; but here, [with Income Tax] a spy comes not only into the house but opens the bureau of every man and becomes acquainted with his most secret concerns. A man must show to this spy his bills, his notes, his bonds and all his securities. This is monstrous.

(Mr Taylor, 1798)

[It] would tend to crush the independent spirit of the people and is a measure partaking of the spirit of absolute government. There is a great objection also to this Bill upon the ground that government must necessarily become acquainted with the circumstances of every individual in the kingdom ... This is a thing that is quite improper for any government to know for it will be an encouragement to the minister to go on with a scale of ruinous expense and there is nothing to oppose the desire of the minister whenever he wants to lay hold of any of this [wealth].

(Sir William Pulteney, 1798)

It could also, according to another ingenious argument, erode the morals of the family.

Has it never occurred to the House that it has a bad effect on a man's children to know early in life that they would become possessed of large fortunes on the death of their parents?

(Sir William Pulteney, 1798)

It might happen that a father should be very unwilling to have the state of his affairs made known to his son lest the knowledge of the wealth he was to inherit might damp the efforts of the youth in the pursuits he might wish him to engage and make him neglect to exercise his talents.

... Son is set against father, and father against son. ... It even goes so far as to bring forward ... the wife against the husband. Thus it appears that every social tie is disregarded.

(Lord Holland, 1799)

Our modern conception of personal confidentiality was not reckoned with at the outset. That a tax collector would not seek to augment his (likely to be) miserly government salary by exploiting his privileged knowledge about people's business affairs went unquestioned. It was a foregone conclusion that he would be tempted to do so. Following from this assumption, there was presaged a crippling distortion of the nation's commercial affairs.

> As to commercial men, the disquiet they must experience at having their concerns laid open to the world [means that] it is probable that a large proportion of the commercial interest must now be liable to heavy losses [since] it follows that a trader must either pay five per cent on a supposed profit or go to the commissioners and confess [that his business is losing money]. Rather than do [the latter] numbers will pay the tax so that it will be a tax not on income but on loss.
>
> (Mr Smith, 1816)

However far-fetched it sounds today, this was a real fear at the time – that in preference to having their trading position exposed to the world, businesses would stump up the tax even if they were in fact trading at a loss, for fear that revelation of the loss would further compromise their affairs. A growing sense of paranoia enveloped the argument. It was not surprising then that when, just four years after the tax's introduction, an interlude of peace arrived in the War, and with Pitt out of office, it was dropped. The rationale for its termination was logical. Income Tax was still regarded as an emergency measure, as the new Prime Minister and Chancellor, Henry Addington told the House on the tax's abolition in 1802.

> This burden should not be left to rest on the shoulders of the public in time of peace because it should be reserved for the important occasions which, I trust, will not soon recur.

One happy member was confident that the nation had seen the last of it for good.

The nation has so unequivocally expressed their indignation at the degrading and oppressive nature of the tax that I am sure no minister will ever dare to reinflict it on the country.

(Mr Jones, 1802)

Hope springs. ... With the resumption of hostilities, it in fact returned at the very next Budget, in 1803, to the disgust of some.

Can any man who feels the pride of independence endure such a measure?

(Mr Smith, 1803)

Hated though it might be, the exigencies of war prevented any serious prospect of another abolition, but with Napoleon's eventual defeat at Waterloo many looked to the new peace-time government to give up once more this emergency tax. In fact, it showed absolutely no inclination to, having come through the years to appreciate the simplicity, and potential scope, of the tax for the future. So, in one of the greatest displays in Parliamentary history of the House exercising an independent view over the Government of the day, the Commons promptly voted down the motion introduced in 1816 to continue the tax.

The tax will never by any detail, by any modification be rendered palatable to individuals or beneficial to the public.

(Mr Smith, 1816)

The central underlying theme – and one borne out all too evidently in the years which followed – was that it was too dangerous to leave in the hands of government, with all its predelictions for expansion and greed, this open, and effectively bottomless, honey-pot.

No-one who has the least experience of the conduct of government can fail to see that instead of producing a redemption of the [national] debt it will produce wasteful establishments and extravagant expenditure. It will only be by ridding the country of the tax that ministers can be induced to practise any economy.

(Mr Baring, 1816)

So, by 238 to 201, they abolished Income Tax themselves. The revolt was remarkably successful, and no government attempted to re-impose the tax for twenty-five years. Perhaps inevitably, it could not last. The antiquated indirect tax system, which by the 1840s raised public revenues by levies on no fewer than 1046 separate commodities, was simply creaking and grinding to a halt. Newly-installed Prime Minister and reformer par excellence, Sir Robert Peel, grasped the nettle. His Budget of 1842 started the process of blowing the cobwebs away. He reduced tariffs on three-quarters of the goods. But he had to make up the difference, and he chose the bold move of reintroducing Income Tax. Although it was at the (by modern standards) exceptionally modest basic rate of seven old pence in the pound (or 2.9 per cent) – compared with as high as ten per cent under Pitt – the outcry was unrelenting to a measure which was:

so obnoxious, so disgusting and so repugnant to the feelings of the country.

(Mr Duncombe, 1842)

The peace time conditions made the tax's abominable nature impossible to bear.

Such is the odious nature of this tax that it is one to which no free people ought to submit but under [exceptional] circumstances to which the present circumstances of this country have not even the remotest analogy.

(Sir W. Clay, 1842)

So harassing, so mischievous, so revolting to the feelings [is the tax] that it can only safely be resorted to in one of those last emergencies in which a nation is apt to think and feel as one man.

(Mr Christie, 1842)

Machinery [of the tax] is extremely cumbrous and extremely inconvenient; [it] contains a variety of powers which no man can wish to see lodged in the hands of any government except in a case of absolute necessity.

(Marquess of Lansdowne, 1842)

A clever angle on the argument was proposed by one opponent who suggested that foreign powers would draw completely the wrong conclusions.

It has always been considered everywhere as a tax to be resorted to only as a last resource. What must [we] think of the condition of England if it is to suffer after many years of peace the imposition of a tax which has always been essentially a war-tax – a tax which the people will not tolerate after the very first year of peace. The imposition of such a tax will produce a conviction [abroad] that we have no other resources, that we have been obliged to resort to a tax as if the nation is making a struggle for existence and that we will be found unprepared for war.

(Lord John Russell, 1842)

While the government pondered the prospect of an imminent invasion from across the Channel as soon as the tax was reimposed, opponents kept up the barrage of arguments against the principle of the case. An important strand was that unlike the indirect taxes on goods, Income Tax was unavoidable.

> If you impose a window tax, a house tax or a tax upon commodities, it may be met in cases where the pressure is greatest by retrenchment, by sacrifices which it is possible to make; but from the Income Tax, there is no escape.
>
> (Viscount Howick, 1842)

> Indirect taxation is to a very great extent in the hands of the individual who is taxed. It depends upon the amount of consumption and he who chooses to abstain from the consumption of taxed articles might to the extent of his abstaining escape, however opulent, from the public burden. Direct taxation however has this evil – it put in the hands of the executive government a most despotic power and created an instrument that can be but imperfectly controlled by public opinion when the tax is once set on foot. It invests the functionaries who collect it with an overbearing authority and influence.
>
> (Dr Bowring, 1842)

The ripple effect on the poor would be highly injurious.

> How many of our artisans are employed in producing not the necessaries, not the comforts but the luxuries of the rich. Will not the demand for those luxuries be diminished by this tax? And will not the employment of such artisans be taken away from them?
>
> (Mr Wood, 1842)

The argument that the shift from taxes on goods – which all paid – to one on incomes – which would fall predominantly on the better off – was not the simple panacea it at first seemed.

A great deal has been said about the merit of the tax in enabling us to avoid taxes on consumption and thereby not pressing on the working classes. But this is a tax, if not directly on the working classes, [then on those] who employed them. ... I believe it will lead to a still greater number of the working classes being thrown out of employment.

(Mr Buller, 1842)

This opponent was confident that, put simply, the British people would not stand for it.

I have seen such indications of public feeling against it that I am sure that when it comes into operation and the people feel its pressure you will have a constant agitation going on against it – an agitation which will be continued until it is successful in its effort to procure the abandonment of this impost.

Others agreed.

Its vexatious and oppressive character will not have been long practically felt by the country before the disposition to get rid of it [will] become universal and if [the Chancellor] endeavours to maintain it, he will, like the Minister in 1816, see even his truest friends go out into the lobby against him on a proposition to abolish it.

(Viscount Howick, 1842)

Nothing can be more injurious or unwise than placing the national credit on an impost so odious as this. Let the system but once come into operation – let the secret inquisition be sitting and bankers and others called on to disclose their private affairs and I am firmly of the opinion that so loud an expression of the public dissatisfaction will reach this House that it will become a question whether any government, however strong, can resist it.

(Mr Hawes, 1842)

Although an Income Tax might now be passed by persons ignorant of the effect it produced when it existed before ... my firm conviction is that it will be impossible to maintain it.

(Mr Wood, 1842)

The tax would encourage the darker side of human nature to come to the fore. How could such an effect be for the good of the country?

Is it mere imagination to suggest that this tax is unjust, inquisitorial and immoral? Does it not while in operation teem with evil? Is it not fertile with falsehood and fraud? [Tax inspectors will] put the conscience of every honest man to the question while to every prevaricator, every shuffler, every equivocator, every perjurer, an impunity proportional to his utter destitution of all principle is scandalously secured. ... The evils of the Income Tax are so monstrous that it is almost impossible to heighten them – they set hyperbole at defiance.

(Mr Sheil, 1842)

The tax is one which, of necessity, more than any other gives all sorts of encouragement to fraud, enabling men to deceive, giving some the opportunity of returning themselves as more prosperous than they really are and inducing others to return themselves at less than they actually are worth.

(Mr Buller, 1842)

This system of the Income Tax is a positive penalty on honesty and it is a positive premium on dishonesty.

(Mr Lewis, 1874)

A frequent argument was that the inquisitorial nature of investigation demanded by the tax was out of keeping with the British way of doing things. Never would so much antagonism be created for so little reward.

[It was] a scheme of taxation which was alien to the habits of the people of this country [and] which must be carried into execution in an inquisitorial manner and therefore which must be attended with vexatious proceedings infinitely more annoying than the amount taken from our pockets.

(Mr Labouchere, 1842)

One opponent, rather wishful one thinks, tried to get the government to see that it was in fact making a rod for its own back.

It appears to me unwise in a country which takes so large a portion of a man's income for the public service to let each individual see too clearly the exact amount he pays. [Although people might pay the same through indirect taxes] they blamed their butcher or their baker for it and do not complain of the government for the amount thus taken from them. ... I feel it wise to raise as large a revenue as possible from indirect taxation.

(Mr Buller, 1842)

But through all the diversions and the byways of the campaign, the one pervasive fear remained the unrestricted scope now presented to Government for indiscriminate fundraising. There opened up a vista of ceaseless claims for more and more – for evermore.

Once this tax is imposed, this power created, I greatly fear that hereafter the proposal of making a penny or twopence in the pound addition to the direct taxation will be found so simple and unembarrassing that [income tax] might become a permanent measure. Nothing, when the machinery of collection is created, could be more attractive to a Finance Minister than to strain the cord a little tighter and so to add to the Treasury receipts.

(Dr Bowring, 1842)

Don't we all know it now!

> We have in the instance of this tax a machinery established of
> the most prodigious force – ay, and which does not disdain
> even the meanest fractions; a machinery which has been justly
> compared ... to the force of the elephant whose trunk can raze
> oaks and can pick up the minutest article, a needle or a pin. We
> have a machinery established which enables the Government
> without the slightest difficulty, without any delay, without any
> new measure, without any adaptation of new means to a new
> end, but by the simple turning of a screw to raise £100,000 or
> £200,000 or ... to raise hundreds of thousands and millions
> with the same facility. This is a tax with which I would trust no
> Government ... To no Government would I give if I could
> possibly avoid it the management of such a dreadful machinery
> as this.
>
> (Lord Brougham, 1853)

Although for thirty years after Peel's re-introduction Income Tax was renewed for varying periods of three, five or even seven years, maintaining the fiction that it was still of a temporary nature, there was never any real prospect of Government relinquishing such an uncomplicated way of acquiring funds. Once the great social reforms beginning in the 1870s ushered in huge public financial commitments, the ritual complaints switched from the principle of the tax to the battles over the rates at which it was charged, arguments with which we remain to this day all too familiar. The last time the House toyed with abolition was in July 1874, but unlike 1816 this backbench effort failed. In the General Election of that year, though, both main parties – Conservatives and Liberals – had abolition of Income Tax as a manifesto pledge. Once in power, however, the realities of life proved irresistible. The Conservative victor, Disraeli, found he could only reduce it – from threepence to twopence in the pound, a mere 0.8 per cent and the lowest it ever reached. Since then, it has been a predictable, inexorable and shameless rise. The siren voices from those battles lost long ago continue to ring all too true to the modern taxpayer, like this prescient observation from the final campaign.

> A point which shows the impolicy of retaining the tax in this time of peace is that it is a direct encouragement to the Government to waste the public money ... for if any Government find themselves in a strait they can always fall back upon it as a resource and get out of the difficulty by putting on an extra penny.
>
> (Mr Lewis, 1874)

Quite. And we've been paying the price ever since.

'Immoral In ... Tendency, Impolitic In ... Principle'

Lotteries

There had always been other ways to raise money for public uses, although they were by no means any more popular. With proposals current in our own day for the resurrection of one long-unused method, it is perhaps appropriate to look again at one of the previous means favoured by Government – the lottery. Before Income Tax offered the instant solution to sudden needs, administrations resorted, for example to meet emergencies in the Napoleonic Wars, to lotteries as a sure-fire way of raising cash quickly from the people's pockets. People liked them, there was no doubt about that. Their unpopularity lay with that most troublesome of thorns, the self-appointed moral inspectors of public life keen to expose any potential activity which might blight the purity of the body politic. They were less evident in the war years – after all, even they accepted that desperate times called for desperate remedies – but come peace time they renewed their opposition to any attempt by governments to use the method for money-raising for the ordinary civil purposes of life. Critics had made their views quite clear even before any proposal was put to Parliament. They gave fair warning to the Government not even to think about trying.

I strongly object to this scheme of finance as inconsistent with the principles of public morality.

(Mr Whitbread, 1815)

I feel the fullest conviction that no pecuniary consideration

should reconcile Parliament to the existence of a measure so
peculiarly calculated, as the system of lottery in all its branches
is, to debauch the morals and corrupt the character of the
country – to spread mischief and misery through every town,
village and hamlet. I know the baneful effects of this abominable system and I hope that the benevolence and wisdom of
Parliament will soon put an end to its existence.

(Mr Bennet, 1816)

No consideration of financial advantage should induce the
sanction of a measure so pregnant with mischief to the morals
of the people. ... By the establishment of state lotteries, the
Government of this country has encouraged and provoked a
spirit of gambling which, degrading the character of the people
and weakening their habits of industry, must abate the moral
strength of the state and ultimately diminish its financial
resources.

(Mr Lyttelton, 1816)

Slave-trade reformer William Wilberforce was a leading
light in the opposition to lotteries.

There can be no excuse for a lottery because it is in itself a
vicious transaction. It tends to the destruction of domestic
happiness, by tempting the subject to deviate from those
habits of sober industry which, persevered in, could not fail of
bringing their possessor comfort.

(1816)

Regardless of such a clear measure of antipathy, the Government tried in 1818 to raise £250,000 through instituting a
lottery. The actual amount represented a minute proportion
of public funds needed – something like half of one per cent –
which it was hoped would make opponents mollify their
reaction. In fact, it had the very opposite effect.

It is immoral in its tendency and impolitic in its principle. ... It is a most shabby and dishonourable plan for cheating the people out of their money ... a system so base and disgraceful. ... If the [Government] is disposed to sacrifice public morals for the paltry gain of £250,000 I am not inclined to agree with ... such dishonourable and fraudulent practices.

(Mr Lyttelton, 1818)

One Member took a recent pronouncement of the Government's commitment to financial probity and turned it back on the administration.

If His Majesty's ministers said that we should be slow in tampering with the revenue of the country ... Ministers should not themselves tamper with the morals of the people.

(Mr Morland, 1818)

The thin end of the wedge argument was, as usual, never far away.

If the principle of raising money by lottery is once established, we might upon the same justification proceed to raise a revenue from licensing brothels and gaming houses. The system of lotteries goes to ... subvert the morals [and] impair the industry ... of the state.

(Mr Lyttelton, 1818)

The ripple effect would be widespread.

To raise money by lottery is not only to do that by public authority which it is held reprehensible to do in private life, but it is to act unhandsomely, unfairly and ungenerously to that public whom the laws ought to defend and protect. It is one of the grossest violations of its moral duty which a government could commit. In lotteries, all that is base in the practice

of private gambling is recognised and adopted by the state.
                                        (Mr Lyttelton, 1819)

It was a particularly pernicious feature of lotteries that whether
one won or lost the effects was always to encourage more, not
less, gambling. Winning only set a bad example to neighbours
and encouraged them to feel they could emulate the successful winner (and of course encouraged the winner also to ride
his luck again); losing, while obviously costing money at each
failure, also in its own way encouraged further gambling, on
the grounds that the more one lost the more one intuitively
felt one had used up one's stock of bad luck and that fortune
was getting closer and closer. The same psychology has worked
magnificently to the advantage of slot gambling machines
ever since their invention. Mr Lyttelton had seen the:

> sad effects in a village or small town of the fatal good fortune
> of some speculator whose example, encouraging other adven-
> turers, ... spread disappointment and ruin, ... [where] a spirit of
> gambling raged there with redoubled ardour and the industri-
> ous habits of the people completely destroyed.
>
>   (1819)

Nothing could reconcile him to the concept.

> Lotteries absorb the earnings of the poor; and what is worse
> they absorb their principles of honest industry, for it is well
> known that when a man once engages in gambling specula-
> tions he becomes averse to the performance of his ordinary
> duties and indifferent to the petty earnings of his original
> avocation. The whole of the lottery system is one of fraud,
> seduction and specious robbery, intended to intoxicate the
> minds of the poor and ignorant to inflame their passions and to
> excite their cupidity.
>
>   (1819)

Surely the British nation was above such stooping.

> With regard to the observation that lotteries are resorted to in other countries it might be said that so are expedients at which it is impossible for Englishmen not to be shocked.
>
> (Mr Wodehouse, 1819)

Indeed, it was pointed out, lotteries were inconsistent with other aims of government policy.

> I think it inconsistent that the Government should encourage savings banks with one hand and gambling habits with the other.
>
> (Sir M. Ridley, 1818)

The Government had taken great efforts immediately after the Napoleonic Wars to cultivate public confidence in savings banks and a whole welter of new regulations had just been passed to promote further the idea in the nation's consciousness that spare money should be saved. Now, perversely, the same Government could be seen encouraging its frittering away.

> [Lotteries] create a spirit of gambling which would not otherwise be found in operation ... The encouragement of saving banks with one hand while on the other the lottery-office keepers are permitted by every scheme and mode of deceit to induce the people to throw away their little savings in the lottery is a solecism in legislation. It is urging the honest man to spend his little savings in mischievous and ruinous adventure.
>
> (Mr W. Smith, 1818)

We give the last word to Wilberforce who argued, with some cogency, that lotteries, having once been illegal (presumably for good reason), could hardly be declared decriminalized without some risk that the same principle would soon be running riot through society.

> If the practice of raising money by lottery was once allowed to be criminal, it cannot be defended upon any ground that would not justify other crimes. [Lotteries] tend to destroy every good principle, every industrious habit, more perhaps than any other circumstance whatever.

(1818)

'A RECORD LOW FOR ANY STATESMAN IN THIS COUNTRY'
PREMIUM BONDS

The attempt to raise money by the lottery failed, and the mechanism was to be dropped for public finance for nearly two centuries, until the 1990s, in an exercise yet to reach fulfilment. Critics, though, thought they espied a partial relapse during the First World War when an idea surfaced which today may be viewed as a harmless part of society's financial furniture, but at the time resurrected all the old fears – the humble Premium Bond. The idea of a public Government-sponsored bond, bearing no interest but with prizes on offer to holders as an inducement to save, emerged early in 1917 as one solution to the growing crisis over financing the war. The Government of the day professed an open mind and set up a Select Committee to investigate. It came out a year later against the scheme on the grounds that the amount likely to be raised would be disproportionately small compared with the contentious nature of the change. Almost two years later, in December 1919, the House had another chance to express its opinion – on a free vote, the Premium Bond was rejected by the considerable majority of 276-84. A strong vein of opinion, redolent of the lottery campaign of a century before, assailed the idea without mercy. It helped that the Chancellor himself was opposed to it.

> In my opinion the result of your issue of Premium Bonds will be not that you will make a man save who has not saved before but that it will induce a man to gamble who has hitherto saved. ... There is a great deal too much of the spirit of gambling in the

country today, too much of the disposition to get rich quickly.
It is not that spirit that will help us in our difficulties or carry
us to safety. What we require is sober, steady, honest work and
the more you turn the people's attention to chance the more
you take them away from strenuous effort and from continuous
hard work.

(Mr Austen Chamberlain, 1919)

The price was not worth paying.

I believe they are corrupting in their effect. ... Above all, at a
time when the one lesson you have to teach everybody is that
there is no salvation except in work you teach them to look to
chance. If you do that, no amount of money you may get,
whether it be much more than I anticipate or not, will com-
pensate the country for the damage which will be done.

(Mr Austen Chamberlain, 1919)

For another opponent, the Premium Bond fell fatally between two stools. It could not succeed because it was
neither one thing nor the other: it was too poor a bet for the
gambler; too scant a reward for the investor.

This is a proposal that the Government should borrow money
by a combined appeal to the investing instinct and the gambling instinct. I am sure it will never succeed. Insofar as people
are investors they are not gamblers; insofar as they are gamblers they are not investors. It is true that there are certain
speculative investments but to the speculative investor those
investments will be incomparably more attractive than Premium Bonds. You will never stand the smallest chance in
competing against the regular speculative investment. ... The
sort of man who gives money to the Government is the sort of
man who values security. He will not look at an investment of
this kind. It offers him much less than he could get from an

equally secure Government proposal. On the other hand you shrink yourself from running it as a great gambling appeal. You are not going to paint the streets with incitements to the gaming instinct. Insofar as your appeal is an appeal to gaming it will be a moral disaster; insofar as it is an appeal to investment it will be a financial failure.

(Lord Hugh Cecil, 1919)

Without offering interest on the bond – the interest foregone was one's entry fee for the draw – it could appeal only to the baser instincts in society. Personal futures were now to be secured on distinctly fragile grounds.

Everyone who invests in Premium Bonds will hope to get rich by chance. It will fail the great majority of them. But it is the nature of this instinct that once stimulated it is not satisfied by failure but tries again and again. If not Premium Bonds it will be something else and step by step you will stimulate the gambling instinct. ... You cannot encourage thrift by encouraging gambling.

(Lord Hugh Cecil, 1919)

The whole concept had the seeds of fatal consequences for the social spirit.

There is no better type of citizen than the man who is struggling to buy his own house and a very grave responsibility would rest upon those who will divert money from that object. ... I can conceive of nothing which would be so demoralising [as the Premium Bond]. I can conceive of nothing which would more certainly shake the foundations of this country and, I believe, so far as raising money is concerned, it will be an absolute failure.

(Mr Thomas, 1919)

The leader of the Labour Party also opposed the idea. His analysis of the popular psyche was incisive and full of foreboding.

> All those who have mixed with the masses in the workshops, in the factories, in the warehouses, have been compelled to recognise the fact that gamblers do not come in the first instance to the coarser methods of gambling and then transfer to what may be called the finer methods. All experience goes to prove that it is exactly the other way. They begin with what may be described as the finer methods and then the spirit within them develops until they do not care very much how coarse the method is. ... I am opposed to [Premium Bonds] because I am convinced that [they] will interfere with that standard of productiveness which is so essential in the national interest. ... The effect of ... gambling produces a spirit of restlessness and excitement that is altogether antagonistic to that consistent steady toil out of which alone an increased standard of productiveness can be secured.
>
> (Mr Henderson, 1919)

After a mauling like that Governments consistently refused to consider the scheme again – for almost forty years. Then, out of the blue, in the Budget of Chancellor Macmillan in 1956, it popped up again, not as an idea floated for discussion but as a solid brick in the financial and budgetary wall. It took everyone by surprise. The country, it seemed the Government thought, after years of austerity now deserved a little fillip to its life, a small gleam of allure to brighten up the post-war years. Opponents were far from enamoured. Harold Wilson, then Shadow Chancellor, responding immediately after the Budget statement, called it:

> a squalid raffle.

At least one thought he saw through the flannel about the

scheme being no different as a saving method than any other Government bond. He was quite clear where he felt the country was heading.

> I have too high an appreciation of the quality and dignity of this great country of ours to think that it cannot get out of its difficulties without running a lottery. The Government are reducing the country to the level of a South American republic.
>
> (Mr Hobson, 1956)

Difficult though it may seem to us today, the level of agitation over what is now regarded as an innocuous, almost trifling, aspect of life was unrestrained.

> I regard the Premium Bond as a record low for any statesman in this country. It is an appeal to the least desirable instinct in the community, the instinct of getting something for nothing.
>
> (Mr Simmons, 1956)

Quoting a previous Chancellor (Cripps, in 1949) exhorting the nation to 'renounce and denounce the easy-going, get-rich-quick attitude to life that in all levels of society has found its post-war devotee', he continued:

> We shall destroy that spirit by introducing Premium Bonds and we shall not touch greatness as a nation again....
>
> (Mr Simmons, 1956)

Heady fears indeed, but he was not alone. Even the Archbishop of Canterbury felt moved to pronounce. In the House of Lords he intoned words of even greater gravity.

> [The Government] has chosen not a dazzling but a rather second-rate expedient which may attract savings but which adds nothing to the spiritual capital of the nation and which

insinuates on a large scale this ... undignified and unedifying
adulteration of public duty by motives of private gain.

... Private gain divorced from responsibility, whether in
management of workers or anywhere else is anti-social. The
Government's great concern must be that money gained shall
be truly earned and that money earned shall be used reasonably, thoughtfully and for the general good. The Chancellor's
action ... contradicts that social principle.

On lighter levels, sarcasm was equally successful in hitting
home. One Member quoted the observation of a Scottish
professor which had been widely reported.

'[It is] regrettable that when people could not be induced to
invest in the future of their country they should be asked to
have a flutter on it.'

(Dr Mabon, 1956)

Another even feared for the nation's international stature.

When I heard [the Chancellor] announce his Premium Bond
scheme I was rather shocked, though not on religious grounds.
It seemed to me to be rather cheap. It seemed a wee bit 'off
white' for the Mother of Parliaments. ... It seemed to me that
the Mother of Parliaments had come down in the world when
she had to depend for the stability of Sterling upon a Premium
Bond scheme. ... We are proud that men and women who come
from newer Parliaments in other parts of the world tend to look
to us for guidance and stability. It seemed to me, therefore, that
the suggestion was lowering the prestige of this House.

(Mr Osborne, 1956)

He concluded that in the modern world the scheme probably wouldn't work anyway. He foresaw problems in at-
tracting savings. In the old days, one put something away

for rainy days:

> But in the modern State, under a welfare system, where we may
> say that there will be no more rainy days it will be very difficult
> to get people to save. That is one of the problems which faces
> us in these modern times and it will not be easily overcome.
>
> (Mr Osborne, 1956)

The storm quickly subsided though, and the genial old Premium Bond, the satisfyingly homely named computer, ERNIE, and the weekly draws, became a corner stone of the British way of life, ironically becoming rather a steadying, reliable facet of the nation's tradition, far removed from the cataclysmic future once painted for it.

'Confusion In Every Market Town In England'

Decimalization

'We'll never get used to it' was a familiar refrain in all these reforms. To end, perhaps the most fundamental reform of all – decimalization. Surprisingly, for a reform not realized until the 1970s, it has a much longer history than might be expected. It had in fact been formally approved by the House of Commons as early as 1855, when the conclusions of a Select Committee into the idea were debated. The Committee had returned a positive verdict and the House voted in favour of the principle. Indeed, these pronouncements themselves came more than fifteen years after a commission of experts appointed by the Government had become the first official body to endorse decimalization, in 1838. Its findings in fact had prompted the introduction in the 1840s of the florin – the two shilling piece – as the precursor to the changeover. As one tenth of the then twenty shilling pound, the florin can in fact be considered as effectively Britain's first decimal coin.

Inevitably progress became stalled – there were always weightier matters commanding politicians' attention. Governments recoiled from such a fundamental change to the way of life if there was no pressing urgency for it. There was never any surge of great interest in turning the House's pronouncement into practice. Whenever the issue arose there were always good reasons why it should be yet again deferred. A steady band of traditionalists were also always on hand to paint the miserable picture of life in a decimal world. Essentially, the main strand of the opposition went: why go through all the upheaval of change for no good reason? The argument that if it wasn't broken, don't mend it was persuasive.

> To establish a system of decimal coinage would simply be to introduce confusion because it would interfere with that which is the standard of value in the minds of the people. ... We are all familiar with the score and the dozen; but there is no similar word in any language I know for a group of ten; and human nature does not work by decimals.
>
> (Mr Stevenson, 1881)

The arguments inevitably became entwined with those against the parallel effort to decimalize the country's weights and measures, metrication, and it was in this context that another Member had graphically endorsed Mr Stevenson's point.

> I will ... take the most familiar instance and show that although a great deal has been said about the advantages of the French subdivisions, yet after all our subdivisions are more natural for the ordinary purposes of life. If a boy has to divide an apple ... [he] cuts it into two parts if he wants to halve it and those halves into quarters if he wishes to make four parts. In the same way, if a housewife has to cut up a loaf for her family, she divides it into two, into four, into eight or into sixteen parts. ... Supposing the loaf to weigh originally a pound, each of these sixteen divisions comes out an ounce. Such is the rationale of our system of measuring. ... Founded on continual halving and proved by the common senses of mankind before the great era of enlightenment inaugurated in 1789 to be the most convenient and natural one.
>
> (Mr Beresford Hope, 1868)

He might have stood a better chance of convincing advocates of 'arbitrary' counting systems if he could have shown money to follow the same natural principles – but unfortunately it did not. For those too young today to remember, the twelve-pence shilling turned into the twenty-shilling pound (or the twenty-one shilling guinea). Even he could not rationally explain that. But, inexplicable as it might be, it had stood the test of time and experience, as another argued.

> I cannot regard the decimal system as a revelation from Heaven or believe that the present method could have grown up without possessing some convenience or advantage.
>
> (Mr Hubbard, 1863)

The same commentator agreed, two decades later, with Mr Stevenson's thesis.

> Commodities are naturally divided by the hand into halves, quarters and eighths; but division into tenths and hundredths is virtually impossible. ... There is no doubt that for the purposes of division our own system is infinitely more convenient and more practical.
>
> (Mr Hubbard, 1881)

Any mathematician would tell you likewise.

> Obviously 12 is a far more convenient number than 10. 12 can be divided by four figures, [6,4,3,2] while 10 can be divided only by two.
>
> (Mr Scourfield, 1871)

Surprisingly, however, metrication was to make greater progress at first than decimalization of the coinage. No fewer than four attempts were made in 1863 and 1864 to introduce compulsory metrication. Eventually proponents got an Act passed making metrication permissable – traders were now legally able to transact business in metric measures. It went onto the Statute Book in 1868. A Bill to make metric measures compulsory passed the House of Lords in 1904, but ran out of time in the Commons. The measure is still awaited to this day, whereas decimalization of the currency has been with us compulsorily for over twenty years. The defeat of the old pound, shillings and pence would have been a bitter blow to their nineteenth century defenders, as well as the prediction that the change would:

> create confusion in every market town in England.
> (Marquess of Salisbury, 1864)

The mechanics of the decimal were prone to error.

> Those who work in decimals know what stupendous mistakes are made by placing the decimal point in a wrong position and it is easy to place it in a wrong position in a long row of figures.
> (Mr Haworth, 1907)

In contrast, one of the more curious arguments held that there was good reason intellectually for having a complicated system like pounds, shillings and pence.

> Our present arithmetical system is defensible as an intellectual exercise which develops the minds of scholars and the decimal system would not be an advance from an educational point of view.
> (Mr Hubbard, 1868)

This early forerunner of the 'if it isn't hurting, it isn't working' philosophy was, in Mr Hubbard's view, an inestimable asset.

Admitting that the more complex rules now requisite for

children to learn occupy an additional portion of their school life, is the time so expended wasted? Is it not rather well bestowed in improving their intelligence?

(1863)

As late as 1907 the same notion was still being advanced.

A good deal has been said about the suffering a child has to undergo in learning unnecessary tables; but a child has to develop its memory and in this way its memory is developed.

(Sir G. Scott Robertson)

If all this has perhaps generated a nostalgia for the rigour of the good old days, the following should quickly dispel it. Although not a criticism of reform, rather a panegyric for change, it is one of the best and most overpowering accumulation of argument there could possibly be to demonstrate just how taxed our ancestors' young minds actually were.

For measures of length we have the ordinary inch, foot and yard. In cloth measure we have yards, nails and ells. There are four different sorts of ells. For nautical purposes we have fathoms, knots, leagues and geographical miles, differing from the common mile. The fathom of a man-of-war is six feet; of a merchant vessel five and a half feet; of a fishing smack five feet. We have also the Scotch and Irish mile and the Scotch and Irish acre. There are several sorts of acres in the United Kingdom and there are a great variety of roods. We have in almost every trade measures of length specially used in those trades. For the measurement of horses we have the hand; shoemakers use sizes; and we are compelled to adopt gauges where the French use the millimetre. The gauges are entirely arbitrary. The custom of the trade is the only thing which would decide the question in case of dispute. For measures of capacity we have twenty different bushels, we can scarcely tell what a hogshead means. For ale it is 54 gallons; for wine 63. Pipes of wine vary in many ways; each sort of wine seems to claim the privilege of a different sort of pipe. For measurement of weight we have about ten different stones; a stone of wool in Darlington is 18 pounds, a stone of flax at Downpatrick 24 pounds, a stone of flax at Belfast 16 ¾ pounds, but it is also at Belfast 24 ½ pounds, having in one place two values. The hundredweight may mean 100 pounds, 112 pounds or 120 pounds. If you buy an ounce or a pound of anything you must inquire if it belongs to Dutch, troy or avoirdupois weight.

(Sir Minto Farquhar, 1863)

Phew! Anyone still harbouring doubts about change?

FIVE:
WORLD OF
WORK

'Freedom Under An Interdict'
Working Hours

Getting rid of the evils of child labour was, as we have seen, a troublesome enough concept for many to accept. Far longer, then, would it be before some of our other basic tenets of working life came to pass. Reasonable hours of labour, unemployment benefit, old age pensions, holidays with pay, all fundamental principles of modern society, were each subjected to an ordeal of fiery opposition before acceptance.

We have already had a foretaste of the battle over hours with the debates on reducing the working time of children. The arguments were largely similar when it came to adults – not surprisingly, according to the critics, who accused philanthropic agitators of treating adults exactly like children.

Can any mortal who calmly reflects on the subject really screw up his mind to the belief that it is for the interest of the workmen and work-women to have their hours of labour reduced to ten when they are able, willing and anxious to work for a longer period? Can anyone believe that it is really not for their interest to be told that they are free ... that it is not for their interest to be told, 'Make such contracts as you please with your master, carry your labour to the best market, where you can get the greatest share of that abundance which Providence has prepared for you' ...? No [say the reformers] do not let him be free to carry his labour to the best market and get the most he can obtain by it from his employer – do not let him profit as much as he can and work as much as he is willing and disposed and anxious to work – put your legislative shackle on him ... do not treat them like free men and women, but like children ... or ... like slaves.

> ... You put his freedom under an interdict ... clothe him in
> the shackles of an Act of Parliament and prescribe to him what
> neither nature nor his own judgment nor strength has pre-
> scribed to him, the hours beyond which you will not allow him
> to work and labour.
>
> (Lord Brougham, 1844)

Government would get sucked in to endless regulation.
The classic 'thin end of the wedge' warning about taking
the smallest or most well-meaning action was played for
everything it was worth.

> [The Hours Bill] is liable to the argument ... [that] you have
> interfered once and you must now in consistency take this
> additional step. This is one of the many miseries of the system
> of interference, that you are liable to be taunted with incon-
> sistency if you will not push it to an extravagant length.
>
> (Lord Brougham, 1844)

Any such interference, a 'most dangerous and unprecedented
principle' according to our old friend Mr Labouchere, would
end up only bringing harm to workers in the eyes of many.

> Let no man think that the working classes will thank [the
> proponent] and bless him for a measure which, reducing their
> hours of labour, diminishes also their wages; far from it – such
> a man will speedily become the object of general obloquy
> amongst the working classes.
>
> (Mr Cobden, 1844)

Cobden was certainly no reactionary lackey. At the very time
he was making such observations he was also engaged in the
monumental campaign for the abolition of the Corn Laws,
the greatest economic reform of the period. As founder of the
Anti-Corn Law League, his reforming credentials are fairly

pure, and demonstrates then that, as seen at the time, the issue of workers' hours was far from a clear cut one. Another prominent radical also, on this topic, professed doubts.

> Why, I ask you, will you interfere in concerns in which the labourers can best judge for themselves and by a crude and restrictive legislation, attempt to make laws respecting matters with regard to which individuals and private interests can best form an opinion?
> (Mr Roebuck, 1844)

Sir Robert Peel, still another who had shown remarkable willingness to cut through tradition where he judged it to be in the wide public interest – his reforms of the legal and criminal law system in the 1820s were landmarks in British history and it was he who, as Prime Minister, sacrificed the unity of his own party for a generation to steer through the contentious Corn Laws reform – worried about the nation's outlook if the thin-end-of-the-hours-wedge was inserted into the Statute Book. Such interference would:

> end by entirely changing the character of the British people. You may make them entirely dependent upon Government interference; you must then, indeed, have an army of inspectors and sub-inspectors. And the only protection against your interference is this, that your Bill may become so odious that the whole mass of the population will rise up against it.
>   ... Suppose that [workers] are unable to do that which constitutes the independence of their moral character, viz, to earn their subsistence by honest industry; suppose you drive them to the workhouse; ... suppose you diminish the hours of employment and lessen the power of individuals to earn their subsistence by honest industry; supposing all that, have you then promoted the moral character or social comfort and welfare of the people? I haven't a doubt about your intentions ... but I want to show you that by your unnecessary interference, by

legislating to supply the parental place and to enforce morality by law, that by so doing you incur the hazard of defeating your own object, of diminishing the physical comforts and of lowering the moral character of the people.

(1844)

It was a critical moment in the development of society which, if a wrong turning was taken, would lead the country up a fatally debilitating path.

Doctrines of interference in the private affairs of people would:

lead to the establishment of inquisitions into almost every trade. ... We are not content ... merely with the production of wealth but [now] are to watch over the habits and morals of the people. ... I want to know by what mode [proponents] will set about carrying out these principles of provident and beneficient legislation. Looking at the moral character of the people – looking at their sense of wrong, at their hatred of oppression, at their philanthropy, at their charity, at their religious feeling which have grown up with independence and freedom of action, depend upon it, your attempt to substitute legislative interference for that independence and for that freedom of action will change materially the character of the people.

(Sir Robert Peel, 1844)

The essence of the issue was articulated clearly and directly by one opponent.

The working class has a distinct right to use their labour as they please and whatever number of hours they choose to work Parliament has no right to attempt a limitation.

(Mr Parker, 1844)

It would be simply impracticable to organize.

If you adopt the principle of interference generally, and say that in all cases the labour performed throughout the country shall be subject to the vigilance of the Government you must do this – you must turn one-third of the people of England into commissioners to watch the other two-thirds. Is this, Sir, I ask, a thing to be tolerated? Why, Sir, it is against the genius of the country – it is opposed to common sense – it is utterly impossible to carry into effect.

(Mr Labouchere, 1846)

The crucial complaint, as always in this kind of debate, was that it was very easy for the reformers to be progressive at someone else's expense.

The measure is merely a mockery of the sufferings of the working classes. Their cry for relief is met by something intended to be benevolent but which ... might be taken for the most bitter irony. They demand diminished suffering by toil. It is generally accorded to them. But at what cost? Why, diminished remuneration. Is it right to raise sanguine expectations of benefits to be obtained and then to create feelings of such disappointment?

(Mr Trelawny, 1846)

But as if this was not enough, the ramifications were much wider. Although legislators aimed only at factory workers:

All labour [will be] affected. The able-bodied labourer, driven out ... will seek other occupations and artificially beat down the prices of other classes of labourers and thus the injurious effects of this measure will be multiplied in every direction. ... Pronouncing that men should only work a certain number of hours, and therefore diminishing wages, you will necessarily extend the bounds of the destitute class whom you must relieve because you will have arbitrarily denied them the right to help themselves.

(Mr Trelawny, 1846)

At the heart of the matter was the question of who should be in control of a worker's destiny – the Government or the worker?

> Is it just so to legislate that a working man, disposed to labour in prosperous times when business is brisk all the hours that he is allowed to work or that his strength will permit for the express purpose of saving his over-earnings to meet the oscillations of trade which must come and which, when they do come, will suspend his labours, shall be prevented from thus pushing his industry to the utmost and labouring long hours if he pleases?
>
> (Sir J. Graham, 1847)

Sir Robert Peel again ventured into the fray to pose the acute question: how could one improve the working person's condition through a measure whose only purpose was to deprive him of a significant amount of work?

> If you could convince me that the present measure will tend to the moral and intellectual improvement, to the general, to the social welfare of the labouring classes, I should be tempted to make the experiment. ... Sir, I do not doubt the advantage of leisure; but I greatly doubt whether there be any better means of improving the condition of the labourer and of elevating the character of the working class than to give them an increased command over the necessaries of life. You say that by this Bill you will not diminish wages. But will it not be a most marvellous event in legislation if you provide by law that five days in the week shall be the maximum of labour in this country and yet can induce the master to pay the same amount of wages?
>
> (1847)

Another stalwart against regulation summed up the position faced by the working poor.

What effect will [restrictions] have upon the moral condition of these poor people? I believe there is not a more sound principle ... than this, that poverty is the root of many evils – that distress, that uncertainty of possessing the common necessaries of life – that fear of want continually haunting the mind – is just as injurious to the mental organization as it is to the physical health of a man. To deprive a man having £6,000 a year of £1,000 will be doing him little harm; it will not at all interfere with his comforts and little with his luxuries; but take away from the labourer the sum which such an enactment as this will take away will be to cut into not his comforts but the necessaries of his existence. ... And if we now all of a sudden expose our labouring population to the chance of poverty and all the cares and anxieties by which poverty is accompanied, we must be prepared for the consequences which this will have upon the moral condition of the people.

(Lord Brougham, 1847)

Of course, the various Factory Acts of the first half of the nineteenth century were passed into law, and the nation became used to Parliament probing the minutiae of daily life and exacting legislative revenge on any and every perceived inadequacy in society. The frustration of one opponent of such intrusion was voiced as early as 1850, with concern about the growing influence of the State over its citizens.

I wish the people not to depend upon Government. I wish them, by means of their own savings, to provide a sum for their own wants. [These new ideas] are getting the working classes into a habit of thinking that those things will be done for them which can only be done by themselves.

(Mr Trelawny, 1850)

'Indolence Super-Induced'
Unemployment Benefit

It was a theory that had long been pursued in a complementary arena, that dealing with the other side of the coin to the labouring class: the unemployed. A foretaste of the arguments that would be brought forth here came early in the nineteenth century, immediately after the Napoleonic Wars had ended throwing countless thousands of demobilized soldiers back onto the streets to fend for themselves in civil society. Unemployment rose inexorably, exacerbated by the increased use of machines to replace human hands. Combined, these forces led to periods of dangerous instability and much social disorder in Britain in the decade after 1815. Aside from the bread riots and the machine-smashing episodes, a more serious underlying impact of the post-war situation was the crushing effect the masses of out of work and penniless people had on the rudimentary social security system of the day, the centuries old Poor Law. The system, created in Elizabethan times, put the onus of supporting the destitute on village and town authorities, which raised the money through rents and rates on its land- and house-holders.

By 1815 it had become a complex and unwieldy system, with each of the country's 15,000 parishes and villages having their own local arrangements, rules and regulations. What was, however, abundantly clear cut was the growing cost. It had risen by the second decade of the century to absorb as much as one third of the rental collected in the entire kingdom.

With reform on the table, voices were not slow in emerging to query the very principle behind poor relief. It was to be a precursor of many a critique down the years,

right down to the modern day, which held that the State
could be too kind for its own, and its people's, good. The
same argument could be heard at the beginning of the
twentieth century when old-age pensions were debated
and frequently in our own era from critics who complain
that State handouts demoralize the human spirit and sap
bodily will. What follows, although dating from the earliest
days, stands well for a timeless principle applicable, in the
eyes of opponents, as much to us now as them then.

> The system of giving relief to every person merely because he
> is poor is expressly contrary to the law of nature and the law of
> God which declares that each individual shall earn his bread
> by the sweat of his brow; and it is impossible that mankind can
> be maintained upon any other principle. Our system [of Poor
> Law] ... causes a man to have an interest in enjoying the fruit
> of the land but no interest in the labour that produces it.
>
> ... The time must come when every healthy person must
> live by the produce of his own labour. ... It is utterly impossible
> that we could, by taxation or any other means, provide for the
> increasing amount of rates which will be required while this
> system prevails and from which I really think the greatest
> danger threatens the community.
>
> (Mr Lockhart, 1816)

What effect did the knowledge that immediate relief of
poverty was available have on a person?

> Economy and forethought are banished; improvidence and
> immorality encouraged. To restore the respectability and the
> happiness of the inferior classes they must be brought back to
> those manners from which they have swerved. Their general
> good sense I think of as highly of as any man but [they have
> been] misled ... by depending on parochial relief.
>
> ... The relief bestowed on [a recipient] may remove in-
> deed the cravings of hunger but it is at the expense of all the

best feelings of his nature. To restore independence of mind to
the labouring classes is an indispensable ingredient in every
plan for bettering their situation. Need there be any other
proof requisite of this than the superiority of our people, on the
whole, over every other nation. Whence does this arise? Is it
not among the blessed fruits of our free Constitution, inspiring
independence of mind and action, giving consequence in his
own eyes to every member of the community? Hence has
arisen the glory, the pre-eminence of England. Extinguish the
vital spark of liberty, destroy the political character of the
people and we shall soon sink to a level with countries groan-
ing under despotism.

   ... Relief takes away a principal incentive to right action
and lessens the influence of moral principle which places the
reward of merit in the esteem of the virtuous.

(Mr Curwen, 1816)

The same guardian of the public morals returned the
following year with ever more alarming news of how others
saw us.

Foreigners contemplate with astonishment the sums provided
in Great Britain for the poor which with the addition of
endowments to charities exceed nine millions annually, a
revenue possessed by few sovereigns in Europe. What are its
effects? ... Does it produce happiness, content and gratitude
among the poor? No, Sir! Discontent, gloom and misery per-
vade all who partake of it. Not a particle of gratitude [nor]
contentment is to be found.

(1817)

He had been on his travels and sought to show how the British
mainland poor compared badly with the Irish peasantry.

We commiserate the situation of those whom we see deprived

of what habit leads us to view as the first necessaries of life. Their clothing scanty and worn out; their cabins mean and in disrepair; the earthen floor a few boards and a wretched straw pallet their bed; a stool or two and an iron pot forming their whole menage; their sole food potatoes; salt and buttermilk their luxuries. Such are the outward objects in view. But those who have the courage to examine more minutely into the condition of this hardy race ... may draw conclusions very opposite to those which first strike the eye. The inhabitant of this wretched abode will be observed cheerful: kind hearted, affectionate, charitable in the highest degree, with the strongest sense of his duties as a son, a husband and a parent and happy in their execution. In the midst of his privations his independent, unsubdued spirit supports him. It is the mind which imprints the stamp of happiness or misery. The Irish peasant amidst all his wants and sufferings appears far superior to the unhappy victim of pauperism in this country.

... The effect of the Poor Laws [in England] is to destroy all the best and most kindly feelings of the heart. It jaundices the eye and prevents it from deriving comfort from what it possesses; every benefit granted to one is considered by others as an injury done them: thus envy and jealousy are perpetually engendered.

(Mr Curwen, 1817)

Perverse though the outcome of the logic might be, the argument carried enough plausibility to make the neutral observer stop to think. Illuminating – or at least suggestive – it might be of what was actually happening out in the country, the trouble with the diagnosis was that it contained no obvious politically acceptable prescription for putting matters right. The policy which logically flowed from the analysis was to make everyone poorer and the human spirit would somehow then shine through. Other commentators, perhaps troubled by this philosophical dilemma, chose to adopt a far less rosy view of human nature which, nevertheless, could still hold out for exactly the same objective – the ending of State relief.

> By the indolence super induced from the security of sustenance the pauper loses even the power of great bodily exertion; or, if not, spends the surplus with which the opportunity of extra-exertion occasionally supplies him in enervating drink and dissoluteness.
>
> (Sir Egerton Brydges, 1817)

The Foreign Secretary, and chief Government spokesman in the Commons – Prime Minister the Earl of Liverpool sat in the Lords – gave the official expression of concern about the prospects for the country if the extravagant relief then available was not curtailed.

> [I] take as gloomy a view of the influence of the Poor Laws in breaking down the national character as [I] can possibly do; and if no means can be found of elevating the national character by inspiring the population of the country with the wish rather to live on their own labour than on what they can draw from the labour and prosperity of others, I firmly believe that the English people will not in future ages be what they have been in times past.
>
> (Lord Castlereagh, 1817)

Two evils were at work, he continued.

> The present system not only goes to accumulate burdens on the country which it cannot continue to bear but to destroy the true wealth of the poor man, the capability of making exertions for his own livelihood; for if pecuniary relief goes on with the laxity which now prevails, and all the cunning of uncultivated minds is to be directed to the means of escaping from labour and enjoying the fruits of the labour of others, a national calamity might be said to be overtaking us by a double operation – in the increased burdens imposed on the country and the diminution of the

industry from which its resources are derived.

A foretaste of the work-for-work's-sake schemes which were to be popularly subscribed to in our own century appeared to be the only solution.

> I would rather employ the labouring poor to dig a hole one day and make them fill it up again the next than allow them to remain idle and expose themselves to the danger of losing the use of their hands and legs and the power of making themselves serviceable to themselves and the country. Though this labour might not be immediately productive, it at least keeps the labourers in a state which renders them capable of future efforts and thus averts one great danger to be apprehended from a great proportion of the labouring poor subsisting without effort at all. If the law does not receive some correction in its administration, the evil will at last become too strong for the law.
>
> (Lord Castlereagh, 1817)

Even worse prognostications came later. Was it not obvious that if the poor were given a sense of security it would only encourage reckless behaviour.

> My fear is ... that the poor will marry ... improvidently when their children are to be provided for [by public relief].
>
> (Mr Lamb, 1818)

> It will promote early marriages and make people utterly regardless of their children. At present they do take some little care of them and how they might provide for them is a consideration with many before they marry; if the clause [providing for child assistance] is carried, they will be deprived of every motive both for abstaining from marriage and for taking care of their offspring.
>
> (Mr Cripps, 1830)

One of the most comprehensive assaults on the system came in 1821.

> The effect ... operates as a premium for poverty, indolence, licentiousness and immorality. By the doom of nature man must earn his bread by the sweat of his brow and nothing can be more injurious to a country than the adoption of a principle in legislation which holds out to any considerable portion of the population an exemption from such sentence and disconnect the ideas of labour and profit. The poor laws hold out to the labourer a prospect of relief, not in old age, not in sickness, but a refuge from the consequences of his own indolence. They have a tendency to degrade the character of the man who receives relief under them, to lower him in his own estimation, to diminish his industry and thus to involve by degrees in their fatal circle the whole mass of the labouring population.
>
> ... The relief is scarcely considered in the light of charity: there is nothing of grace about it; it is bestowed without compassion and received without gratitude.
>
> (Mr Scarlett, 1821)

Moreover, it fudged the hitherto clear cut lines separating the classes, although the language in which he made the point made it sound as if a valuable social connection was being lost. In reality it was the loss of a valuable social distinction that was being lamented.

> There is another consideration which is paramount to all others – it dissolves between the poor and the rich those ties which have formerly bound together the different orders of society; there is no longer gratitude on the one hand or real charity on the other; the poor receive without thanks what they are entitled to receive and the rich give without compassion what they are compelled to bestow.
>
> (Mr Scarlett, 1821)

There was now to be one form of life for the working man and a completely different – and more onerous – one for the rest.

> Why is not the labouring man to be impressed with the same necessity for husbanding his resources for his family that is felt by other classes in society? It is obviously of the same advantage to all classes that such an impression should prevail and that a most immoral system must be the result of any particular relaxation from so just and provident a responsibility.
>
> (Mr Scarlett, 1821)

It was left to another Member to muse on how society could possibly proceed on honest foundations in such a state.

> The inevitable effect of such indiscriminate and wild prodigality of relief has been – as it must be from the nature of man, and woman also – to remove and put away from the minds of the lower classes those feelings and habits of sober, prudent, domestic economy and frugality.
>
> ... [For the pauper] it is indifferent ... whether he comes ... fuming from the alehouse ... or reeking in the effects of the most laborious toil if he is entitled to demand and receive equal relief, without distinction or inquiry whether his wants are owing to his vices or his misfortunes.
>
> ... Many have doubted and not without grave authority to support this opinion, whether the distressed and impotent poor are entitled to any assistance from the public as a matter of right. ... The necessitous poor are entitled to some relief: but it is of the most stinted and penurious kind ... it is limited to such relief as may prevent their dying from want of sustenance. ... [It was never considered] that the poor man, without work, was to live with his family a co-rival in comfort and respectability with the honest provident labourer who derived his support from his personal industry.
>
> (Mr Nolan, 1822)

'THE COMPULSORY CHARITY OF OTHERS'
OLD-AGE PENSIONS

The Poor Laws were reformed in 1834, making receipt of relief conditional upon claimants entering the workhouse, a deterrent intended to ward off all but the most desperate cases. It was to be another half century before legislators again got agitated on the subject of State-supported citizens and the same theme of public welfare *versus* private thrift when the issue of old-age pensions came on the scene. Reforms in Germany – Bismarck had introduced pensions for all in 1891 – sparked urgings for the same in Britain. The concept was not in fact a completely foreign import. A Bill providing for publicly funded pensions for the aged had been passed by the Commons as early as 1773, but had been rejected by the Lords. The idea suffered the same fate in 1789, and further efforts in 1796 and 1817 also failed. The issue lay dormant until Bismarck's innovation.

In Britain the notion was revived in 1893 with the establishment of a Royal Commission to examine possible schemes. Unfortunately for the proponents it reached a negative conclusion on the practicality of the idea two years later. It recommended looking at a wider variety of methods. A Parliamentary Committee was set up in 1896 and studied over a hundred different plans for a system. In 1898 it too concluded that it wouldn't work. It was to be another decade before the old-age pension became a reality, swept into being by the indomitable vigour of the then Chancellor of the Exchequer, Lloyd George who simply refused to accept no for an answer.

The practicalities of such a gargantuan undertaking were the principal reasons for the doubts and delays down the years, but for many a greater, philosophical issue was at stake. It paralleled the concerns aired over poor relief, and aimed squarely at the effect on the nation's attitude towards the management of personal finance. Advanced as early in the debate as 1894 by the Government spokesman, the argument was not without a shade of logic.

> Will it promote thrift or encourage a man not to spend his wages if he knows that at 65 he will have a pension of a certain amount, reducible by the income to be derived from what has been saved? Will not that condition stimulate a man to get rid of what he has saved as he approaches the age of 65?
>
> (Mr Shaw Lefevre, President Local Government Board, 1894)

Joseph Chamberlain, Colonial Secretary, had been the first front bench Member to produce a scheme, that on which the Royal Commission deliberated. By the end of the five years of study by the best brains in the country and with the expense of the Boer War looming endlessly into the future, he found himself obliged to set out the official case against pensions with what were clearly intended to be terminal objections.

> Any universal scheme for giving pensions to everybody is ... beyond the resources of the State. It would cost such an enormous sum and would involve such an entire disintegration of our whole financial system that it is perfectly impossible to contemplate it as practical legislation and even if possible it would be equally open to the objection – in my opinion, fatal objection – that it would make no distinction whatever between the provident, thrifty and industrious man and the drunkard and the spendthrift. I think, Sir, that any scheme which may be proposed must encourage thrift and independence or else it would do more harm than good.
>
> (1899)

Single-handed attempts by individual Members to introduce the measure were treated to unrestrained scorn. Few reached the ferocity of this, in March 1902.

It is based on a false theory. I think it would be unjust in its operation, certainly extremely difficult of application and highly probably deleterious in its results on the social character of our people. What is the theory which underlies this Bill? It is that every child who is born into a civilized community, by the mere fact of honouring that community with its presence, has the right to be supported by his fellow citizens until he is capable of work and of fulfilling his own destiny and that he is entitled, when no longer able to perform that task to special accommodation and recognition for the services he has rendered to the community.

... That is not the motive, however, which prompts the honest working man to labour. The motive which prompts him is the instinct of social preservation which induces him to consider that he and his family ought to owe their livelihood to his personal exertions rather than to the compulsory charity of others. That is a view which I believe to be deeply engraven on the English character. It is a wholesome view and one which conduces to the preservation of a high ideal amongst our people and I regard with great suspicion any legislation which seems in the least degree likely to impair it. It is impossible, I think, seriously to contend that a man who, at the age of sixty-five, when hard labour becomes impossible for him, finds himself without adequate means of subsistence – pathetic as that spectacle is and anxious as we all are to relieve him – it is impossible, I say, to contend that because he has kept himself for sixty-five years he is entitled as a matter of right to special consideration on the part of his fellow citizens.

[Knowledge of a pension entitlement] will not induce to the formation of provident habits among our people or the preservation of that disposition to thrift, of the growth of which during the last century we have had such gratifying proof. I believe the spirit is growing up amongst the people in the direction of providing for themselves against all the ordinary contingencies of life. ... I am convinced that [pensions] will tend in the direction of stopping that steady progress.

(Mr Bond, 1902)

Joseph Chamberlain returned to the battle the following year, having evidently moved further from his early support of the idea than even his contribution of three years before suggested. Referring to 'these wild doctrines' and 'extreme and extravagant proposals', he stated his new view concisely and apocalyptically.

I believe ... it would be undesirable to give [pensions] in that form [i.e., universal] because ... the promise of universal pensions to everyone, without reference to previous character would be the greatest blow ever struck at thrift in this country.

(1903)

Stripped of the rhetoric, the issue was plain: universal pensions available to all regardless of character or need struck opponents as financially and, indeed, morally irresponsible – but the problems which flowed from any attempt to discriminate were equally unpalatable: did one give a pension only to those who had demonstrated thrift, and had savings – those who thus by definition were least needful? The perversity of that solution needed only to be stated to be ruled out as a sensible policy; or did one give it only to the poor, thereby, according to the critics, penalizing thrift and responsibility and rewarding the financially carefree and prodigal? That too seemed illogical. Caught in the psychological cleft stick, certain only of the knowledge that a comprehensive scheme could not be afforded, governments dallied, allowing opponents to continue to heap up the moral arguments against the scheme.

> On whose behalf are old age pensions asked for? They are asked
> for on behalf of those who have made no provision for them-
> selves. But why have they made no provision for old age?
> There are only two possible reasons. Either because they have
> not earned sufficient to enable them to do so or because they
> have misspent their earnings. ... I am told that a sum of £170
> million a year is spent on drink. That would supply all the old
> age pensions we want. But how can we secure that fund except
> by appealing to the man to abstain from drink and provide for
> his old age. If, however, we say to any workman, 'Drink away
> as much as you like for when you grow old you shall be
> supported in comfort at the expense of your colleagues who
> have not drunk,' then clearly we are subsidising drunkenness. If
> we do that we are taxing men who spend their money well in
> order to subsidise the men who spend their money ill.
>
> (Mr Cox, 1907)

There was no difference in principle with the common
arrangement already in hand whereby workers got paid, for
six days' work, a sum intended to support the earner for
seven. No-one was proposing that the State should pay
workers on Sunday when they did no work.

> If ... there was the obligation upon a man to earn enough by six
> days' work to keep him for seven days, surely there is an
> obligation upon him to earn enough during his youth and
> prime to provide for old age. If we give a man an old age
> pension, we relieve him from this obligation.
>
> (Mr Cox, 1907)

The same year the same observer used another analogy to
repeat the point.

I contend that it is part of the duty of life to make provision for
old age. The State compels education; surely it has also the
right to compel thrift.

There were of course already State pensions, almost exclusively reserved for distinguished public servants who had
performed particular feats of service to the nation. There
had been a time when those seeking wider application of
pensions saw them as some form of reward for hard work.
That was long past.

The demand now is for pensions to be given to everybody who
arrives at a certain time of life who has not done any special
service to the State and without regard to any special merit or
even special need. In my opinion, pensions of that sort are
worse than a waste of public money; they are the greatest
possible incentive to the absence of self-reliance and thrift.

(Viscount St Aldwyn, 1907)

One argument was that giving pensions at the end of a
working life rather than raising wages throughout it and
from which responsible people could make provision for
old age, perpetuated rather than solved the stigma of
poverty.

What I object to in all these schemes of State charity is that
instead of aiming at the abolition of poverty they tend to
perpetuate poverty by treating it as a permanent institution.

(Mr Cox, 1908)

One critic was convinced that the shape and character not
only of the nation but of politics itself would be irredeemably
sullied.

[Old age pensions] will endanger and sap the foundations of

our political fibre. ... And is there not reason to fear that once we have established this system ... there will be a race between the political parties as to who should go furthest? We give five shillings; the next party will give seven shillings and sixpence; then they will get it up to ten shillings; the age of seventy will slide down to sixty-five or sixty.

... Step by step the age will fall and the pension will increase and step by step one party will be compelled to bid against another to gain the ear of the electors. This is a prospect which I for one cannot contemplate with equanimity.

(Sir H. Craik, 1908)

His vision, at least, bears some resemblance to the eventual reality which ensued.

'A Ruinous Principle'
Holidays

Improving the lot of working folk took one other major route in the last quarter of the nineteenth century – the advent of the public holiday. Until 1871 workers enjoyed just two statutory holidays – Christmas Day and Good Friday. The path-breaking Bank Holiday Act of that year, which established the essential framework which still exists today, introduced four more – Boxing Day, Easter Monday, Whit Monday and the first Monday in August. The reform was initially of advantage only to the salaried classes such as clerks and professionals, as the Act simply declared the days 'closed' for trading in bills of exchange and financial transactions. Daily-paid labourers were merely deprived of a day's work – and pay. It was to be some time further before the vast majority of employers acknowledged the justice of paying workers for the official holidays, and even longer before additional personal holidays without loss of pay were provided. Not until well into the second quarter of the present century did the annual paid holiday become an accepted staple of working life. The concept of any break – paid or unpaid – was deprecated by critics as weakening the national spirit of industry. Even the extra public holidays would, they maintained, have dire consequences. Compared with the generally lackadaisical French and Mediterranean countries:

> It is well known that the paucity of holydays [sic] in Protestant countries is regarded as giving us a commercial advantage.
>
> (Mr Baring, 1868)

If the House enforces idleness by Act of Parliament on the

working classes of this country, we will be initiating a ruinous principle which will tend still further to give the advantages which foreign countries are now obtaining over us in all our great national industries for which, up to this time, this country has been pre-eminent. I object to men being forced to idleness by Act of Parliament and thus having to use extra exertion on the following day to make up their loss.

(Mr Wilson, 1875)

And, he concluded:

I believe the Bill will be found to act injuriously by giving the working classes increased facilities for drinking.

It was all a most disturbing pattern.

I ... am afraid we are running philanthropically mad in endeavouring by Acts of Parliament to interfere with the ordinary course of business.

(Mr Norwood, 1875)

In the late 1920s attempts were made to introduce compulsory paid holidays, but without success. By then just a quarter of the workforce – an estimated three million out of twelve – were receiving paid holidays from their employers. Holidays which were taken by most workers were paid for by saving up during the year. This was to some a morally uplifting aspect, encouraging thrift and frugality, foresight and responsibility, all of which would be lost if the holiday came, in effect, 'free'.

You will take away from all these people the incentive to save for their holidays. You may say they will have an equivalent in that they are going to be paid for their holidays, but is this the same thing? Do you not think that something for which you have saved up, a pleasure to which you are looking forward, is very much more worth while and much more interesting than the knowledge that you are going to draw just your week's salary or wages from your employers?

(Captain Hudson, 1929)

The men in the mills of Lancashire contribute something each week throughout the year for their holidays. They accumulate large sums and have most excellent holidays ... but to get something for nothing by law seems to me to be a very unusual procedure. I can understand people getting something for nothing by good will or by trickery but not by law – not a week's pay for no work rendered. That, I think, is going far beyond any idea of what is fair as between employers and employed. [Compulsion] will destroy goodwill and embitter relations between employer and employee.

(Sir James Reynolds, 1929)

Captain Hudson could only view the prospect of the notion with doom.

The results are problematical if not actually dangerous. (1929)

It was not until 1938 that the Holidays With Pay Act settled the matter once and for all. Lucky workers managed to get their first holiday in before the War intervened to put them on hold again for another six years.

SIX:
THE MOTOR
CAR

'THESE SLAUGHTERING, STINKING ENGINES OF INIQUITY'

Of all the technical innovations of the twentieth century, few have transformed our lives, attitudes and environment as rapidly and spectacularly as the motor car. Within a generation, the byways of Britain were changed beyond recognition, but as always thoughts and outlooks were constantly one or more steps behind the technical advances. The advent of the petrol-driven 'highway locomotive', the speedier and much more agile relation of the steam traction engine, provoked vivid descriptions of its effect both on people and their livelihoods of doom-laden, stifling proportions. Freed in 1896 from the restrictions imposed upon the steam engines – the infamous Red Flag Act of 1865 which required every engine to be preceded by a person waving a warning to all in its path – cars took on an aura of their own.

> In all the places where they have been introduced, they are absolutely found to have become a nuisance.
>
> (Dr Tanner, 1896)

The new breed of motorists and their machines were an indisputable menace.

> They claim the right to drive the public off the roads. Harmless men, women and children, dogs and cattle have all got to fly for their lives at the bidding of one of these slaughtering, stinking engines of iniquity.
>
> (Mr Cathcart Wason, 1903)

As late as the 1930s they were still rueing the day.

This invention has within it possibilities of greater evil and unhappiness for the human race than any invention that has ever been discovered. ... Wherever it has gone it has completely destroyed all the beauty and the peace of life.

(Lord Buckmaster, 1932)

The noise of cars had, according to eminent men in the medical profession, the effect of:

produc[ing] a neurotic and nerve-racked race.

(Lord Buckmaster, 1933)

Dr Farquharson enquired whether something could be done:

to relieve the rural and suburban districts of London from the annoyance caused by motor cars which dash along in defiance of the comfort and convenience of those who use the road, poisoning the air with fumes of petroleum and destroying the vegetation of trees and hedgerows by clouds of dust which also render safe steering difficult or impossible.

(1904)

The government spokesman, Mr Long, President of the Local Government Board, replied succinctly:

I am afraid I do not see my way to any effective action in the direction suggested.

This complete surrender to the pestilence raised spectres of a fundamental change to the nation's way of life.

In villages every door and window has to be shut and the occupants cannot even sit in their gardens on account of the dust which is raised by these motor cars. The consequence is that the whole value of their property is destroyed. This also applies in county districts to glass houses used for the cultivation of fruit and flowers. ... The tremendous dust raised by them settles on the glass obscuring the sunlight and the fruit and flowers cannot ripen or come into full bloom.

(Sir P. Muntz, 1905)

And it was not only bystanders who stood to suffer.

[O]f all the forms of motion, the motorbicycle is the most despicable. ... I am quite convinced that if ... every citizen spent his time on, and got his life shaken out of him by, a motorbicycle, we will have the worst physique in the whole world.

(Mr Redmond, 1903)

Wider concerns occupied one peer. The insidious undermining of tradition seemed to worry him more than anything else.

The noise of these machines is a public nuisance for they groan, grunt, shiver, shake and stink. The wearing of glasses and leather coats is an affectation and the use of the word 'chauffeur' is intolerable and should be prohibited. The introduction of these needless foreign expressions is odious.

(Earl of Wemyss, 1903)

And agriculture too he thought would be decimated.

If it were not for the fact that [horses] are needed for the infantry and cavalry and other purposes I am afraid they would die out. This constitutes a bad look-out for agriculture. We grow corn, oats, hay and straw. Motors do not eat oats, they do not eat hay and they do not lie on the straw and when horses are done away with, it will not be worth while our growing these agricultural articles of consumption having lost our best customer.

(1903)

There *were* the optimists, though, who had no doubt that the motor car simply wouldn't catch on.

Depend upon it, if these motorists and motor cars are not kept in order they will have to leave the roads altogether because in the long run the people will never submit to the intolerable nuisance which has been created.

(Mr Cripps, 1903)

Others were less worried, convinced otherwise that come what may the motor car was no threat to the traditional forms of locomotion.

The hon Member also referred in his speech to a fear that motor cars would supersede horses and do a great deal of harm to horse breeding. I do not believe the introduction of motor cars will ever affect the riding of horses; the prophecies that have been made are likely to be falsified as have been those made when the railways were introduced in this country.

(Mr Scott-Montagu, 1903)

There really could be no competition, surely?

When you are driving a horse, there are two brains at work – that of the horse and that of the man – and very often that of the horse is much the best in the event of difficulty. But with the motor car, there is only one brain. We hear a great deal about the development of roadside inns. I venture to say that a motorist who has been ... taking a glass at several of them will be much more dangerous to the public than a man who has been doing the same thing but is driving in a trap and who will be taken care of by his steady old horse.

(Mr Soares, 1903)

The fears for the horse's future went to the heart of the security of the nation.

> [The car] has had a very bad effect on horse breeding and the displacement of a large number of horses will probably give serious cause for alarm to those who are interested in maintaining the armaments of this country.
>
> (Lord Willoughby de Broke, 1908)

The War Office had a crystal-clear vision of the future, though.

> I doubt whether at any time the reduction of horses will be as great as one might anticipate. I take it that under no circumstances shall we ever want less than 40,000 for the Expeditionary Forces.

That was Lieutenant-Colonel Seely, Under Secretary of State at the War Office assuring MPs on behalf of the government. Astonishingly it was as late as April 1911. A colleague had earlier made it quite plain how the War Office saw things.

> The spectacle of a regiment of motor cars charging, no doubt would be inspiriting but I do not think such a scheme will be likely to prove any permanent advantage to the Army.
>
> (Lord Stanley, Financial Secretary, War Office, 1901)

Same brave spirits ventured, albeit with evident caution, a view of the future.

> It is quite possible that there may be developments of the industry both as regards the employment given by the manufacture of these cars and as to the use to which they may be put in this country which will give the common people a

much greater interest in the motor car than they have at present.

(Mr McArthur, 1903)

But it was never going to be a headlong rush.

The Postmaster-General has had reports upon the recent trials of motor cars ... but he has not come to any conclusions upon the question whether they can yet be used with advantage for the mail service.

(Mr Austen Chamberlain, 1901)

Down the years the greatest source of conflict between the supporters and antagonists of the motoring fraternity was the vexed question of speed. Since the great release ushered in by the Locomotives on Highways Act of 1896, the question was never far from the top of the agenda. The 1896 Act imposed a limit of 14mph. Within seven years, pressure was growing for it to be increased – to the formidable heights of 20mph. The catastrophic implications were clear.

If this Bill passes as it stands, we shall have to give up the use of the roads entirely to the motoring fraternity.

(Mr Soares, 1903)

Others disagreed. One of the more remarkable aspects of the debate in the early years – and which was still to hold some currency until as late as the 1930s – was the argument that the solution actually lay in the opposite direction, that speed limits should in fact be abolished rather than tightened. The logic was compelling: artificial speed limits only encouraged drivers to drive up to them.

The imposition of an arbitrary speed limit is a tactical mistake and will not serve the real purpose its advocates have in view.

(Lord Balfour, 1903)

Motorists desire the abolition of the speed limit in order that reckless motorists and professional motorists ... may not imagine that because a certain speed is mentioned that that speed is always permissable.

(Mr Norman, 1903)

Notwithstanding such views, the 1903 Act passed. The regressive impact on the nation's general morality was deplored.

The police efforts are devoted to proving that the man was going beyond the statutory 20 miles an hour and thus have led to what I regard as a most undesirable practice known as the police trap, which is contrary to British methods.

(Mr Long, 1908)

If anything could make [matters] worse, it is the system ... of police traps. ... It is the worst way of enforcing the law, purely arbitrary, fortuitous and uncertain, the very way to get the law despised and disobeyed.

(Viscount Cecil, 1928)

By the end even the Government's chief law officer agreed.

It is deplorable that three policemen should waste their time on a comparatively straight road upon which vehicles can run in perfect safety in order to catch someone who is exceeding the speed limit.

(Sir William Jowitt, Attorney-General, 1930)

Parliament was never short of imaginative ideas on how to control speed, and thereby accidents, short of imposing arbitrary limits. One Member believed he had put his finger on the obvious solution. Far from arming cars with ever more powerful warning horns, the answer lay clearly the other way – abolish them completely! It was not without some logic since the present situation showed that:

> At the present moment the traffic on our roads is conducted in the same way in which the railway traffic used to be conducted many years ago in America. Railways in America were unfenced. The engine rang a bell and if anybody got in the way it was said, 'Oh well, he ought not to have been in the way; the engine rang the bell.' That is very much the idea which is prevalent among motorists today. They blow their horn and they think that it is sufficient and if you do not get out of the way you are run over.
>
> (Lord Banbury, 1928)

So, the answer was obvious.

> If the use of the horn or warning signal by motorists was forbidden, they would have to take the same chance as drivers of horse vehicles; they would have to go much slower round corners and through populous places and would not be able, by blowing a horn, to order everybody else out of the way. Their speed would be greatly reduced, they would have to pull up oftener and they would be forced to be a little more considerate of other people.
>
> (Lord Willoughby de Broke, 1908)

Another idea – perhaps even now worthy of modern adaptation – was that the motorist should be made to reveal to the world their misdemeanour.

> One [idea] for which it always appears to me there is a great deal to be said [is] that every vehicle ... should have an

automatic whistle warning the public when they are exceeding
the speed limit.

(Mr McKenna, 1914)

The notion was updated in the 1930s, and doubtless could
be once again even today.

My suggestion ... is that there should be a mechanical indicator
on the motor car which would make it quite clear when the
driver was in fact breaking the law. I cannot see any great
hardship in that. It merely provides that there shall be at the back
of the car a dial divided into quarters, the first quarter showing
when the car is within the limits of the law, the second when it
is a little beyond it, say thirty-five or forty, the third when the
speed is between forty-five and sixty and the fourth when it is
above sixty. It would give a test which anyone could enforce.

(Viscount Cecil, 1934)

He told his fellow peers that he had been told that such a
device could be fitted for as little as £3. Large electronic
displays on the backs of cars today? Now there's a thought.

Recognition of the problem of speed was widespread by
1930. But the solution was quite incredible. Far from
imposing even more rigorous controls, logic drew the legislators in the opposite direction. The seminal Road Traffic
Act of that year simply abolished the speed limit for private
cars – on the refreshingly pragmatic grounds that nobody
was taking any notice of it.

When a law becomes out of date and ridiculous, when members of the public no longer desire that a certain law should be
enforced ... the police have to adapt themselves to modern
conditions.

(Mr Herbert Morrison, Minister of Transport, 1930)

[Speed limits] should be abolished and no sensible or reasonable person can really have any doubt about it. ... The speed limit has created an entirely new class of offence; it has brought before the Courts of this country people who in the ordinary way never break the law; it has choked the Courts with these cases to the detriment of the ordinary business.

(Earl Winterton, 1930)

The Government had trailed the argument the previous year setting out the basis for the abolition with disarmingly forceful logic.

The psychological effect of a fixed speed limit has been thoroughly bad. Ever since 1896 it has hypnotised the public and it has thereby diverted attention from what really matters – that is, dangerous driving. ... I am convinced that if there had never been a speed limit and if attention had been directed to the real matter from the first, the tale of killed and injured would have been far smaller than it is.

(Earl Russell, government spokesman, 1929)

The same end was argued by others, but the logic was not always as clear cut. That of the delightfully named Sir Gervais Rentoul was less fathomable than most.

Arguments in favour of the retention of the speed limit leave me entirely unconvinced. We all recognise the appalling total of casualties that take place on the roads at the present time, but they all take place while we nominally have a speed limit in force and I fail to recognise that any evidence has yet been forthcoming to show that that appalling total would be in any way increased by the suggested abolition of the speed limit.

(1930)

The argument that if present speed restrictions were not

reducing the number of accidents, then the controls should be abandoned altogether rather than enforced more rigorously was one shared by others too.

> I am not one of those people who believe that speed per se is really going to make for dangerous driving on our roads today. ... I do not believe the retention of the speed limit will really have any effect in helping to reduce the number of accidents.
> (Lord Erskine, 1930)

Indeed, some held it positively contributed to them.

> The speed limit does not make for safety ... It directs attention to the wrong thing. ... We do not want [drivers] to try to drive with their eyes fixed on the speedometer but with eyes fixed on the space in front of them.
> (Earl Russell, 1930)

The Minister of Transport outlined the case for abolition.

> Supposing we indicate that the speed limit should be increased to 30, 35 or even 40 miles an hour, what are we saying? We are saying that in the ordinary run of driving a motor car it is reasonable to run at 30, 35 or 40 miles an hour. I venture to say to the House that that is an exceedingly dangerous thing to say and that it is dangerous to get it into the motorist's head ... that generally speaking 30, 35 or 40 miles an hour is a reasonable speed at which to travel.
> (Mr Morrison, 1930)

The solution as the government saw it was not to inflict the weighty arm of the law but to encourage the sweet reason of the motorist.

> Let us examine the psychology of the motorist. ... If you lay

down a maximum speed of 35 miles an hour the whole psychology of traffic control and dangerous driving will tend toward the idea that the man who is driving at 35 miles an hour is driving reasonably on the King's highway. For myself, I shrink from laying down such a principle in any statute. ... This problem is not going to be solved so much by compulsion as by education, by the inculcation of a genuine social conscience. We must make the motorist feel that when he is discourteous and inconsiderate on the road he is not a British gentleman, and that we are not going to regard him as such. When we have reached that stage by the inculcation of good conduct, we shall have done far more than by setting up a standard of 35 miles an hour which may be a matter of utmost danger.

(Mr Morrison, 1930)

So the speed limit was abolished. What followed was, in the description of one 1930s observer, a 'holocaust' on the roads. The number killed in road accidents (over 7000 a year during the early '30s) was more than the total would be thirty years later when the number of cars on the road was six times greater. The mayhem was halted, in legislative terms, extraordinarily rapidly. Just four years later another Act was passed reimposing a limit. The 1934 Act established the foundations of today's road laws on speed, imposing a 30-miles-an-hour limit in built-up areas — although moving still ever cautiously, it was initially only for an experimental five-year period. It reopened all the old arguments again, but on slightly different tacks.

Personally I do not believe that the 30 miles an hour limit will do what it is intended that it shall do. ... I believe a speed limit of 30 miles an hour in certain areas will give a false sense of security to certain people. A speed of 30 miles an hour in crowded areas for certain types of drivers is always far too high a speed limit.

(Mrs Tate, 1934)

When we have a speed limit of 30 miles an hour, what will be the result? I think that many people when they are driving at 30 miles an hour will think it is perfectly safe and that they need not bother very much and then, with people getting careless and not keeping a good lookout we shall perhaps see many more accidents.

(Sir G.Fox, 1934)

I submit that a speed limit actually does in fact encourage a wrong mentality. If you have a speed limit – you can fix it at any figure you like, twenty, thirty or forty miles an hour, it does not matter which – that maximum is almost automatically looked upon as the minimum by many motorists.

(Earl Howe, 1934)

The pernicious effect was plain for all to see.

I do not think it is a good thing for Parliament to start making a lot of criminals and prosecuting thousands upon thousands of people all over the country because they happen to go more than 30 miles an hour. ... It is all nonsense. It will mean absolute chaos. It is a perfectly ridiculous suggestion. It will not do the slightest good. It will only annoy a large number of people and do a lot of harm.

(Sir W. Brass, 1934)

You create a bad atmosphere and the police instead of being the friend of the motorist, instead of trying to help them, will be looking out for breaches of the speed limit while motorists, instead of watching the road properly, will be looking round to see whether there are traps.

(Sir W. Brass, 1934)

There could only be chaos and confusion.

Already the restrictions and regulations affecting the motoring public are very many in number and very drastic in practice. ... The enforcement of the speed limit will be, of course, by the obnoxious speed trap. ... The chief result in my opinion will be a large increase in prosecutions for non-observance of the limit in places where danger to the public is practically non-existent. ... The definition of a built-up area will unquestionably cause a great deal of trouble and create a great deal of confusion and many anomalies.

(Mr McKeag, 1934)

The whole idea smacked of molly-coddling by a 'grandmotherly' state.

I consider this to be absolutely reactionary legislation. We have to adapt our conditions to the changes that take place in the world. It is no use getting alarmed over these figures. Over 6,000 people commit suicide every year but nobody makes a fuss about that. It is true that 7,000 people are killed in motor accidents but it is not always going on like that. People are getting used to the new conditions.

... Older members of the House will recollect the numbers of chickens that we killed in the early days. We used to come back with the radiator stuffed with feathers. It was the same with dogs. Dogs get out of the way of motor cars nowadays and you never kill one. There is education even in the lower animals. These things will right themselves. It may well be that we have to go to the peak of road accidents and that even within a year or two people will realise the extreme change that has come over our life and that very much greater care must be taken.

(Lieutenant-Colonel Moore-Brabazon, 1934)

Besides, the good, honest integrity of the British motorist would always be the ultimate salvation.

To those who suggest that it is an unreasonable hardship to motorists not to drive above 30 miles an hour in a populated area, I would reply that a careful driver has no pleasure in going faster than that.

(Mr Anstruther-Gray, 1934)

The Minister of Transport felt the whole business would only be of temporary duration. Perhaps one of the most optimistic (and misguided) of prophets, his faith was undaunting.

I firmly believe that a time is coming when many of the problems we are discussing today are going to solve themselves automatically with quickened reaction, with inherited caution, when an ingrained sense of safety is going to take the place of many of these restrictions and regulations which we now have to impose.

(Mr Stanley, 1934)

His deputy, concluding the debates on the Bill, still held out optimistically too that they could all soon be back taking all the limits off again.

It may well be – and I hope profoundly that it will be so – that the automatic check to speed caused by the institution of marked crossing places for pedestrians, by a general improvement in the standard of driving, by a better attention to warning signs and by a greater development in road sense and in road manners on the part of all users of the road may ultimately do away entirely with the need of any limitation of speed.

(Lieutenant-Colonel Headlam, 1934)

As hinted above, the landmark 1934 Act heralded many other of the now familiar motoring controls. We shall come to pedestrian crossings shortly, but perhaps the next most important reform brought in by the Act was one which, surprising as it may seem to us now, had been fiercely resisted by governments of all political persuasions since the dawn of the motor age – the driving test. As early as 1902, the President of the Local Government Board, the government's roads spokesman, was voicing official doubts.

> I am afraid there would be much difficulty in giving effect to the suggestion.
>
> (Mr Long)

The recurring theme of the objection to what we now take as an essential part of life was the view that accidents were not caused by novices but by the reckless old hands. For decades opinion was adamant that testing would serve no purpose.

> It has not hitherto been considered necessary or desirable to amend the law in this respect. ... Accidents with motor cars are rarely traceable to incompetence to drive while they are not infrequently associated with undue confidence or occasional recklessness on the part of skilled drivers.
>
> (Mr Burns, President Local Government Board, 1911)

> As far as I am aware there is no evidence to show that any substantial proportion of accidents in which motor vehicles are involved is due to any want of capacity on the part of drivers such as would be disclosed by a driving test. A universal test of the kind proposed by my rt hon Friend would clearly be expensive and might become perfunctory.
>
> (Colonel Ashley, President, L.G.B., 1927)

A proposal to introduce tests was expressly voted out of the 1930 Act. Again for the Government:

> We are satisfied that driving tests have absolutely no value.
>
> (Earl Russell, 1929)

The view was shared in the Upper House.

> My own belief is that the more skilful a man is, the more dangerous he is because he takes greater risks. What really is wanted is road sense and you will not get that by having examinations. ... All you prove by an examination is that you know when to put on the brakes and when to put in the gears.
>
> (Lord Banbury, 1929)

Tests focused on the wrong target.

> The reason [some drivers] drive safely is because of inexperience. They take no risks; they go slowly and very carefully. The driver who causes the accident ... is the driver who thinks he can do anything and tries it once too often. ... I hope your Lordships will not be led away by the fallacy that imposing these tests would do anything to diminish accidents. That really is a fallacy. I think we should get nothing by it.
>
> ... The man who can drive really well, if temperamentally reckless, becomes dangerous. It is a matter of temperament and not of skill. ... We shall get an entirely false sense of security if we impose this suggested test. We may improve road manners, we may teach people not to keep so much to the centre of the road but I do not think we shall seriously add to the safety of driving by imposing this test.
>
> (Earl Russell, 1929)

The simple point was that the test could never eradicate bad driving.

> In my view, drivers' tests are no use. ... Unfortunately, it is not the learner who is really dangerous on the roads. It is the man

who can drive a motor car, and perhaps can drive it well but who does not observe the rules of the road. ... Perhaps he passes on bends, drives past tramcars too fast when people are getting out, drives past schools without realising it is the time of day when the children are about to come out. No driving test, however severe, will enable you to get over that particular difficulty.

(Lord Erskine, 1930)

No less than the Government's chief law officer, the Attorney-General, came out again on the side of opposing such misguided concepts.

The cause of accidents, really, is not inability to drive the vehicle but is much more often the fact that an experienced driver disregards precautions which he ought to take or, perhaps, a lack of what is termed 'road sense'. You cannot see whether a man has 'road sense' in a test of half an hour or an hour, and there are some people who even if they drive all their lives never seem to get 'road sense'. ... I do not believe that inexperienced drivers do much harm.

(Sir W. Jowitt, 1930)

And then there would be the practical difficulties of administering such tests.

If skill and physical fitness are to be assessed, it will mean regular re-examination and great expense. [We] doubt whether in effect it would be found satisfactory unless a special service of highly-skilled examiners was set up which would maintain uniform standards. We are not convinced that such an extension of bureaucratic control is necessary.

(Mr Neal, Parliamentary Secretary, Ministry of Transport, 1921)

His successor also deplored the vast number of people who would be needed.

> I do not think that the imposition of tests for drivers would be a practical means of giving effect to the hon Member's wishes and would entail a large number of officials.
>
> (Lieutenant-Colonel Moore-Brabazon, 1923)

And *his* successor too.

> Any advantage which at first sight might appear likely to result from the institution of tests on the lines indicated would be outweighed by the expense, difficulties and disadvantages inseparable from any such system.
>
> (Colonel Ashley, 1925).

The scope for malfeasance was obvious.

> My friends who have had to go through these tests abroad tell me that they are very largely superficial and that the ease with which one goes through the test is in proportion to the size of the fee which one gives to the man who is administering the test. ... I do not say that that would happen in this country but I agree ... that tests are quite unnecessary and will not carry us any further.
>
> (Colonel Ashley, 1930)

To the end there were professions of doubt.

> I wish I could persuade myself that it will have some effect in solving this problem but I cannot see what good we are going to get. ... I do not advocate any test at all because I do not think there is much in it. I know that some of the most brilliant men in business today have been incapable of passing examinations, not because they have not had the knowledge but simply

because they cannot pass examinations and I can conceive of the man who has been through a course of instruction in driving being unable to pass a test just as I can conceive of a man being able to pass a test with flying colours and yet be a public danger on the road.

(Mr Roberts, 1934)

I think [the test] would be absolutely useless. An ordinary sensible person can drive a car quite capably after two or three hours' tuition and all those people would be able to qualify for a licence. It is only six, seven or eight weeks after, according to the amount of mileage driven, when the new motorist thinks he has control of his vehicle and a sudden emergency arises that it is possible to tell whether he is going to be a menace or otherwise to his fellow users of the road.

(Mr Glossop, 1934)

While [it] may eliminate a certain number of people who ought not to be permitted to drive a vehicle in any circumstances, I doubt whether very much good will be accomplished commensurate at any rate with the inconvenience, the red tape and the expense that will be occasioned. One thing, however, is certain: that this test will create another large horde of officials.

(Mr McKeag, 1934)

Speed limits and proficiency tests were not the only pillars of our modern motoring edifice to be dismissed with similar official disdain in the early days. Almost every now commonly accepted aspect of driving was objected to, usually on the grounds that it would increase rather than decrease the number of accidents. The suggestion for compulsory third party insurance for example. It was neither feasible:

I am afraid my hon Friend's suggestion is an impracticable one.

(Mr Neal, 1921)

> To carry out a general scheme of insurance would involve great difficulties. I do not believe it will be possible to come to an agreement with the insurance companies.
>
> (Colonel Ashley, 1927)

If one thought about it, nor was it likely to be advantageous.

> It seems to me that the only result of compulsory insurance would be that nobody would care and accidents would increase.
>
> (Lord Banbury, 1925)

As always, the logic behind the contention was on the face of it plausible.

> I can understand a proposal that *no* motor should be insured against third party risk. That, I think, is an arguable case because then every person driving would take special care not to inflict damage to life or limb ... but I can also understand the frame of mind of a man who ... says, 'Well, I am insured against all risks; it does not matter,' and he will go ahead for all he is worth and as likely as not will cause an accident.
>
> (Viscount Ullswater, 1925)

The theory that once protected by insurance drivers would become careless about how they went about the road was best encapsulated by Lord Banbury the following year.

> The [proposer] says that motorists are in favour of it. Of course they are. What the Bill means is that if the [advocate of insurance] runs over me and kills me he does not suffer in the least, for some third person pays my heirs. ... If [he] himself had put his hand into his own pocket and paid my

heirs something, it might possibly console me for having been run over but it can be no consolation to me that some other person pays for the faults committed by [him]. It is quite natural that all motorists and certainly all reckless motorists should be in favour. ... [H]aving paid [their insurance] they are free to do what they like. They may go at any pace over dangerous or non-dangerous roads. They may, when they see a pedestrian, content themselves with blowing their horn and expecting the pedestrian to get out of the way; and if he does not get out of the way and they run over him, somebody else will pay for the damage which they have done.

(1926)

Put like that, how could the idea ever have got off the ground!?

Similarly, a proposal so apparently sensible to require cyclists to have lights on their bikes would, according to critics, have the paradoxical effect of increasing the likelihood of accidents. Ridiculous? Read on.

If the claim of the motorist is that he cannot go at the speed he would like for fear of running down the cyclist, and that that fear would be removed if a red light or reflector were displayed ... would it not mean that ... the motorist would feel that he could speed up and that therefore there would be an increase in recklessness rather than a decrease?

(Mr Snell, 1927)

Couldn't the Government at least make speedometers compulsory so that drivers would know how fast they were travelling? An elaborate solution without necessity, according to Home Secretary Herbert Gladstone, with an argument charmingly typifying the halcyon days of motoring.

Drivers ... cannot exceed the speed limit of twelve miles an hour fixed for their vehicles without knowing it since to do so they must consciously make an excessive use of the accelerator.

(1908)

Any idea of mechanical aids to signalling were also given the official thumbs down.

Signals by the human hand and arm [are] sufficient and satisfactory. Any attempt to prescribe a form of mechanical signalling device will, obviously, give rise to numerous difficulties.
(Colonel Ashley, 1926)

When they did come, nothing like today's versions were seen as practicable for the motorist to cope with.

It seems to me essential that there should be simplicity of operation of these signals and that the signals themselves should be simple to understand. Anything like coloured flashing lights which may distract a driver's attention is a bad thing.
(Lord de Clifford, 1932)

Government priorities seemed to lay in other directions. Early car radios caused considerable agitation, again from the fear of distraction. At the outset, there was the real chance that they would be banned altogether. In response to one critic, the Minister threatened action if necessary.

If wireless sets on motor vehicles prove to be a source of danger or of annoyance to the public, I may have to consider the prohibition or restriction of their use. I shall watch the matter carefully.

(Mr Stanley, 1934)

Two months later, further roadside distractions were summarily dealt with. The Minister announced a regulation providing that:

> 'No person shall in any scheduled street either wholly or mainly for the purpose of advertisement wear or cause to be worn any fancy dress or other costume.' The object of the regulation [is] to relieve congestion and facilitate traffic.
>
> (Mr Stanley, 1934)

Other innovations to feel the cold blasts of official doubt at first were the now omnipresent white lines. Introduced by private initiative – a Kent alderman had the idea in 1914 to mark dangerous stretches on the London-Folkestone road at Ashford – the marking of the road surface was initially frowned upon by the Ministry.

> I am inclined to think that in certain circumstances the use of the white dividing line tends to facilitate the flow of traffic and to diminish the risk of accidents. I am of opinion, however, that the greatest care should be exercised to limit the use of these signs as their indiscriminate use will only defeat the object in view.
>
> (Colonel Ashley, 1925)

A foretaste of the future was memorably offered by one critic.

> There is a real danger ... of turning motoring into a sort of game of chess. With all these devices on our roads, motoring will be made too complicated. ... If we are to have our roads painted with all sorts of signs they will have no effect at all.
>
> (Captain Gunston, 1934)

Any modern driver arriving at a junction in the wrong lane

will easily acknowledge how right the Captain didn't know he would be. And not only *on* the road, but signs by the roadside threatened to be a major cause of grief.

> The country will be literally plastered with signs of all sorts and descriptions. Indeed, motorists will be kept so busily occupied on looking for signs and notices about [for example] speed limits that they will be unable to give due care and attention to their driving and the police will have it both ways. If the motorist tries to read all the signs that will be erected, he will be charged with not driving with due care and attention; and if he drives with due care and attention he will not be able to follow the signs. Happy indeed is the lot of the motorist in these progressive days.
>
> (Mr McKeag, 1934)

> [There is] the utter need of taking every measure possible to prevent motorists' attention being drawn off the road itself. With the plethora of signs that one sees on the roadside and the host of distracting colours ... it is impossible for a motorist to give that concentration that ought to be given to the road itself.
>
> (Captain Strickland, 1935)

The third great innovation of the 1934 Act after speed limits and the driving test was the pedestrian crossing. Again, in the early days the Minister had his doubts.

> I am aware that in certain cities abroad pedestrians are not permitted to cross the more important streets except under control and at prescribed points. I do not think that it would be practicable to introduce such a system in London.
>
> (Colonel Ashley, 1928)

The English character was essentially to blame.

Suggestions have been put forward with regard to compulsory crossing places and subways in congested parts of large towns. I do not think that the mentality of the English people is in favour of subways.

(Mr Glossop, 1934)

And the impracticabilities were immense.

I do not like the idea of painting the crossings as is proposed because that means that they would have to be painted afresh every week.

(Sir W. Brass, 1934)

For twenty years crossings were to be marked by metallic studs rather than zebra stripes. To enhance their visibility even more, the innovators of the day hit on the strange artifact which allowed at least one Transport Minister to be remembered forever – the Belisha Beacon, coined after the traffic supremo of the day, Leslie Hore-Belisha who held the position from 1934 to 1937. Although at first they did not flash, nor even were they illuminated, their distinctive addition to the nation's skyline had the critics up in arms.

These decorations are really rather stupid and very unnecessary. ... [It is] a fantastic scheme of beacons all over the place with these orange balls in clusters around the town.

(Sir W. Brass, 1934)

'Fantastic' had a rather different connotation back in the Thirties. Then it meant distinctly 'unbelievable' rather than our modern weaker usage of 'brilliant.' He continued:

[They are] a veritable danger as well. ... A pedestrian standing by one of them can of course see the beacon and also thinks that the driver of an oncoming vehicle can see it as well. He cannot but the result is that the pedestrian ventures on to the road thinking that the driver of the vehicle can see the beacon and an accident is the result. These beacons therefore instead of increasing the safety of pedestrians will definitely do exactly the reverse.

(1934)

He ended his tirade by pleading with the government not to:

litter London with 'orange groves' and make us the laughing stock of the world.

Lest it be thought that he was a dyed-in-the-wool reactionary, the same character was at the forefront four years later of advocating another device familiar to us all now but which got the usual official cold shoulder.

In order to induce pedestrians to take more notice of traffic lights, [would the Government] consider experimenting with small red, amber and green pedestrian lights attached to the columns of the main traffic lights, these pedestrians lights working in conjunction with the main lights but in the opposite sense.

(Sir W. Brass, 1938)

This early view of the red and green men signals so common to us all got this reply,

I do not consider that additional signals of the type suggested are necessary, and indeed might be confusing.

(Mr Burgin, 1938)

The antipathy to control was even-handed. A backbencher,

Mr Logan, as early as 1933 advocated the return to 'self-control' instead of these 'Hitler lights' – and this at a time when just ninety-four intersections in the whole of the London metropolitan area were controlled by traffic lights!

Congestion was an ever-present problem right from the dawn of the motoring age. It was begun to be tackled in the 1920s with the creation in London of experimental – and quaintly named – 'parking places', the forerunners of our modern car parks. Their organization still left a little to be desired. So crowded did they become that a bizarre requirement of the early parker was that he had to leave his vehicle unlocked and with the windows open – so that attendants could manhandle the cars which were found to be blocking the movement of others. Two motorists were actually prosecuted in 1929 for locking their cars and this led to the following extraordinary exchange in the House.

> *Colonel Ashley*, Transport Minister: I am not inclined to amend the Regulations as it might prove necessary in certain circumstances that cars should be capable of being moved from their position on a parking place.
> *Sir H. Brittan*: Is it suggested that every time a car is parked, the doors should be left unlocked and the windows open?
> *Colonel Ashley*: Certainly, it has to be because if it is not done in many cases no car can get out of the parking line at all. They are so close that unless a car which is left unattended can be moved, others cannot get out.

How times change – official Government instructions to leave one's precious property unsecured!

The rule lasted until 1932. It was not the first bizarre injunction to be inflicted on London's motorists. In 1928 the Reversing Prohibition Order was introduced banning cars from reversing inside an area of the capital stretching for a three-mile radius from Charing Cross. Quite how it was presumed that such a rule would help, rather than hinder, the movement of traffic is not clear. Sending traffic once more round the block and adding to the congestion every time one missed one's stopping point seemed a curious way to go about it. Regrettably, we do not know how long the regulation lasted.

We might be forgiven for getting the distinct impression that in these early days of motoring the stranger the solution, the better chance it had of getting passed into law. Some, equally outlandish, did fail to get past the barrier, though not on any account of lacking originality. One aimed to bring home to pedestrians their own responsibilities in keeping to the rules of the road.

> To make pedestrians realise the risks they incur by carelessness in crossing thoroughfares, [I suggest] marking with a black cross on the street the spots where any pedestrian has been killed or severely injured.
>
> (Sir W. Davison, 1932)

The Minister replied diplomatically that.

> I doubt whether public opinion in this country would be in favour of it.
>
> (Mr Pybus)

For one Member, the answer had been clear since as early as 1903.

> Perhaps the Government could do with motor cars as was done with certain other conveyances, restrict them to travelling between the hours of six o'clock in the evening and

six o'clock in the morning.

(Mr Harwood, 1903)

The future was equally clear to another in 1935. With the alarming increase in the number of cars on the nation's roads – 224,000 then and increasing at twelve per cent (meaning a doubling in eight years):

> My own view is ... that ultimately we shall have to ration cars. We shall have to have a waiting list and people who want motor cars will have to wait their turn. ... Short of some such method ... I see great difficulties ahead.

(Mr Lovat-Fraser, 1935)

For the record the number of motor vehicles on Britain's roads had, by the late 1980s, reached 20 *million* – and still no sign of rationing.

The vexed question of drinking and driving was not to be tackled until 1967 in legislative terms. The problem was always there though, and in the 1930s it was dealt with under the reckless driving provisions. In the days before the breathalyzer, the standard methods of detecting drunken motorists had one Member squarely on his feet.

> I hear that tests are imposed upon motorists who are thought to be under the influence of drink and I am alarmed for my own safety because I hear that suspected persons are subjected to tests of tongue twisters. I find the greatest difficulty when I am sober in saying, 'Round the rugged rock the ragged rascal ran,' and I am sure that many people who are accused of being drunk would when asked to say something like that find very great difficulty in saying it.

(Mr Taylor, 1936)

After the Second World War, the major controversies

were confined to the impact on the rural way of life of the vast swathe of motorways being planned and the increased congestion of the cities. The next Road Traffic Act was in 1956, which sought to tackle urban congestion by the introduction of an American practice, the parking meter. The scheme could only be a failure according to Opposition views.

> I am not very favourably struck by the provision about parking meters. ... [The objective] is the need for maintaining a free movement of traffic; but is it going to attain that end? Shall we see a free movement of traffic or shall we merely see reshuffling of cars every few hours with people having exhausted their right to stand at one parking meter driving round the block and finding another and doing exactly the same thing again? That is not going to relieve congestion. ... It is only going to add to congestion ... I cannot myself believe that the provision of parking meters is going to do much more than take a few more shillings out of the motorist's pocket.

That came from Prime Minister to be, James Callaghan, in 1955.

One bright spark's contribution during the debates on the Bill was to set another ball rolling.

> There is something to be said for having a special corps of traffic enforcement officers for London....
>
> (Mr Davies, 1955)

... but only the future will tell what place that innovation will have in the roll-call of motoring history.

SEVEN:
THE MEDIA

The rise of the modern, technologically based mass media troubled Parliamentarians with a degree of uncertainty, foreboding and urgency not replicated in any of the other innovations we cover here. It was the very speed of the developments which provided the greatest challenge to the legislators, rather more used to a leisurely caution when it came to reform and adaptation to change. But the luxury of taking forty-four years (as with slavery) or forty-two (as with the Secret Ballot) simply was not available in the early decades of the twentieth century when in rapid succession the scientific boffins repeatedly threatened to outrun the defenders of the public morals with inventions with every-increasing implication for society. First with moving pictures, then with wireless sound and ultimately with their combination – pictures through the airwaves – Parliament quickly felt overwhelmed by the rapidity of change. This tended to increase exponentially the doubts, and the greater the doubts the greater was the absurdity of the response which followed. Given such doubts, it is hardly surprising that Parliament chose to leave itself till last in coming to terms with these foundations of the modern communication society. It was not to resolve its anxieties about the broadcasting of its own proceedings until almost the present day (1975 for radio; 1989 for television in the Commons; for once the Lords were ahead of the game, letting in cameras in 1985). The first suggestion for radio broadcasting of the Commons had come as early as 1923 and was turned down by Prime Minister Bonar Law with the curt objection that:

I do not think that the hon Member's proposal is desirable.

It was an objection that was to hold firm time after time while in those early years Parliament doggedly stuck to wringing its collective hands over the effects these inventions were having on the nation at large.

'TOO MUCH PASSIVE ENJOYMENT'
CINEMA

The moving picture – and the cinema – was the first of the terrible triptych to confront Parliament, and it took on an aura of greater dread because it was essentially a foreign influence. While Europe bloodied itself in crisis, war and reconstruction in the first quarter of the century, the Americans in sunny southern California made films. By the time of the first debate to be held in Parliament on the subject – in the House of Lords in May 1925 – there were already 4000 'picture theatres' in Britain frequented by a staggering 20 million cinemagoers every week. On average around ninety per cent of the fare was American. It was too much for one member of the Upper House, whose observations perhaps carry a familiar ring to modern ears. The Americanization of Europe had begun in earnest, and similar standard bearers for the British way of life would still be arguing sixty or more years later that Britain had lost its national identity to the power of the yankee dollar. Although politically the United States was to remain strongly isolationist until the Second World War, through the medium of film it achieved as much, if not more, in the pre-war years through its cultural invasion of Europe. If you could call it culture.

> The fact is the Americans realised almost instantaneously that the cinema was a heaven-sent method for advertising themselves, their country, their methods, their wares, their ideas and even their language and they have seized upon it as a method of persuading the whole world, civilised and uncivilised, into the belief that America is really the only country which counts.
>
> (Lord Newton, 1925)

It wouldn't be so bad if what was on offer was any good. The Lord Newton again.

> I should not object to this wholesale invasion of American films if they were all good but as a matter of fact, to speak quite plainly, they consist of rubbish. I am told rubbish is the only thing which pays. If that is so, all I can say, and I am sure noble Lords will agree with me, is that if our people are content to witness perpetual rubbish let it, at any rate, be English rubbish in preference to American rubbish because in producing English rubbish the money will at least be spent in this country.

He despaired for the future of civilized arts, but could never feel surprised.

> Unfortunately, rubbish is what the public wants and the taste of the public in the case of cinemas is, as in everything else, about as bad as it can be. Look at the public taste in literature and art. I suppose for every 30,000 who read *The Times Literary Supplement* at least a million read *Tit Bits*.

> What I gather is that the public want to see expensive and attractive females ... and there is very little demand, so far as I am able to ascertain, for really high class productions.

It was not long before positively sinister motives were being found, against which the whole Empire stood vulnerable.

> If you consider the effect upon the millions of young people who frequent cinemas in this country and if you deplore, as possibly you do, the effect which is sometimes created, imagine what the effect must be upon millions of our coloured fellow citizens in remote parts of the world who perpetually have

American films thrust upon them which frequently present the white man under the most unfavourable conditions and in addition are often of an extremely mischievous character.

(Lord Newton, 1925)

Less than two years later, the government legislated to deal with the tide of imports. Sustained concern about the impact of American films led to an Act in 1927 imposing on cinemas a quota arrangement: at least twenty per cent of film exhibited at each had to be home produced. It was, though, still quality – or lack of it – that worried the nation's guardians.

I can conceive nothing more horrible and nothing less valuable from the point of view either of entertainment or of instruction than these dreadful American cowboy films with their mushy sentimentality and their adventures entirely foreign to this country and to the spirit of this country.

(Earl Russell, 1927)

A spiritual spokesman found much to deplore in American 'popular' films, particularly as the manufactured glamour of film stars and the hype surrounding the industry had now reached something of an art form in itself.

[The films] deliberately inculcate false values. Virtue with them has no rewards but wealth and kisses – the two things which in this world it has most to do without. Envy is neither sinful nor foolish when it is directed by poverty towards luxury; no-one who is beautiful ever pays ultimately for her folly.

(Bishop of Southwark, 1927)

The insidious gnawing at the moral fibre of the country and its empire still raised a siren voice.

I do not suppose that there is anything which has done so much harm to the prestige and position of western people and the white race as the exhibition of films which have tended to degrade us in the eyes of peoples who have been accustomed to look upon us with admiration and respect. I am sure that everybody would like to see something done which would tend to get such a production of British films as would overwhelm the exhibition of depraved pictures which come from other parts of the world and, unfortunately are looked upon by eyes that do not sufficiently understand what is being exhibited.

(Sir Robert Horne, 1927)

Or perhaps understood too well! At least one recognized that any hope of emulating Hollywood was sheer fantasy.

It is impossible to expect that films produced in this country where people have to wait for a great many days before they can get fine weather can be produced so as to compete on equal terms with films made in other countries more fortunate in their climate ... and where there is less rain and more sunshine.

(Earl Beauchamp, 1927)

Somehow the nation survived, and perhaps it could be expected that the worries would cease as we got used to the diet. A generation later, a new phenomenon agitated one old diehard who got himself worked up over the ostensibly harmless innovation shortly after the Second World War of Saturday Cinema Clubs. They were to be a central formative experience of millions of childhoods – the raucous, barely controlled chaos of the weekend children-only matinee. Mr Skeffington-Lodge in 1946 saw potent calamities ahead from the:

atmosphere of mass hysteria which is induced by the communal shrieking. I think we shall develop citizens with a false set of values. We shall have a nation of robots and automata for whom 'glamour' offers an escape from the duties and responsibilities of life.

Warning of 'the social danger of too much passive enjoyment', he railed that children should be shown:

decent pictures and not ... the portrayal of luxury-living film stars who, duly surrounded by the glamour I have mentioned, become in the eyes of their beholden simply people to emulate and follow.

Perhaps his last word remains as true today as he thought it was when he spoke again on the subject in 1948.

Hollywood's good gifts to us in the shape of Walt Disney and the Marx Brothers are few compared with the long list of films which act as a social narcotic and which have merely a brassy vulgarity.

'Bound To Fail'
Radio

By 1948, characters like Skeffington-Lodge were more an eccentric aberration than the genuine voice of Britain. Public anxiety about cinema had dropped away quickly in the late 1920s, though, as with all neurotics, this was only because another worry had displaced it. It was now radio which, in the late '20s, occupied centre stage in the national worry-in. The private British Broadcasting Company had begun regular transmissions in 1922, and came under public control just four years later when the British Broadcasting Corporation was created under royal charter. At the outset as a public authority the BBC looked as if it would not be allowed any leeway to influence the nation's minds as cinema was doing. As well as being forbidden to editorialize, in other words to offer its own views on issues, an injunction which still largely holds to this day, it was also not permitted to broadcast: 'speeches or lectures containing statements on topics of political, religious or industrial controversy'. It was, then, to be a diet of bland public information programmes, drama plays and classical music. In those days when the presenters were under strict instructions to dress in dinner jackets and bow ties to address the microphone, getting in tune with the population was a difficult affair at first. One early public critic painted a picture of the sort of station that had been created.

> The public like more variety and they like it light. They also say that they find the programme intolerably didactic and the music, I am told, is mostly chamber music and more highbrow than the ordinary man likes to hear.
>
> (Mr Macpherson, 1928)

The restriction on references to controversy lasted only until the spring of 1928. There had been a real feeling that if it was not to widen its horizons it simply would not last.

> Not only in private conversation but in every newspaper the utmost indignation is manifested against the Corporation. ... The Corporation is dismally failing. I prognosticated at the time it was instituted that it was bound to fail.
>
> (Mr Hore-Belisha, 1928)

The murmurings of discontent with single-channel output were voiced with unselfconscious frankness.

> There are quite a lot of people who because they have limited brains call everything they do not and never will understand high-brow. ... The suggestion I have to make is that we might recognise the demand for the low-brow entertainment, jazz orchestras and the rest of it, and also the demand of those who want the educational lectures and classical music. ... [Two stations] would meet the objection that large numbers of people have to the mixed programme and it would give more opportunity for those who ... want the educational and the classical rather than the jazz and the common things.
>
> (Mr Montague, 1926)

The relaxation of conditions on what could be broadcast was by no means an open licence. Indeed, as the 1930s began the power of radio was recognized by some for its political possibilities (which were to be exploited to their fullest in the dictatorships on the continent). It led to one Member arguing for closer, not reduced control of programming.

> It cannot be doubted that transmission by broadcast is now one of the most potent political forces in the world and if political

issues are to be selected for the country we believe they ought
to be selected in the House of Commons and not at Broadcasting House.

(Sir Stafford Cripps, 1933)

Cripps was a Labour front bench spokesman at the time in
Opposition to the coalition National Government. The
official view of the party carried a foretaste of the future
direction of broadcasting when the media would deter-
mine, rather than reflect, what was important.

Obviously if matters for debate over the broadcast are selected
by the British Broadcasting Corporation, there is a danger that
they may create issues which perfectly justly they may think
are the major political issues at the moment but in regard to
which Members of this House would not agree.

(Sir Stafford Cripps, 1933)

As with cinema, there remained those who still had to be
convinced that there was any virtue in the invention at all.
After a temporary suspension of light music broadcasts
immediately after the war to save electricity during one of
the gravest economic crises of the century, one Member
saw some advantage to the situation.

It is also interesting to wonder whether the break which has
taken place ... may be a blessing in disguise. ... It is by no means
certain that a break of some kind in the non-stop programmes
on the wireless may not be in future a feature of our programmes for the sake of our culture; because it is by no means
certain that the continual soaking of the mind in adventitious
noise from outside may not, at the end of the day, be to some
extent injurious to concentration and to connected thought,
just as the over-indulgence in alcohol during long hours on
licensed premises can be.

(Lieutenant-Colonel Elliot, 1947)

He was not alone in pointing the finger at radio as the fount of all our social ills.

> We who make the laws are perturbed at rising costs in the divorce courts, at the homes for illegitimate children, about foster parents who have to be found for the children of those who have regarded their duties and matrimonial responsibilities far too lightly, those who are encouraged by the entertainment programmes of the BBC, by their band shows and crooners ... to regard that sort of thing as the highlight of happiness.
>
> (Mrs Mann, 1947)

What they might have thought of the modern bill of fare is left to the imagination.

The broadcasters were to provide Parliament itself with the most traumatic challenge the institution has had to face. It was not so much any pressure to bring the microphone or the camera into the House – requests were ritually rejected from day one: radio was ruled out the year after public broadcasting began; similarly, just a year after public television started in 1936 Ministers rejected a call for television coverage of proceedings. Rather, the central issue troubling Parliament was how broadcasters should cover political affairs. Parliament, as the main forum for political dialogue in the country, feared that television would rival it or, horror of horrors, supplant it as the nation's debating chamber. The problem did not come to the fore until after the Second World War, when the deferential air of the early days was breaking down. Both radio and, after its resumption from wartime suspension, television, were finding their feet and coming of age with a rapidity that took officialdom by surprise. The decade after the War saw an awesome tussle between the newly invigorated media and the traditional moderators of politics each fighting for their own vision of how public affairs in the future should be reported. It was to produce one of the most bizarre regulations ever conceived by Government, one which to modern citizens might seem ludicrous in intent and inoperable in practice but which, hard though it is to believe, was still in force less than forty years ago.

The so-called Fourteen Day rule began at the BBC's own initiative as an unwritten, gentleman's agreement reached in 1944 with the Government to try to keep the Corporation out of political controversy. The agreement was that the BBC would avoid broadcasting discussions on any issue which was being, or would imminently be, debated in Parliament. The idea was to declaim any intention on the part of the broadcasters of dethroning Parliament as the national forum for such matters. The Corporation interpreted 'imminent' as within the next fortnight. So, astonishing as it sounds, a cordon of silence was drawn around every topical issue once Parliament had indicated its intention to hold a debate on it. With the end of the War and the media flexing growing muscles, the unwritten understanding was codified into a written agreement in 1948 which also added further restrictions for good measure: that not only were up and coming debates included but *any* subject on which a Bill had been laid before Parliament. The ban lasted from the time of the Bill's introduction to when it either received the Royal Assent or was withdrawn. Given that that could span the best part of the Parliamentary year, it is hardly credible today that such a self-denying ordinance was entered into by a broadcasting organization – but agreed it was, and it was destined to operate until as recently as 1955.

As it grew more and more confident, television in particular jibbed at the restrictions. It was to take the greatest crisis to hit the Government since the War – and television since its inception – to blast the archaic rule to smithereens. When the Suez debacle unfolded in 1956, broadcasters simply ignored the proscription about mentioning anything of the political turmoil that was sweeping the nation. The Government, which as late as July 1955 had turned the rule into a legally binding obligation on the BBC, found itself powerless to uphold the anachronism in the face of public ridicule. It formally suspended the rule, notionally for six months, and then permanently.

One of the most adamant proponents of the rule was Winston Churchill, who detested television and was the last Prime Minister never to have granted an interview on television. His profound belief in the threat the media posed to the traditions and dignity of Parliament was unshakeable.

> On the whole it will be found to be in the long interests of the House of Commons to observe the practice which has been observed for a considerable time.
>
> (1955)

When asked to reconsider:

> I will never reconsider it. It would be shocking to have debates in this House forestalled time after time by expressions of opinion by persons who had not the status or responsibility of Members of Parliament.
>
> ... I am quite sure that the bringing on of exciting debates in these vast new robot organisations of television and BBC broadcasting to take place before a debate in this House might have very deleterious effects upon our general interests. ... Honestly, I think the House would be well advised to stay where it is before it yields up a great deal of the significance and dignity of the debates.
>
> (1955)

A week later, he was even stronger.

> I am a convinced and obstinate opponent of a change. I think
> that the liberty of the individual must be sustained. It must be
> sustained against the tyrant, it must be sustained against the
> mass and it must be sustained against the machine.

Churchill was still Prime Minister when he uttered his
condemnations. But not for much longer – a month later
he retired, bequeathing the new, modern nature of politics
to those arguably better minded to deal with its challenges.
His successor, Anthony Eden, appeared equivocal at first,
acknowledging that, although not a perfect arrangement,
we:

> ... rumble along after a reasonable fair fashion.
>
>   (1955)

Hardly a ringing declaration of faith in the system, but his
troops were to be on hand to put a more stirring defence of
the rule when the House debated the issue in November
1955 – and voted overwhelmingly to retain the restriction.
The Postmaster-General, the Government Minister in
charge of broadcasting, set out the rationale as best he
could. He started by quoting the words of the BBC's own
Director-General in 1949.

> It would be highly undesirable for [the BBC] to become a
> simultaneous debating arena with Parliament. There should
> be explanation, debate, controversy before, and possibly after,
> Parliament has dealt with an issue but Parliament is the only
> grand forum of the nation. Once the matter at issue is under
> actual discussion there, it should not also be being contested
> on the ether.

Television, the Postmaster-General contended, was an unnatural environment in which to conduct public affairs.

> Comparisons have been made between broadcasting and the public meeting. There are obvious differences. ... At a public meeting the audience need not be silent. It can show its dissent. On the air, the speakers have the substantial advantage of talking to an audience which cannot answer back.
>
> (Dr Hill, 1955)

He feared the disproportionate effect that a few telegenic Members would have.

> If ... the limited number of those who appear are selected for special qualities not necessarily related to the knowledge or authority with which they speak on a topic, then is there not a real danger that if a few selected persons are free to broadcast on matters shortly to come up for discussion in this House, if they are to broadcast free of restraint and responsibility ... Parliamentary discussion will be prejudiced and the authority of Parliament will suffer?

Nothing could present a worse recipe than:

> anticipatory or simultaneous discussions on the air by a few people selected by [broadcasters] without any responsibility to Parliament or the nation for the statements they make or the views which they express.
>
> (Dr Hill, 1955)

To give some idea of the burden under which the growing band of Parliamentary broadcasters laboured, one Member graphically complained in the debate that whenever she went into a studio she had thrust into her hands:

2 ½ pages of subjects on which we dare not comment.

(Mrs Mann, 1955)

Dr Hill was unrepentant.

If it be true that the maintenance of Parliament as the principal forum for the discussion of national issues, the maintenance of the prestige of Parliament, is an important element in the preservation of liberty, then limitation though this is, it is not unreasonable to say that this limitation is in itself a contribution to freedom.

Tortured though the logic might be, it was nevertheless a bi-partisan view on the front benches at least. The Leader of the Opposition, Clement Attlee, also supported the rule.

Here in this Chamber when they make their speeches leading statesmen are conscious that they are in the preserve of critics. They can be answered at once not only by leaders but by backbenchers who frequently intervene. I think that that has a very salutary effect on the speeches they make. It is true that people can switch off the wireless but they cannot interrupt speakers on the wireless and a period of time must always go by before there is a reply.

(1955)

He also was worried about who got on the air to pontificate.

I do not quite know how the people who appear on the wireless are selected. I am told that the selection is based on their entertainment value. ... These matters should be put before the public by people with responsibility.

The days of the probing, even aggressive media interview-

ing of politicians was very clearly still some way off when
Attlee spoke. He could not conceive of anything like what
was to come. By curious coincidence, mirroring Churchill,
his words were also some of the last he uttered in his post.
A week after the debate, he retired as leader of the Labour
Party.

Others, though, did have clear visions of the awful future
ahead.

> Parliament ought to be the place where Members of Parlia-
> ment build their political reputations. We put Parliament into
> danger if hon Members begin to look elsewhere for the best
> place to make their speeches.
>
> (Mr Gordon Walker, 1955)

> Surely it is unfair and improper that one should seek, through
> the medium of broadcasting and television to 'jump the gun'
> over fellow Members of Parliament and seek to discuss these
> controversial issues before we have had the full benefit and
> guidance of all the information which necessarily cannot be in
> the possession of individual Members until a Minister, from his
> knowledge and consideration of the subject, has been able to
> deploy before the House and until responsible leaders of the
> Opposition have put their points of view?
>
> (Mr McAdden, 1955)

Such sentiments seem naive in today's bruising world of
television inquisitions where the broadcasters as much set
the political agenda as report it. It would have been the
stuff of nightmares to Parliamentarians of just two generations ago.

Not all was bad though. At the outset there was at times an
equally naive optimism about the power of the box in the

corner of the room. Far from being the destroyer of all we cherished, at least some thought it would be the opposite. The view is worth quoting for its astonishing strength of conviction which, in the video age, may yet still come true.

Make no mistake about it, the repercussions of this new invention are going to be real. I believe they are going to be very wholesome because they tend to keep the home together. That is very fundamental and very serious. Do not let us deny that it is a rival to the cinema; but it does mean that people stay at home. It is a rival to beer; it means that there is entertainment in the home instead of only in the public houses.

(Lord Brabazon of Tara, 1950)

For instance in the Midlands, the average youth used to go out four or five nights a week whatever the weather. But with the coming of television he now stays indoors three or four nights a week. Those who are worried about the problem of growing juvenile delinquency should take some comfort from the fact that here is a medium which can attract the young.

(Mr Rodgers, 1953)

'A TERRIFYING PROSPECT'
TELEVISION

More common, however, was the negative theme. If the Fourteen Day rule was an existing safeguard that could not be allowed to be relinquished, the guardians of broadcasting purity had an even greater bugbear in their sights which had to be prevented from ever coming into existence: commercial television. Simultaneously with fighting the rearguard action to keep politics off the screen, they opposed vigorously the efforts to introduce commercial competition to the BBC. Some had experienced what they took would be the result in America.

> Sponsored television is a menace to our national standards. [It will] pollute the domestic atmosphere of every home, pervert the minds of the children. ... Unless we are very careful commercial television will pervert and reduce the standards of taste, morality and culture in this country for a generation.
>
> (Mr Fletcher, 1953)

> The revenue [of the commercial companies] will largely be influenced by the magnitude of the audience rather than the quality of the programme. ... The chase for mass viewing will inevitably bring standards down because the chase will be for the maximum numbers.
>
> (Mr Morrison, 1953)

> I say respectfully but with complete conviction that the effect of introducing this plan will be a progressive lowering of standards. ... The purpose of advertisers is to sell their goods and in this case to sell them at home and to promote domestic

consumption mainly, I should think, of non-essentials. It may prove fatally easy to persuade the crowd to follow the band that makes the biggest noise. ... I am profoundly apprehensive.

(Viscount Waverley, 1953)

The Television Bill of 1954 was the legislative basis for the creation of the Independent Television Network. The main argument against it was simple – that if television had to rely on advertising for revenue there would be an inevitable drift downwards to secure the biggest audiences, the lowest common denominator argument. Critics said that the advent of more channels would *reduce*, not increase, variety of output. The logic was, in pure economic terms, invincible. Paradoxically, competition would narrow the choice of programme, since where two stations competed both would be tempted to try to get the biggest share of the biggest group of viewers, on the economically sound principle that fifty per cent of the majority of viewers was better than one hundred per cent of tiny pockets of minorities. Inevitably this would drive broadcasters downmarket, building their output on the widest appeal. It had already led, in America, one Member told the House, to all four local channels in the city he visited showing all-in wrestling because sponsors dared not let competitors have a monopoly of programmes which attracted large audiences. The 'sport on all channels' argument was to be a familiar one to British viewers before long too. Where this left the cultured minorities was anyone's guess.

The object will be to get not a cultural or educational programme but one which will appeal to the lowest common denominator of the greatest number of people. ... I should have thought there were in existence already plenty of mediums for advertisement. There is the Press, the cinema and, unfortunately, the horrible signs which disfigure some of our most charming country roads and villages. Why not leave the BBC and the television service alone?

(Mr Scholefield Allen, 1954)

We think that there will be a natural tendency in these programmes to find a generally lower level. [The stations] will be pursuing profit and not public service and they will gradually lower the standards.

(Mr Gordon Walker, 1954)

Mr Ness Edwards summed up his view succinctly.

We regard this Bill as a great danger to the mental and cultural outlook of the people of Britain.

(1954)

In the days before the deluge of crass game shows which fill the modern screen, some had their eye firmly on the future.

We are sincerely concerned that this Bill, if and when it becomes an Act, will unleash on our way of life influences against which we shall find it very difficult to fight back.

(Mr Goronwy Roberts, 1954)

[Commercialism] will not make for the kind of programme that we need because the creative people will surrender their integrity, conform and thereby get rich or else they will starve.

(Mr Mayhew, 1954)

In my view a spate of mediocre entertainment will encourage vacuity and increased vacuity will result in the demand for even more mediocre entertainment – and so on until the jungle finally closes in. ... I oppose this Bill because in my opinion it is philistine and retrogressive. It is philistine because it seeks to widen the gap between education and enter-

tainment, the separation of which is one of the major weak-
nesses of our present age. ... I feel sure that if this Bill becomes
law future historians will deem it to be one of the most
irresponsible measures of modern times.

(Lord Strabogli, 1954)

He was doubtless in full agreement with the American
observer who coined, in 1955, the most graphic and per-
ceptive metaphor to encapsulate the impact of television.
At times, John Mason Brown wrote, it was little more than
'chewing gum for the eyes.' What troubled others was a
deeper moral implication. Provision of television ostensibly 'free' to the viewer (in comparison with the stumping
up of the licence fee for the BBC) would assault the
character of the British citizen.

> It is not going to cost anything and the people of this country
> are going to get something for nothing. ... They will *not* get
> something for nothing. They will get something – they will get
> certainly another programme – but at the cost of self-respect.
> ... Is it really a hardship for the owner of a television
> licence ... to put a few coppers into his savings box ... a week or
> at regular intervals? ... Is it really impossible ... for the workers
> of this country to make a small contribution towards their
> entertainment over the year? ... Surely that is the better way of
> doing it. That is the way the proud Englishman, the proud
> Britisher would prefer to do it than to have it said to him,
> 'We give you this for nothing,' at the cost, I say, of your self-
> respect.
>
> (Lord Kenswood, 1954)

In the critics' eyes, advertising on television was a regrettable innovation whichever way one looked at it. Succeed
or fail, advertising was damned in their view. If it was
ineffectual, it simply wasted money; if it wasn't ineffectual,

it would lead to a rise in consumer spending, encouraging everyone to live beyond their means and detract from exports (in the days when Britain made and exported consumer goods; today the argument is the other way round – rises in consumer spending suck in extra imports). Lord Moyne was of the view that there was precious little difference between:

> whether ... money spent by the nation on television advertising will be ineffectual in promoting sales in the aggregate and so, nationally speaking, wasted or whether [it was] likely to increase the sales of consumer goods at home and so aggravate our present economic difficulties.
>
> (1954)

For another it was the straw to break the camel's back.

> This is an age of mass perception and through various media of public communication such as elements of the Press, a considerable amount of corruption of consciousness has already taken place; and commercial television will just about sink the ship.
>
> (Lord Noel-Buxton, 1954)

He quoted an American television critic's observation on the condition of America, a view not far removed perhaps from thoughts many must have had since about the fare available on this side of the Atlantic.

> I was not put out by the actual commercial 'plugs.' Advertising is interesting; without it, life would lose a lot of colour. It was the entertainment between the 'plugs' which was appalling. It was unimaginative drivel, obviously designed to appeal to a huge naive audience with no standards of judgment. A nation fed on this pap for one generation might as well scrap its

educational system and spend the money on asylums.

(Lord Noel-Buxton, 1954)

Possibly the most memorable critique came from the acknowledged father of public broadcasting, Lord Reith, who, while admittedly not an unbiased observer on these matters having been the first Director-General of the BBC, chose to employ some scathing words against the upstart commercialists. He likened the advent of commercial television to the introduction of history's other socially evil imports into Britain, smallpox and Bubonic plague (and, curiously, something to which he clearly held a personal antipathy – dog racing). In the 1954 debate, he moderated his tone – slightly.

> [The proponents] will have sunk a maggot – a quite unnecessary maggot – into the body politic of England.

A more reasoned, though no less astringent, opposition came from Lord Hailsham, who inveighed against his own Government with what must have seemed convincing logic at the time.

> You do not give people what they want by aiming at the highest common factor of what they will put up with. ... When people are advertising a product, and using television as the medium for advertising, they are not so much concerned to give people what they want as to have at the time of the advertisement the largest viewing audience. The fallacy of the Government's case is to suppose that these two things are necessarily the same.
>
> ... When the honeymoon of television, when [viewers] look at anything, is over, what they want is a series of programmes which really satisfies them. It may well be that in each one of these programmes they are a tiny minority ... you may be a stamp-collector ... or you may be a pigeon fancier. ... The aim of the

advertiser is of necessity not to give the people their first choice but to give them as many second choices as possible. The real vice of commercial television is not that it is lowbrow but that, of necessity, it aims at giving the maximum number of people something they do not really want but what they are just prepared to listen to.

[I am] trying to get a system which is concerned with giving them what they do want and [I] believe as a matter of fact that commercial television does not do that. ... When you have a cricket match on one programme you may want a serious piece of music on the other. What you do want ... is to have something which affords real and genuine choice between two things utterly dissimilar and not a competition between two things each trying to present the same kind of programme in opposition and trying to capture the same maximum audience. ... It is only where you have cooperation in the matter of programmes and not commercial competition that ... you can give an effective variety of choice.

(Lord Hailsham, 1954)

Perhaps the last, shattering words should go to Lord Simon of Wythenshawe, who summed up for many the dreadful prospect ahead.

Watching a thing on television impresses one's memory far more than reading it in a newspaper. What is going to be the effect on the population of several hours of triviality, put over day by day in that very impressive form? Think of the deadening effect of hours and hours of that sort of thing on adults, the citizens of democracy who are going to carry on this country and still more, upon the children. It is to me a terrifying prospect.

(1954)

Case rests, m'lud. Each and every viewer can make up his or her own mind whether the fears have turned out to be unfounded.

EIGHT:
THE ART OF
WAR

Technology challenged every aspect of society. In the vast majority of cases it demanded that people change *their* ways to suit *it* rather than the other way round. Centuries of tradition, practice and deeply-imbued assumptions about how to do something were, in a matter of fleeting moments, overturned. We have seen the effect in many of society's arenas already. Perhaps the motor car was technology's greatest and most wide-reaching assault on the norms by which life had been lived since time immemorial. It justifies a chapter to itself. Technological advances in transport were also to have an impact on a more narrow area of society, one which because of its peculiar penchant for tradition, fixed thinking and abidance by tried and trusted means rather than by innovation, felt the cold draught of fresh air with rather more uncertainty and anxiety than most – the military.

Always renown as the branch of society least open to change – the military wears its resistance to novelty almost as a badge of integrity – the army and navy never welcomed the new fangled inventions of the scientists which threatened to upset the carefully constituted web of existing allegiances and organizational arrangements which had seen the country right for so long. There would be many battles against the sweep of change. All the modern mechanisms of war – the machine gun, the land mine, the aerial bomb, the ironclad battleship, the torpedo, even barbed wire and a host of others came in for damnation at some point in their gestation. Having to be selective, we focus on perhaps the three greatest challenges to the settled order of the military domain: the submarine, which thrust a dagger at the heart of centuries of naval tradition; the tank, which did likewise for the land-based commanders; and the areoplane, which created a brand new theatre of action all of its own.

'A MISTAKE'
THE SUBMARINE

The senior service was, rather appropriately, the first to confront the major technological and operational challenge to the status quo. The submarine had been around in primitive form since the seventeenth century, and had been used in battle as early as the American War of Independence in 1776 when a revolutionary American patriot used one to attack the British flagship at anchor off Staten Island. The mission was an abject failure, but the seeds had been sown. It was to be the 1880s before a design had been perfected which offered the prospect of the submarine as a practical weapon of war. Britain began its submarine fleet with its first launch in 1885, but for more than a quarter of a century we, and the other navies of the world, toyed with them, no-one quite sure exactly what the implications were for the well-honed battle tactics of the surface ship. It would be the First World War which was to unveil the role and impact of submarines. Just as on land, a fundamental shift in the military balance had taken place: on the Western Front the machine gun had tilted the advantage to the defender, who could now pick off thousands with a well-placed gun battery; on and below the high seas the balance had shifted to the offender with submarines, undetectable and virtually impossible to be attacked, able to be predators at will. On land it was to take another technological leap forward – the tank – to break the grip of the machine gun. On water, no such counteracting remedy was at hand.

It had, in fact, all turned out rather differently than the experts had predicted. The earliest assumptions, expounded on the first occasion the House discussed the tactical implications for defence, was that the submarine could never be an instrument of attack and would only be used as a hidden defence in home waters. Quite how they came to this final conclusion is unclear, but the limitations on range of early models seemed to be the problem that looked likely to remain insuperable. No less than the First Lord of the Admiralty seemed to be all at sea.

> The submarine boat ... would seem, so far as the immediate future is concerned, to be essentially a weapon for maritime Powers on the defensive. ... The question of the best way of meeting an attack is receiving much consideration and it is in this direction that practical suggestions would be valuable. It seems certain that the reply to this weapon must be looked for in other directions than in building submarine boats ourselves for it is clear that one submarine boat cannot fight another.
>
> (Mr Goschen, 1900)

Four years later and even this prospect seemed unlikely for one doubter.

> My own impression is that the use of submarines for a great naval country like this is altogether doubtful. ... I am unable to see that submarines will be of any great value to a great naval country and I think the defence of our ports should be secured by over-water boats.
>
> (Mr Bowles, 1904)

The following year, having been told by the Prime Minister, Arthur Balfour, that it seemed 'hardly practicable' to contact all foreign governments with a view to abolishing the submarine as a weapon of war, the same doubter consoled himself with the satisfaction that nothing would come of the invention anyway.

My own view is that the submarine is not our weapon and that ... it is a dangerous weapon to those who use it. It is very doubtful whether it will be of any use in war, either for defence or offence.

(Mr Bowles, 1905)

The reason was obvious.

A submarine is really a mechanical fish with this difference, that we cannot put into it the eyes of a fish to show where it is going. The periscope is a most ineffective instrument and I doubt whether [the submarine] will be really serviceable for naval purposes.

(Sir John Leng, 1905)

Right up to the eve of the Great War, voices were urging the government not to put too much faith in the weapon.

I hope [the Government] is not going to be taken in by the value of submarines. They are entirely theoretical. It has been put about that submarines can do the work of battleships and cruisers. They cannot. They are entirely theoretical. What beats a seaman at any time is when he is in a fog. The submarine is always in a fog. Though I quite agree with them for defence, for offence I am sure they are a mistake.

(Lord Beresford, 1912)

Of course, when it all started attitudes changed – they could hardly not do so as ship after ship was picked off by Germany's unrestricted U-boat warfare in the Atlantic. The strain of argument persisted, though, that the weapon was still contrary to military decency and the unwritten code of honour among warriors. The Prime Minister, Herbert Asquith, felt that submarine warfare was:

[a] systematic violation of all the established conventions and practices of international law. ... I am certain ... it is carried on by men acting against their will but under instructions of a superior power which compels them to defy all the rules with regard to capture and prize which have hitherto been held sacred in maritime warfare.

(1916)

There were to be imaginative efforts to counter the submarine's greatest asset – its invisibility. In 1915 the authorities took a group of sealions from the London stage and tried to train them to find German U-boats. The scheme was unsuccessful. The creatures appeared ('shrewdly' in the words of one historian) to appraise the submarines as inedible and 'declined to waste effort upon them'. An even more bizarre attempt was made to train seagulls to search out and land on periscopes to make submarines detectable. That idea met a similar fate. The legacy of the First World War was that the submarine successfully passed its apprenticeship and henceforth would have to be included in the calculations of tacticians in the defence ministries. As late as 1921, though, there was still some who thought that the worst had already been seen.

There are those who look to the development of the submersible battleship but that means an enormous increase in the size of the submarine and as the submarine increases in size so do the difficulties of handling it increase out of all proportion. In fact, I believe the definite limit to the size of the submarine has already been more than reached and later developments will be a submarine of a smaller type.

(Viscount Curzon, 1921)

'QUITE IMPOSSIBLE ... TO BE USED WITH ADVANTAGE'
THE TANK

If the submarine challenged centuries-old philosophies of the navy, the army had its own contest with modernity which was to be of greater ferocity. It was to be fought against mechanization in general, and boiled down to a battle between the upstart tank and the tried, tested and trusted cavalry. The pioneering of the tank on the Western Front offered a glimpse of the future nature of land warfare. In history's first massed mechanical offensive, at Cambrai in November 1917, 400 tanks forged a six-mile intrusion into German lines in two days, the greatest distance that had ever been gained in one assault since 1914. A few committed advocates espied the future in that brief moment. Although there were to be other tank attacks before the War ended, peace came in 1918 with the tank's credentials still far from assured. The real test of the tank's durability came in peace-time, in the corridors of power in Whitehall and the chamber of the House of Commons.

The new House, elected just weeks after the Armistice, was filled with a generous band of ex-military officers who had served in the War – generous in size, not in opinion. They fought a rearguard action for the type of army they knew best, which had served mankind since the day the first soldier mounted a horse: regardless of what novel gimmickry the mad inventors had contrived, for them the cavalry was the only safe repository of national security. Major-General Seely, who had been Secretary of State for War from 1912-14 and the government minister personally in charge of the tank development programme, proved that inside knowledge was no guarantee of greater insight: he had spent the War commanding a cavalry brigade. Despite the advantage of having seen both instruments in action he drew different conclusions to the modernist.

> I believe that [the Secretary of State's advisers] are entirely wrong in thinking that they can substitute tanks for cavalry. ... That seems to me to be a most extraordinary misreading of the lessons of the War. ... It seems to me that it would be the most extraordinary misconception of the truth to imagine that in applying science to war the first thing to get rid of is the horse. On the contrary, every advance in science has made the horse a more and more indispensable weapon of war. Heavy artillery fire, heavy machine gun fire, gas, aeroplane observation – all of these make rapid movement more essential.
>
> (1921)

Unlike the sustained devotion needed to perfect horsemanship, how would the 'mechanical rider' of the future make good use of their time?

> How long will it take him to learn about a tank? One year? Not that. What is he going to do with the rest of his time? He will not be allowed to parade; you cannot go parading about in tanks. The men will be drawing good pay, probably as mechanics, and they will sit and look at their tanks for 21 years.
>
> (Sir K. Fraser, 1921)

A further five years on, another still remained unconvinced.

> It is asserted nowadays that tanks and aeroplanes are to take the place of cavalry. ... It is obvious that a tank making a very great noise will give many opportunities to the enemy to conceal themselves. It is quite impossible for tanks to be used

with advantage in such terrain as marshy ground or for crossing a river when the bridges have been blown up.

(Captain Holt, 1926)

Even as late as 1931 Government ministers still saw the need to offer assurances.

Until we are thoroughly satisfied that horses, so far as troops are concerned, can be dispensed with – and I think it is a fairly long time ahead before they can be dispensed with absolutely – the cavalry will remain as it is.

(Mr Shaw, Secretary of State for War, 1931)

Later still, the delightfully named Lieutenant-Colonel Acland Troyte could still be heard arguing that the military chiefs were moving in the wrong direction.

Any reduction of cavalry would be a very great mistake indeed. I have served nearly all my life as an infantry man and I fully realise the tremendous value of cavalry to the infantry. ... The numbers of the cavalry instead of being reduced should rather be increased.

(1933)

His colleague agreed.

If there is one thing which we learnt from the War it is the value of cavalry at the beginning of a War. ... Therefore, it is essential that the numbers should not be further reduced and I hope that ... they will not be mechanised or turned into something else. ... Our field officers are mounted for the one purpose of being able to go forward and find out exactly the situation. Without cavalry we should be unable to fight a war in Europe or anywhere else.

(Lieutenant-Colonel Applin, 1933)

At almost the same time, in Germany, Hitler was being dazzled by the ideas and demonstrations of a young army officer, Heinz Guderian. In 1934 the new German leader sanctioned the formation of the first Panzer tank battalion. Being born was the concept of Blitzkrieg, the art of rapid, mechanical and overwhelming force delivered in a single crushing blow. It would revolutionize warfare and stun the world in 1939 and 1940. Still, on this side of the North Sea, we confidently held to the experience of the past.

> One thing which is very satisfactory is that the authorities feel that the day of the cavalry is not done. In fact, it is there just as much as ever. Cavalry today can be of use at the beginning of the fight and at the end. ... The disorganised infantry will still feel panicky fear when they hear that the cavalry is once more upon them. The cavalry will be able to come into their own when mechanical vehicles have all broken down ... and when possibly the petrol dumps are all exploded.
>
> (Brigadier-General Makins, 1933)

> I am sure my hon Friend cannot support his argument that horses are useless in war because he has seen them blown to pieces by guns. As far as I know, men are blown to pieces by guns but we do not say that they are useless. Tanks are blown to pieces with the people inside them but we do not say that tanks are useless. ... It is of course well known that we cannot break through barbed wire ... but when the enemy are defeated and retiring you cannot complete your victory without cavalry.
>
> ... Cavalry are as necessary today as they have ever been; the men and the horses are always necessary in war if they are properly used.
>
> (Lieutenant-Colonel Applin, 1934)

Not for the first time, knowledge about what was happening abroad was woefully inaccurate.

> There is now considerable doubt as to whether the tank is still
> the useful tactical weapon which it proved to be for the short
> time during the War. ... In view of ... the fact that the Germans
> ... take no interest in tanks at all ... perhaps we ought not to
> undergo too much expense in this respect. I suggest that one
> tank brigade would be sufficient to keep at full fighting strength.
> (Lord Apsley, 1935)

Such views smacked of wishful thinking. Others made no
apologies.

> We are quite justified in keeping a nucleus of cavalry which is
> the finest arm in the service for training commanding officers.
> (Brigadier-General Clifton Brown, 1935)

And even Government could not abandon faith entirely.

> I think we are compelled to retain cavalry if we are to have a
> complete and efficient expeditionary force. ... It is necessary to
> retain the horses and to retain cavalry as we have known it.
> (Mr Hacking, Financial Secretary, War Office, 1935)

As late as 1936 there were undaunted foes of mechanization. Few Members can have begun their Parliamentary
careers with a maiden speech so strident in assertion, so
wrong in perception and so unsuspecting of the future he
was embarking upon.

> I am perfectly convinced that the role of the cavalry is still as
> important today as it has been throughout the ages.
> (Major P.S. Shaw, 1936)

As we stumbled into the Second World War in a generation, the warnings were still there.

> It is only too certain that the time may come when we may require the cavalry arm. ... The total abolition of the cavalry would be a frightful blunder.
>
> (Brigadier-General Sir Henry Croft, 1936)

After that the rest was silence.

'The Bomber Will Always Get Through'
The Aeroplane

The two arms of the military, confronting their own internal problems in digesting new ideas, were taken by surprise by perhaps the most rapid innovation to affect – or afflict – warfare: the aircraft. Of all the innovations which transformed war, none came to have as widespread a psychological grip of terror on the nation than the prospect of aerial warfare. The fear was understandable: suddenly, in the twinkling of an eye, an entirely new battleground had come into play, one, moreover, in which all the advantage lay with the attacker. One early Government observer spoke about the impossibility of defending 'in three dimensions'. The fact that unlike any other weapon of war, aircraft could move vertically as well as the traditional horizontal forwards and sideways gave it, according to early tacticians, unimpeded access behind any defensive lines on the ground. Doubts about how to defend – or indeed whether it would ever be possible to do so – against the aircraft mounted in the 1920s into a national psychosis, epitomized by the famous assertion uttered by Stanley Baldwin, Conservative leader in the National Government, in November 1932.

> I think it is well also for the man in the street to realise that there is no power on earth that can protect him from being bombed. Whatever people may tell him, the bomber will always get through.

'The bomber will always get through' created expectations of the future analagous to those which would become the abiding dread of all living in the nuclear age – that once unleashed, there really were no defences against the new weapon and that absolute, terminal destruction would result. Seen today, a Government information film made to give advice to citizens in the event of air raids evokes almost identically the fear familiar to modern minds of the four-minute warning.

In the Second World War, things turned out a little better in fact than feared, but the nation had to go through the experience with all its doubts and fears first before the nature of the beast became evident. The misjudgment then, so far as aircraft were concerned, tended to lay in the opposite direction to most of the other subjects we have considered. It was not that it wouldn't work that worried people, but that it would work rather too well. This was the tenor of much of the debate in the 1930s. Leaning on the lessons of the rudimentary attacks by airships on British cities in the First World War, catastrophic implications were drawn.

> It is hopeless to attempt to protect yourself against this raid of 300 aeroplanes. It took 32,000 men to protect London against the raids of the 36 machines. ... It will be seen at once that to attempt to prevent an enemy from bombarding your town by preparation in time of peace in the way of land defence is frankly impossible. All that you can say is, 'If you are going to destroy my town, I will destroy yours.'
>
> (Major-General Seely, 1922)

Paralleling our own nuclear age, this is the first exposition of the deterrence theory which would govern the Cold War superpowers forty years later. The development of the aircraft, it was confidently asserted, made warfare either impossible or suicidal. Some awful visions were offered if it did break out.

A force of 500 aeroplanes could in the space of a single night obliterate from the face of the earth a city a kilometre square. ... A force of this size could wipe off the surface of the globe a city as big as Paris in the course of a fortnight or three weeks.

(Sir S. Hoare, a former Air Minister, 1924)

It will be possible in another war for London to be wrecked by aircraft attack in twelve hours.

(Mr Hudson, 1925)

The result was pretty plain. The next war would be over in a matter of days.

The next war is bound to be a short war. Of course they said that of the last War. ... Do not, however, let us always judge what the next war will be by what the last war was. ... I cannot conceive of any country being able to continue a war for a week after its air force, its aerodromes and its petrol tanks have been destroyed. ... The war will be decided ... not in five years, or in five weeks but in five days.

(Colonel Wedgwood, 1934)

Even Churchill, embarking on his wilderness-years role as arch-critic of Government timidity, while voicing against defeatism could himself wildly over-estimate the consequences of war.

I do not accept the sweeping claim of the extreme votaries of the air. I think that a great many statements which are made are calculated to frustrate the purpose of reasonable precautions by presenting the problem as if it were one which was insoluble. But without accepting these claims, no-one can doubt that a week or ten days' intensive bombing attack upon London would be a very serious matter indeed. One could hardly expect that less than 30,000 or 40,000 people would be killed or maimed.

(1934)

In reality, when the Blitz on London and other British cities did come, it lasted just over eight months (from September 1940 to May 1941). In that time, on Churchill's estimate, the death toll should have been in the order of a million. In fact it was 30,000, slightly over half of whom died in London.

For some, in the very early days, the whole idea could be dismissed as a damp squib. In the first debate to be held in Parliament on the new invention – nearly six years after the first manned flight – it was brushed aside with nonchalant scorn.

Ordinary common-sense tells us that such machines will probably never be used for the carrying of large bodies of troops and ammunition.

(Sir Gilbert Parker, 1909)

The prospect of air warfare was literally a flight of fancy.

The idea that there could easily be dropped from such machines explosive materials with any chance of hitting any particular object has been entirely disproved by all the experiments that have been made in that direction. No doubt an explosive dropped from an aerial machine would hit somewhere but that would not be a very useful or scientific method of bombardment. ... I do not think that nations in the future are going to conduct their battles by scattering explosives over houses. That is very unlikely to take place. It would be the very reversal of the rules of war which have now existed for a long time. Nobody expects an enemy to bombard a seaside place like Brighton. With civilised nations warfare is not conducted by simply destroying property and killing civilians or by dropping dynamite about London, Paris or Berlin. Such a proceeding would have no effect at all on the ending of the war. No nation would make peace because the enemy was killing civilians. So long as the naval and military forces were not attacked they would be perfectly ready to go on. It is entirely contrary to all practice to scatter explosives in the way suggested and that such a brutal and futile proceeding would be resorted to is one which we need not contemplate.

(Mr Mond, 1909)

The faith in humanity was touching, if misplaced. The difficulty in weighing up the implications of aircraft was wholesale. Some, including the usually retrogressive Major-General Seely, ventured further to an alternative extreme seeing the aircraft as the panacea for world peace.

I am not at all sure that within a few years air power may not make fleets and armies as we see them obsolete.

(1919)

What is even more surprising is that he was speaking as Under-Secretary for Air at the time, voicing the official view of the Government. He was not alone.

I believe that when we do get air travel thoroughly developed, as it will be one day, it will be a physical defeat for all the people who want to set up barriers between the nations of the world with customs and tariffs. The moment when the air is full of flying machines, all customs barriers, alien restrictions and all these divisions which separate mankind and prevent it being one united family will cease.

(Captain Benn, 1920)

Although not entirely fitting in with the military theme of this chapter, it would be difficult not also to record the early thoughts on the prospects for *civil* aviation which began to be voiced in parallel with the developments of military thinking, if only to show that it was not the case that misguided assessments about the invention were a peculiarity of tradition-encrusted martial minds. Many thought that 'normal' people flying was preposterous. Churchill, in his earlier manifestation as Secretary of State for Air during this highly protoplasmic time for the aeroplane, had his doubts.

> The task of fostering civilian aviation in the British Isles will be attended with much difficulty. The fogs and mists and other climatic conditions are a terrible hindrance. Moreover, the country is covered by a network of railways and roads which constitute a most formidable competition with the air. Travelling by air does not mean travelling from one city to another, but from one aerodrome to another; the aerodromes are on the outsides of the cities and it usually takes from 15 to 30 minutes to reach or return from an aerodrome. Then you have to compete in an aeroplane with trains which carry passengers into the heart of the cities and with motor cars which take them actually door to door. ... Therefore I should not expect to see a very large or a very rapid development of domestic civil aviation within these islands.
>
> (1921)

He was not short of support.

> I do not believe that civil aviation has more than very limited potentialities. I believe it may be made a luxurious and costly mode of travel for a very few rich people. I do not believe it will be able to be brought into use for general transport. You may do something with it for mails but not a great deal. The unfortunate fact is that there is only one way to resist the force of gravity and that is by the exercise of prodigious and unremit-

ting centrifugal force. ... It seems to me the heavier you make these things the more force you have to call in and the more force you call in the more weight you are going to have. While I believe the aeroplane has little or only a very limited future, the whole of its potentialities are warlike.

(Mr Rose, 1923)

We in this island shall never fly commercially for more than sixty miles over the island. It will never pay us to fly from London to Glasgow commercially and so all our commercial flying has to be from London to the Channel or from London to the North Sea and then over Europe.

(Major Hills, 1928)

Even as domestic airlines got off the ground their future was not viewed as bright.

I think that we have possibly made an entirely wrong start in civil aviation by trying to run from London to Paris and from London to India carrying passengers. After all, directly you carry passengers, you increase your responsibilities. The human passenger is the most expensive form of freight that you can carry. You have to provide appliances, you have to provide facilities and you have to provide a useful payload for the machine with trimmings like upholstery and one thing and another. The carrying of passengers is not economical. ...

(Captain H. Balfour, 1931)

Civil aviation will never be a commercial proposition in this country. It may be that individuals will continue to use aeroplanes for business and pleasure purposes to an increasing degree but as a commercial proposition I think we are already too well served by our railways. ... If we take Edinburgh, unless there is a far more highly developed night flying service it will be more convenient to get into the train at midnight and arrive at

Edinburgh early next morning than to occupy a certain portion
of the day in flying to Edinburgh.

                             (Captain Cazalet, 1931)

Not to be out-argued with technical counterblasts, he
anticipated and then destroyed his critics.

Of course you can increase speed. ... It is perfectly easy to
increase your speed if you are prepared to pay more money, but
I understand that if you increase your speed by twenty per cent
you also increase your cost by fifty per cent. It is purely a matter
of pounds, shillings and pence whether you are prepared to
compete in speed with other countries.

In the end the aircraft was to prove rather more resilient to
human uncertainties than anyone could have imagined.